THE Right Job, Right Now

9824

THE COMPLETE TOOLKIT
FOR FINDING YOUR
PERFECT CAREER

SUSAN D. STRAYER, S.P.H.R.

ST. MARTIN'S GRIFFIN ❦ NEW YORK

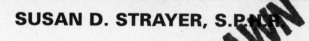

www.stmartins.com

Design by M-Space Design

LIBRARY OF CONGRESS CATALOGING-IN-PUBLICATION DATA

Strayer, Susan D.
   The right job, right now : the complete toolkit for finding your perfect career / Susan D. Strayer
      p. cm.
   ISBN-13: 978-0-312-34926-4
   ISBN-10: 0-312-34926-2
   1. Vocational guidance. 2. Job hunting. 3. Career development. I. Title.

HF5381.S883 2007
650.14—dc22

                                                                      2006051157

First Edition: January 2007

10 9 8 7 6 5 4 3 2 1

To Ellie and Zachary

My pint-size inspirations:
When you stop having fun, it's time to do something else.

CONTENTS

ACKNOWLEDGMENTS

If there is anything I have learned from writing *The Right Job, Right Now* it is that gratitude is truly underrated. First and foremost, I am indebted to Melinda Blau for opening the "author's door." Her ability to gracefully point out my missteps, to thoughtfully turn me in the right direction and take a networking chance on me, is beyond appreciated. Already an incredibly talented and best-selling author, Melinda has many more successful books ahead of her, and I can't wait to read every single one.

To Eileen Cope, whose early commitment to the book proposal and honesty and energy throughout the writing process is, I'm sure, unmatched in the publishing industry, thank you. Thanks as well to Lowenstein-Yost for its agency support on *The Right Job, Right Now*. And, it goes without saying, to Sheila Oakes and the team at St. Martin's—I am forever grateful.

There are also dozens of writers and professionals who gave me advice and guidance in the early stages, including Melinda Blau, Brad Meltzer, Debbie Aiges, and Robert DiRomualdo. Tremendous thanks to them as well as those who trusted me with their networking connections, including Jennifer Martin, Peter Brown, Eric Tamarkin, and Lara Meisner.

The Recruiting Roundtable, a research program of the Corporate Executive Board (www.executiveboard.com), also provided a deep amount of insight for this book. I am grateful to the Roundtable's leader, David Williams, and consultant Donna Weiss, who were especially generous in lending their expertise.

The many professionals I have been privileged to work with, and for, during the course of my career, have contributed to this book in ways they may never know. Martha Youngblood, John Ring, Glenn Richardson, and Paul O'Neill were among the earliest role models I had for being the consummate professional.

The following are just a few of the people who helped me learn that colleagues aren't always only people you work alongside, but can become friends and teachers in their own right: Nicole Fann, Katie Lallande Kalka, Sarah Nowell, Kaori Ogino, Sarah Sandfort Schultz, Cara Scarola, Amy Steptoe, and Kirsten Thor Vartanoff. I thank them and web designer extraordinaire, Jason Novak, who will never admit how talented he is.

Others whom I have learned from in many ways, who supported my business early on and/or who lent their own career woes to this book, include among many others, Rebecca Zucker, Heather Corcoran, Wendy Person, Keith

Stemple, Darby Scism, Scott Crawford, Mike Ward, Penny White, Kathryn Collins, Amy Joyce, Kelly Zafar, Rachel Rowley, Suzanne Duvall, and Kathleen Langheck. And to my many clients who put their faith in me and were committed to finding their own Career Sweet Spot.

I am also appreciative of my friends and peers at the Owen Graduate School of Management at Vanderbilt University for supporting me as I labored on *The Right Job, Right Now* while in the midst of classwork and final exams (self-induced pain, I know). And, of course, to Peter for his constant encouragement and keeping me sane when I didn't think I had any sanity left. That in itself is a feat deserving of reward.

I'd be remiss if I didn't profusely thank my entire family—above all, my parents Joan and John Strayer, my sister Lara Meisner, and my brother John R. Strayer. Support is one thing, but genuine enthusiasm, encouragement, and pride are something else. For that and more, there aren't enough words of thanks.

Finally, and most important, *The Right Job, Right Now* probably wouldn't exist without the commitment and incredible intellect of Sarita Venkat. My earliest collaborator, contributor, and devil's advocate, Sarita's early brainstorming sessions, research, and writing suggestions were instrumental in getting the book off the ground. Perhaps one of the most kind and genuine people I have ever known, and also an accomplished writer, Sarita is in many ways the spark that helped ignite what I hope is *The Right Job, Right Now* revolution.

—SUSAN D. STRAYER
Nashville, Tennessee, December 2006

FOREWORD

When I graduated college a decade ago, the main topic my friends and I talked about was where we were all headed. Cities, jobs, marriages—there was so much to choose from and so much to do. But a few years into that euphoria, reality set in. Is this what we really wanted? Were we satisfied, fulfilled, happy? You know, all that stuff that makes sitcoms so easy to relate to.

Stumbling through my twenties, everyone around me faced daily tests with family issues, relationship problems, and sometimes health crises. Everyone had a different challenge, a different story. What dominated lunch dates or happy hours was a common bond over workplace frustrations: an unfulfilling job, a psychotic boss, ignorant co-workers, a pitifully small paycheck. It wasn't that I didn't know anyone who was happy at work, because many of us were (even if marginally), but there was always a workplace problem that couldn't be solved or a career goal that was impossible to reach.

Although most of us made our choices by default, when I looked back I realized that some of what we did was much harder than it needed to be. Or, on the other hand, we were much more apathetic than we should have been. There wasn't really a trusted resource to go to for advice, so we simply complained to one another. When we tired of that, we turned to our families. We asked our parents for information and insight, but they just hadn't had the same career choices that we have. We refused to listen to our siblings, assuming that we'd figure it out on our own, or just suck it up. What other options were there?

It seemed that the only way to find the best-fit career was to rely on luck—to try one job or one field after another and hope that we'd finally strike gold. It seemed that the only way to solve a workplace problem was to poll as many people as possible and go with what our gut said was the right choice. Sure, intuition and luck play a role in successes of all kinds—there is no doubt about that. But to rely only on luck and your gut is a risky, exhausting way to build a career. I set out to change that, building a business and a career development model that is focused on making realistic and smart career decisions.

I know, the word model sounds academic and boring. But it's not. It's more like a plan, a series of steps that you can follow without feeling like you've just been to the shrink.

In the past few years, as a career coach I have listened to hundreds of career stories and frustrations, and in my role as a recruiter and business professional, interviewed hundreds of job candidates. While many people want to have a fulfilling career, or are willing to work hard to make their on-the-job experience a good one, not everyone has the time or money, or is willing to embark on long journeys of self-reflection. A quick look in the mirror is all we have time for and all we can afford. We're slaves to the Internet and want a menu of options to solve our career problems. We don't need lectures from a mother or father figure whose job-searching techniques were perfected before Blackberrys or Instant Messenging. We often don't have the patience to complete hours of exercises or worry about what kind of economy we might face tomorrow or in ten years. That's where *The Right Job, Right Now* comes in: a straightforward, no-nonsense way to finally get options and answers regardless of whether you can commit to complete career reinvention, or just need quick help.

While a good deal of what is in this book comes from my extensive research and work experience in human resources and business—recruiting, career development, training, consulting—much also comes from a huge collection of stories, choices, and chances I've compiled from listening to successes, failures, and second and third takes.

Regardless of where you are in your career, you'll discover that everyone's got a different career opinion. The advice you get from one career counselor might be different from that which comes from your boss or your mom. But *The Right Job, Right Now* isn't about *one* right way. It's a collection of suggestions from which you can choose the best solution at whatever point you are in your career. There are some clear-cut rights and wrongs. *The Right Job, Right Now* won't sugarcoat them for you. And if anyone tells you there's one silver bullet for finding the perfect career, they're lying.

I wanted *The Right Job, Right Now* to be not just a book, but a tool. As a result you'll find that the book's structure is different from that of other books you may have read. While it can and should be read from cover to cover for the most effective career strategy guidance, it can also be thumbed through to find the topic you need to address right this minute: You're forced to work with a lazy co-worker or have a pending interview and need some quick troubleshooting or immediate advice. *The Right Job, Right Now* is both a guide to a complete career makeover and a reference tool—a book for those who have the time to sit back and think, and for those who barely have time to think about what's for dinner.

INTRODUCTION

The one thing to make clear before we get going is that there is no such thing as the perfect career. Yes, you read it right: *There is no such thing as the perfect career.* But there is a career that is perfect for you. It's one that has all the things that really matter to you at this point in your life, and takes into consideration your priorities and needs as well as what you have to offer a workplace, employer, field, or industry.

You may be completely disgusted, slightly bored, or simply stuck in a career rut. Or you may have a career problem that you're not sure even has a solution. And once one career question is answered, it's followed by another and another. If you're like most people, you'll probably have more than enough career questions in your lifetime and less than enough time to deal with them all.

You can buy ten books, each one addressing one of the issues you're facing. Or you can spend hours combing through a long-winded text to answer one burning workplace dilemma. Instead, you've picked up the first practical career reference guide that can help you find the best-fit job, restart your career, and answer career questions as they arise.

If you need a complete career overhaul, then read the book from cover to cover. If you require help in one specific area, then skip to that section and discover several ways to tackle that problem. Either way, *The Right Job, Right Now* gives you a straightforward, no-nonsense approach to get on with the rest of your career life. Before you dive in, however, there are a few important things you should know.

How *The Right Job, Right Now* Works

The Right Job, Right Now is not your typical career guide. You won't find long, rambling lectures about the one and only right way to conduct a job search or how to weave your spirituality into your job search. There's no preaching here, just a clear path from start to finish on rethinking your career, accompanied by uncomplicated advice on common career and workplace problems. Regardless of exactly why you've picked up *The Right Job, Right Now*, it's important to know what lies ahead of you. Think of this book as a career-planning model crossed with a career toolkit: You can use the book to create a feasible career development plan while you address everyday problems along the way.

Rethinking Your Career Path:
Start at the Beginning

Many people are driven to buy a career book to help them start over from scratch. Or, for you first-time job hunters, to simply start from scratch. Perhaps you've found yourself several years into a career you hate. Perhaps you want to avoid falling into a rut from the beginning. Maybe life has changed and you need a job or career that's a better fit to your new circumstances. Or perhaps you like your career, but have become a serial job hopper who hopes each new company will be a better match than the last. No matter what your career needs, *The Right Job, Right Now* can take you from start to finish. Based on the Kaleidoscope Career Model™, *The Right Job, Right Now* will help you map out a simple and productive plan and make good decisions that address current career issues and long-term plans. You're not just preparing for your next job. You're planning for your career.

To do this, you're going to have to commit some time, but you now have a step-by-step guide to help you think through your options and how and when to take action. If you want to change careers, find a better job, or just figure out where you belong in the career galaxy, there's no better time or way to get started.

Getting Help on Specific Questions:
Get Right to the Point

Not everyone wants to start from scratch. Maybe you were surprised by your boss's request for a copy of your resumé. Perhaps you want quick advice on how to handle an overly demanding colleague. Or let's say you have a case interview for a job you really want and you don't even know what a case interview is, let alone how to prepare for it. At times like these, you don't have time to read an entire book on one topic, or comb through pages and pages to find a few solutions.

If you're facing a specific problem, treat *The Right Job, Right Now* like a toolkit. Use the table of contents to locate your topic of interest and you can flip directly to that section for answers. Keep it in your desk to grab at a moment's notice. You never know when you might get your first poor performance review, and you'll want to know what to do when it happens.

Keep in mind that if you're using *The Right Job, Right Now* for job trouble-shooting, you might find yourself skipping from section to section. With every career dilemma, the book will refer you to other relevant chapters and issues you might need to consider. It might inspire you to start at page one and develop your own new career plan.

Knowing Yourself

Perhaps the most important reminder I can offer before you get started is: Know yourself. Don't worry, I'm not getting all psycho-babblely on you, just keeping you honest. Some people have the patience to read a book from cover to cover, to reflect on every question asked and every exercise posed. Others prefer to jump right to the answers, choosing the one that seems like the best fit. Whatever your personality or your level of commitment, *The Right Job, Right Now* can help you. You have to figure how much help you really want and what you are willing to do to get the help you need.

If you're sick of your job and can barely get up in the morning and get out the door, then you may be more motivated to change than others are. But sometimes a stable paycheck or a long tenure makes it harder to take the first step to leave. Or, let's say you've been interviewing for months for the same type of job, with no result. Friends, colleagues, and I can give you advice until we're blue in the face, but until you take a closer look at your technique or approach and figure out what's not working, nothing's going to change.

You have to be willing to try something different or take a few risks. And for any career or workplace issue to be resolved or overcome, you've got to put in some effort. You need to realize it all comes from you. No one can do this for you and you have to accept that what worked five years ago might not work now.

Be honest with yourself. Do you have the time and energy to invest in a complete career overhaul? Or can you only manage a simple resumé revision? Some people want to take the time to find the best possible career. Others need only some resumé or workplace guidance. Wherever you fall on the energy, motivation, and commitment spectrum, *The Right Job, Right Now* can help. After all, your time is valuable and we don't want to waste it. Just know that you've got to put some effort in to get anything in return.

Step by Step

As you make your way through the entire book, or through a single chapter, every "To Do" will always be listed as "Action." That's your cue that you need to do some work. You'll also be cautioned to "STOP" several times throughout the book if there's an action you need to complete before moving on, or if there's something you have to know to avoid a serious career-limiting move.

For you list-lovers, at the end of each chapter you will find a complete recap and list of Action items. You'll also find "Good to Knows" in boxes throughout the book that should provide answers to many of your questions. If your question isn't answered here, check out *The Right Job, Right Now* online (www.therightjobrightnow.com) for more information and resources.

Getting Extra Help

Maybe you aced your English classes but needed a tutor in algebra. Maybe it was the other way around. The point is, no one can do everything. Getting extra help in an area you're struggling with is nothing to be embarrassed about. In this respect, career development is no different from English or algebra.

Career counseling and coaching is a big business. There is no shortage of professionals who can help you. Whether you choose to employ a professional in addition to reading *The Right Job, Right Now* is up to you. You can find a job on your own, but not everyone has the motivation or ability to go at it without some help.

If you've got some life issues that might be impeding your efforts, a licensed career counselor or psychologist might be a good first step. Let's face it, life isn't always a picnic. And if you are encountering personal, relationship, or mental health problems, a job search is going to be that much harder for you. *The Right Job, Right Now* is full of great advice, but you have to be prepared to take it. If you're unsure about what you need, talk to a licensed counselor or therapist. (See Appendix B for some suggestions on how to find one.)

> **Good to Know:**
> Both counseling and coaching are fields that require specific training and licensure. When considering whether to work with one of these professionals, be sure to ask about all those acronyms on his business card, such as M.S.W. or L.C.C.

If your problem is motivational, or you need help or guidance to assess and better understand yourself, you might want to consider working with a career coach. Like counselors, they have gone through extensive training, but may be better poised to spur you to action or coach you through a specific professional situation. After all, many coaches are often former business professionals themselves.

As part of a session, the coach may administer a career assessment test. You may remember taking some of these in high school or college, answering what seemed like ridiculous questions: Would you prefer to fix a car or hoe a garden? However, many assessments can help you more than you think. It's not just about filling in a circle to choose whether you'd rather wield a sword or bake a cake.

If you're struggling with how to find happiness in your career, an assessment may help point you in the right direction. Some assessments are designed to help you focus your career options while others, like the Meyers-Briggs Type Indicator, help you better understand your own behaviors so you can get a sense of what careers you might and might not like. Either way, don't just take tests hoping for a brilliant epiphany. If you're looking for an assessment that can help narrow your interests or isolate problem areas, Appendix A has some suggestions on where to start, or you can ask your coach or counselor.

More Than a Book

No matter where this book takes you, just remember: It doesn't stop here. *The Right Job, Right Now* online (www.therightjobrightnow.com) is designed to be your real-time companion with live discussions, real stories, and more help if you need it. Careers change, businesses change, times change. What works today might not work tomorrow. So stay on top of your career and what you need to advance it. You're in the right place to get started.

PART ONE

What Do You Really Want to Do?: A Career Plan for the Rest of Your Life

Frustration, confusion, apathy—whatever it is that's driven you to the career edge—you need a plan, a strategy, or, at the very least, someone to tell you what to do.

> **STOP** If you have a quick career question or need fast advice in one specific area, go back to the table of contents and jump to the section that can give you the help you need now. If you need a plan to make a job change, a career switch, or a complete career overhaul, keep reading.

Part I introduces what's missing from most career books: an easy-to-use plan. Called the Kaleidoscope Career Model™, it's a simple method for taking a complete look at yourself and your career. It's not a psychological analysis of all your career misgivings, it's just an uncomplicated way to take an inventory of all you can give to a career or job and determine everything you want in return.

Don't put your feet up just yet. Just because it's easy to follow doesn't mean you don't have work ahead of you. But if you're ready for a straightforward and realistic approach to finally take career action, this is it.

1

Getting Started—Ready, Set, Go

Jason is a thirty-year-old working professional.* His dad's birthday is tomorrow and Jason, total slacker that he is, hasn't bought him a gift yet. His time is limited so he heads over to the local mall on his lunch hour. He wants to get a great gift but he has no idea what to buy. He hasn't talked to his sister to see what she is buying, he hasn't called his mom to ask for suggestions, and he hasn't done any online research for any ideas. Like many men, Jason dreads shopping, so he's not familiar with the shops in the mall. When he gets there, he walks in and starts wandering. He assumes he knows his dad well enough to find something he will like. Jason rambles from store to store looking for the perfect gift.

Time passes quickly and before Jason knows it, he has ten minutes left on his lunch hour and no gift. Finding himself in the department store, he settles for a shirt and tie. He pays quickly and walks out disappointed. He has a gift that he knows his dad will use, but it's not what he wanted. He also knows he didn't get to half the stores in the mall.

There is a way Jason could have made his search for a present much easier. You know those mall directories that have those big "You Are Here" signs on them? Had Jason thought to consult one, he could have figured out where he was in the mall and what choices were nearby. Or he could have looked at all the options, gotten a gift idea or two, and then determined the quickest route to his destination. Jason probably didn't have to settle.

This story isn't about a man's unfamiliarity with the mall. It's about knowing what you're looking for (in this case a gift) but not knowing exactly where

---

*Anecdote courtesy of Karen Weist, associate director of the Career Management Center for the Owen Graduate School of Management at Vanderbilt University.

you're going or how to get there. You can't merely say you need a gift and expect to find the perfect one. You have to research what the recipient might like, look at your store options, and make a plan for the time you have available. In the same way you can't say you need a job and expect to land the perfect one. You have to examine your options, make a plan to narrow them down, and find the right one.

Ready . . .

The Right Job, Right Now involves hard work, commitment, and action. There's no such thing as a silver bullet that will deliver your dream job after you read a few hundred pages. If you are truly frustrated with your career and willing to take action, you *will* get results!

The source of career frustration can be any number of annoyances or difficulties. For Brandon, it's that jerk of a boss who makes waking up every morning equivalent to a trip to the dentist. For Julia, the only passion at work is on the afternoon soap opera video streaming to her computer daily. For Kristine, it's the nature of the work she has to do—the cubicles around her are filled with intelligent, mutually respectful colleagues, but she'd rather socialize by the water cooler than make another cold call to yet another prospective client.

Complaining to anyone who will listen doesn't help. Your mom doesn't really understand what you do. "What exactly do you consult on, dear?" Your friends are about to start a collection to send you to a therapist (or maybe a *new* therapist), and when you talk about your job dissatisfaction your spouse looks at you with a blank stare that says, "I look like I'm listening but, really, I'm drowning you out."

Perhaps you're about to begin your career and afraid to graduate because you can't imagine finding a job you love. Maybe you've moved from one job to another trying to compensate for a bad boss or boring work assignments. Or you stay in the same lackluster position thinking it can't get any better or that you shouldn't cheat on faithful stability. Regardless of the reason, you are probably thinking career perfection is unattainable, that it doesn't exist. Keep in mind, however, that career perfection isn't about rising to the top of the corporate ladder or getting it all (whatever that means). It's about defining and getting what *you* want the most. And that is definitely attainable.

You may want a boss who is a true mentor, four weeks of vacation, and a clear path for growth. Your colleague may want a flexible schedule, domestic-partner benefits, and that next plum client assignment. Hmm, now that you're thinking about it, that flexible schedule sounds great, but the travel that comes with the star client assignment isn't worth it. Everyone has different choices and options. This is where the kaleidoscope comes in.

Kaleidoscopes are instruments of art. When you pick up a kaleidoscope, you're the artist in control of that set of colors. The *slightest* turn produces a new pattern, until you settle on one that pleases your eye.

A career can be thought of in the same way; certain shapes and colors (that is, skills and rewards) create a pattern unique to the individual. No two career paths are identical. I'm going to ask you to create your own career kaleidoscope that will lead you to your perfect career. You don't have to be an artist by nature to make this work. You just need to know how to be creative with your kaleidoscope and make the best choices.

Set . . .

Before we begin, there are six rules you need to follow.

One: Honesty Reigns

Honesty is essential at all times. In order to create the Career Kaleidoscope that's the best reflection of yourself, you have to be perfectly honest. Honest with yourself, your partner, your spouse, your family, and your dog. Well, maybe not the dog, but you get the picture. What you *think* should be important, is irrelevant. It's what really matters to you that matters most. This is no time to beat around the bush. If you can't be honest, you can't play.

Two: Determine Who Else Gets to Play

Art is very personal and you're about to build what might be one of your most personal creations. Is it *your* career? Sure. Does it have an effect on everyone else around you? Absolutely. If you're in a committed relationship, you have to take that into consideration. Remember, you already agreed to be honest and you need to extend this honesty into a very candid conversation with your partner about your career.

You may think you already know what role a career plays in your life, but what happens if and when you have kids? What if you change your mind about wanting to travel extensively for work? While you have to take charge and create the Career Kaleidoscope, you also need to share it with the people in your life who should have a say in how your job affects them. Should you ask your mom's permission before taking a job with an extensive travel schedule? Probably not. But if she's sick or elderly and requires your care, you should consider these factors and have a conversation with her and any other family members who are involved. Bottom line: Be prepared to involve others as you make your career decisions.

Three: In the End, It's Your Choice

You can do all the research you want, talk to family members, mentors, specialists in your field or industry, but at the end of the day, each decision about your career is yours to make. Sure you'll make sacrifices in deference to others in your life. But you have to be the one to decide to make that sacrifice or you'll be miserable.

Four: Getting It Down on Paper

The biggest mistake most people make with their career strategy is keeping it all in their heads. If you were assigned to manage a project at work, what is the first thing you'd do? You'd create a plan. On paper. Keeping your career preferences and choices in your head makes it nearly impossible to compare your options and make good decisions. Imagine going into a project-update meeting at work without any evidence of what you've accomplished. If you work for yourself, you could get away with it, but it won't fly anywhere else. You've got to sit down and commit the same effort and attention to your career strategy as you would to a project at work.

Five: Be Prepared to Do Some Work

Although creating your Career Kaleidoscope is logical and straightforward, you've got work to do throughout the process. The level of effort you apply is up to you. Think about the relationships in your life. The more energy and effort you put into making them work, the more you get out of them. The same goes for your career strategy.

If you put the work in *now* to create your Career Kaleidoscope and your strategy, you'll save yourself a great deal of time, energy, and effort *later* that comes from job hopping, staying in a job you don't like, or through overall career frustration.

Six: There's No Obvious Answer

Unfortunately we live in a world in which people sometimes think "What's the right thing to do?" or "My parents really wanted me to become a doctor" or "I wasn't supposed to become a teacher." If you want to find the perfect career for you, you've got to throw those notions out the window and think for yourself. If you want a job that pays a high salary—indulge your want. If you're not interested in taking over the family business, say so. You have to be prepared to choose what you want without worrying what you should do or what's expected of you. Will you have to make sacrifices and work long hours to earn that high salary? Perhaps. Will it be hard to tell your dad you don't want to run the store? Sure. But a good career strategy requires making the tough choices.

Go!

Now that the rules are established, we're ready to go. The first step is to create the base of the kaleidoscope itself. Let's get in the mindset of values and boundaries. Married? Think about the one trait in your spouse or partner that you know your lifetime mate had to have. Or, think about your favorite food. "I absolutely can't have steak unless I have _____ with it." Before creating any career strategy or plan, it is important to determine any must-haves or any absolutes. This involves defining your values and setting your boundaries.

For example, if a family situation has you attached to a specific geographic area, take that into account before wasting time exploring opportunities across the country. If you know your career will never be your first priority, create that as a boundary and explore opportunities that match this decision. Remember, no one's judging you. It doesn't matter whether your dad thinks your career should be your first priority. It's whether *you* do. This first step might be the hardest because it might be the first time in your life that you think about your career in your own terms. You may have to consider your spouse or other family member's feelings later, but for now think first about what you want.

Hold Your Horses

Some career experts tell you to plan first and then act. Others tell you to act first, trying on different personas and jobs to see what you like. *The Right Job, Right Now* combines these options. Remember, there is no silver bullet and only you can determine what will work best for you. If you're an executive in mid-career, with enough time and money to live on while you experiment with your options, trying on different identities is ideal, but you have to be honest with yourself about how much time and effort is realistic and available (are those your kids screaming in the background?). On the other hand, if you're a new professional, fresh out of college, you may not want to waste those crucial, early years on "trying on" different career options. Imagine for a

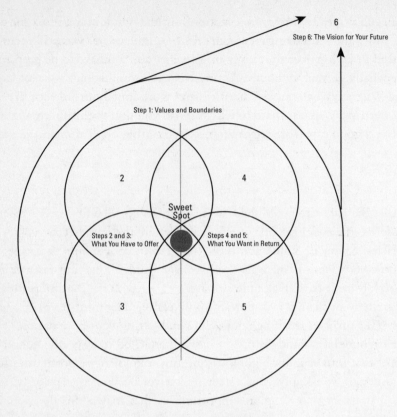

6

Step 6: The Vision for Your Future

Step 1: Values and Boundaries

2

4

Sweet
Spot

Steps 2 and 3:
What You Have to Offer

Steps 4 and 5:
What You Want in Return

3

5

THE CAREER KALEIDOSCOPE

moment that you found the best-fit career the first time you tried it on for size. Your career would grow and advance that much more quickly. However, it's never too late to find the right job. Never.

First, you're going to create some boundaries. Using your life preferences, you're going to narrow down your options and create some parameters. The world may be your oyster, but let's rule out the obvious first, shall we?

You're going to have to figure out what matters to you in your life, what skills you have, what kind of environment you like to work in, and where you see yourself—as a subject matter expert or a manager? Don't stop in the middle. If you really want to make this work, go through each of the following six steps and take them seriously. This is your life, your career. If you don't take it seriously, no one else will.

To start, you'll be completing your own Career Kaleidoscope by tackling each of the steps one at a time. In Step 1 you define your values and boundaries. This will help determine what role you want your career to play in your life right now, along with the absolutes—the factors that have to be present for you to even begin to think about the type of career or job you will accept. In Steps 2 and 3, you'll focus on what you have to offer. What do you have to offer a potential employer and how well can you articulate your strengths and how you actually want to use them? In Steps 4 and 5, you'll decide on what you want in return. For all of the blood, sweat, and tears that go into your daily work, how do you want to be rewarded and in what type of environment? In Step 6, you will focus on where you want to see your career headed. What is your vision?

The information derived from these steps will lead you to the center of the Kaleidoscope—or what I call your career "sweet spot." Think of the sweet spot as the "right job." It combines all of the most important elements of a job. You can't have everything you want, but you can have what matters most.

As you go through Part One and create your Career Kaleidoscope, keep in mind that nothing is set in stone. This is where the "right now" part comes in. As your life changes, as your commitments change, so will your career. Think about what you want right now as you create the Kaleidoscope and as your life changes, go back and revisit the Kaleidoscope. This flexible career tool can be used again and again as your desires, needs, and circumstances evolve.

Step 1: Creating the Base of Your Career Kaleidoscope

The first step is to create a base for your Kaleidoscope that is built on your values and boundaries. Your values are the things that matter most to you in your life and can't be placed on a back burner for the sake of your career. They will certainly have an impact on the choices you make about your job. Boundaries are absolutes that define where and how you are willing to do a job.

To effectively work the system, it's important to start putting pen to paper. Even if you're married to your laptop, get a spiral notebook you can use for all of your initial thoughts. You'll use a computer for the majority of the process, but you can't always pull out your laptop at a moment's notice when inspiration strikes. Write "Career" on the cover and keep it with you—at work, home, travel, wherever.

I'd like to introduce you to Bill McCarrick who is frustrated with his current employment and is starting the process of rethinking his career. Bill is a marketing professional in the healthcare industry. He has an undergraduate degree in science and spent two years as a staff scientist at a large pharmaceutical company before realizing he didn't want to be stuck in a lab for the rest of his life. He liked business and was given the opportunity to move into pharmaceutical sales on a trial basis and prove himself. He did well in sales and spent five years traveling to many doctors' offices, and he made excellent money doing so by exceeding his sales targets. The travel got tiring and frustrating for his family, so Bill moved into the corporate marketing department at the same pharmaceutical firm. He spent two years there before leaving because his boss was unbearable. Now, Bill has the same kind of position at a different healthcare company. He isn't happy but isn't sure why.

Why is Bill's story relevant? You might be in the same boat as he. Bill is completely frustrated at work, and has been for several years. He does his job well, but doesn't like it and hasn't advanced in the past year because his heart just isn't in it. He has decided he needs to start a career search from scratch.

> **ACTION:** Open to the first page of your notebook and write "What Matters to Me Is:" at the top of the page.

Under "What Matters to Me Is," list all the things in life that matter most to you including family, hobbies, and beliefs. Your list might look something like Bill's:

What Matters to Me Is:

1. Having a job I like and feel valued at
2. My wife and her happiness
3. Kids
4. Taking care of my parents
5. Having a stable job
6. Doing home projects
7. Bicycling
8. Ability to relax, take vacations, and enjoy life
9. Working to become financially independent by 55

Bill has a number of things that matter to him—many of which may be important to you as well. There are also items on his list that may be completely different than yours. For example, recognizing that his kids are important to him may cause Bill to make certain choices. If you don't have kids, or don't want to have kids, you might make different choices.

The idea is to get your list on paper so you can define your values and boundaries based on what matters most—to you. For Bill, it's clear that his family matters, as well as his personal interests (bicycling, home projects). He has expressed a desire to contribute financially to his family, and to commit to planning for his

> **Good to Know:**
>
> Step One may take several days and several conversations with key people in your life. Take the time to think through and clearly define your values and boundaries. While they may evolve and change, you'll want to work from what matters most now, knowing that this may change in the future.

long-term financial independence. For some people, money isn't an issue—they can adapt their lifestyle to the amount of money coming in the door. Bill has a long-term goal of being financially free, which may mean sacrifice in other areas.

If what matters to you doesn't inspire much of a list, answer the question: "I am happiest when I am _____." That should help round out your list.

ACTION: Define what you value and your boundaries.

Using the list you've created, think about what the items mean. What are the larger beliefs and guiding principles in your life? What matters most to you? This will help you begin to determine the things you value.

In preparing his list, Bill took his wife into consideration. She is currently working full-time in an industry that isn't popular in many cities. Bill and his wife have had several candid conversations and agree that a relocation is not an option for at least another five years.

Bill uses these aspects of his life to begin to create his career strategy. Determining what you value helps to prioritize and gain clarity on what will be important to you as you advance your career.

What *you* value may include:

- **Recognition:** "I value being recognized for my achievements and successes."
- **Family:** "I value the ability to spend a significant amount of time with my family."
- **Monetary rewards:** "I value being paid well in return for my hard work and commitment."
- **Security:** "I value knowing that things are stable and will be so for the long term."

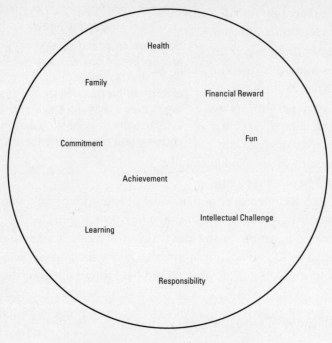

BILL'S VALUES AND BOUNDARIES: DRAFT

If you look at the list of suggested values on the next page, you may think that everything on it is important to you. And that may be true. But go back to your list: "What matters to me?" The items you listed probably represent your most important values. Remember, this exercise should reflect what matters most to you. You can't have it all, so you want to make sure you consider what is most important.

Create a circle to serve as the base of your kaleidoscope and put the things that you value inside the circle. In Bill's circle, he took into account his commitment to taking care of his parents (who are both elderly). When Bill started thinking about how important it was that he take care of his parents as long as they needed him, it reminded him how much he values following through on that commitment. Likewise, Bill thought more about what having a job he likes and feels valued at meant to him. He used the values list to help him describe such a job and included learning, intellectual challenge, and achievement as things he values and as things that are important to him not only at work, but in his life as a whole. Finally, his commitment to become financially independent is exhibited through valuing financial reward.

Other things commonly valued include:

- **Family:** wanting to ensure time with family, making family a priority above all other things
- **Promotion:** anticipating advancement, the opportunity to move up in an organization or in your career
- **Altruism:** helping others, making a difference in the world
- **Belonging:** feeling welcome or a sense of belonging, knowing you are needed
- **Intellect:** being challenged intellectually, academically, or cognitively
- **Socialization:** being around others, the ability to socialize
- **Money:** wanting to receive monetary reward in return for work; financial stability, wealth
- **Commitment:** staying with an organization or group for a long time, a sense of loyalty

Once you have determined what you value you need to define your boundaries. What are the limitations you are willing to work within, and what are the deal breakers? Think about the must-haves and the absolutes for your career or a job. For example, your boundaries or deal breakers might include:

- **Location:** limiting a search to a specific geographic region
- **Ethics:** not considering companies that sell products or offer services that conflict with your religious, political, or personal beliefs (i.e., working for a tobacco company)
- **Time:** amount of time you have to find a new job
- **Job requirements:** not exploring careers that require more education (i.e., because you can't afford the time or money it would take to attain that level of education)

When Bill thought about when he is happiest, he immediately recalled the time he spends with his wife and kids, and the stability, especially financial, he has worked so hard to achieve. Bill also knew there was a geographic boundary. But other than that, there were few other limitations to his search. Bill took these three limitations as his boundaries: family, stability, and geography. He then compared them to the first draft of his circle (page 12), looked for patterns, and narrowed down the things he values and his boundaries to four key areas. Now, as he makes career decisions, he can always ask himself "How does this affect the base of my Career Kaleidoscope?" Serving as the base of his Kaleidoscope, these elements represent the building blocks of his life and ensure that what matters most to him will always remain front and center as he considers any career move.

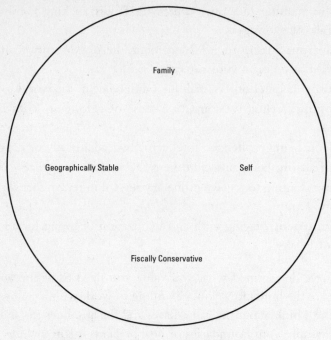

BILL'S VALUES AND BOUNDARIES: FINAL

Now it's your turn. Compare the things you value with any boundaries or limitations you have set and look for patterns. For example, Bill used "geographically stable" to combine his limitation of only being able to look for a job in his current location with the fact that he values stability.

If you take away the base of a kaleidoscope, the colors aren't reflected and the instrument doesn't work. If you remove a key component from the base of your Career Kaleidoscope, it has the same effect. What does your base look like? Let's recap:

1. List the things that matter most
2. Use your list to define the things you value
3. Draw your circle and put the things you value in the circle
4. Determine any boundaries or limitations
5. Compare the boundaries to the things you value
6. Look for patterns, finalize your values

Remember, before you can think about a career strategy you have to make sure you haven't overlooked the major priorities of your life. This step may be the easiest, but may also be the most important. The things that matter most are

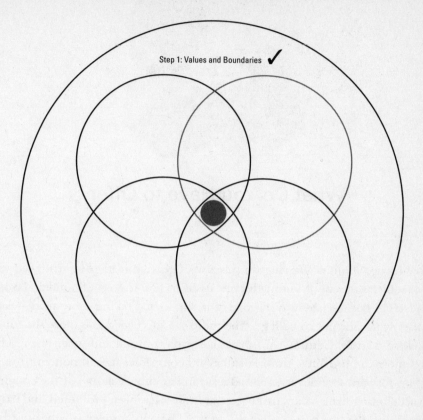

Step 1: Values and Boundaries ✓

often the easiest to ignore. The values and boundaries that create the base of your Kaleidoscope are there for a reason—so you never forget what's most important to you. Whether they include your beloved spouse or your beloved Mercedes, they're your personal priorities and no one's judging them. As you create your Kaleidoscope the things you value and boundaries you define will be reflected in every choice you make. If you look down at the page in front of you, your values and boundaries should be done, and the base of your Career Kaleidoscope and Step 1 are completed.

2

What Do You Have to Offer?

Growing up, Shondra Warrington was always good at math. She struggled with other subjects in school, but math came easily to her. It wasn't Shondra's favorite subject, but because she was so good at it, she started taking more math-related courses when she got to college. The more she succeeded, the more she sought out these courses. Getting "As" made her parents proud and when she reached her senior year, recruiters from Fortune 500 companies started noticing, too.

Fast-forward several years. Shondra sits in her cubicle at one of the country's top accounting firms. She's making great money, has been promoted, and has already passed the first part of the CPA exam. The only problem is, on some days, if she has to look at one more company income statement, she feels like she'll scream. She's really good at accounting, but she doesn't want to do it for the rest of her life.

Sound familiar? Maybe you're in a job where you're performing well, but you just don't like it. Maybe you know you're very good at giving presentations but never have a chance to do it. Perhaps you work by yourself all day and crave interaction with your co-workers. However, you don't want to (or can't) give up working completely—you know you want some sort of career.

Considerations of easy wealth and laziness aside, you need to explore what you're capable of doing well and what you actually like to do. You've already thought about the role a career plays in your life. Now it's time to think about what role you'll play in a career.

Think about the last major purchase you made. Let's use a car as an example. When you decide to buy a car, you're buying it for one major reason—you need transportation. Apart from that basic requirement, there are certain things you need from the vehicle, depending on your style, interests, and budget. If you're the outdoorsy type, you might want a roof rack so you can haul your skis or your bike. If you have enough kids to field your own basketball team you probably need a vehicle with enough space to hold them all.

As the buyer, you usually have a list of characteristics you're looking for in a product and you tend to focus on only those products that meet your needs. On the flip side, car companies have departments full of people who are responsible for getting you to notice their cars. That's why those minivan commercials feature lots of happy kids streaming out of the easy-open doors, and why luxury car commercials showcase their fancy features and well-appointed interiors. Marketing experts are product focused. They know what their audience is looking for and then they promote the features that matter most to that audience.

In order to find the job that's right for you, it's important to get into a product mindset. In this chapter, you're going to determine what qualities you have and what qualities you want to sell. If you have no idea what kind of career or job would be a good fit for you, this chapter is especially important. However, even if you have a good plan for what your next career step is, you can't sell yourself to an employer or a company until you know exactly what it is you are selling.

You probably don't have to think too hard to come up with a few things you are good at. You can probably even rattle them off at will. However, it's unlikely that you have ever taken a complete inventory of your skills. But that's what you're about to do and you're going to write them down. No job or career will use every single one of your skills or abilities. But just as a car company might do with its newest model, you've got to take a complete inventory of all of your features to determine which are the best combinations for you and for your audience.

Cars may have a wide range of features but in this exercise we're going to focus on two specific features: skills and behaviors.

Step 2: Define Your Skills

If asked what you know how to do, you respond with a random assortment of answers: cook dinner, sing karaoke, change a tire, or change a diaper. The list could be endless. We want to narrow the list down to all of the things you can do well in a professional setting. While you might be the pie-eating champion in your hometown, unless you think you might make a career out of it, it won't be a skill to focus on here. This is Step 2 of the Career Kaleidoscope.

While making a list of skills may seem elementary, think about it in business terms. It's essentially resource identification. You don't know what you have to

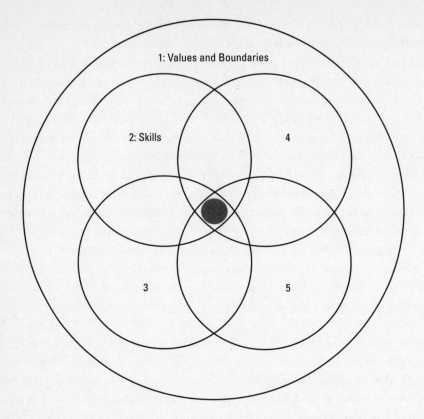

put into a project until you assess all the resources. Putting your skills on paper allows you to see a complete picture of what you are capable of, and more important, what you aren't. One of the biggest mistakes many people make in this process is to apply for jobs they aren't qualified for. Others might be qualified but have resumés that focus on skills not required for that particular role. The goal here is to take an inventory of all your skills so you can decide not only which ones you want to use the most, but to make a better match between what you have to offer to careers that might be of interest as well as to determine what additional skills you might need to attain in order to get the job you want.

ACTION: Make a list of your skills.

Get out your notebook and prepare to start writing. The first step is to make a list of your skills. These are all the things you can do that you think would be valuable in workplace. To give you an example: take a look at this job description from a sales posting:

RESPONSIBILITIES

1. Meet or exceed all sales and revenue targets for your territory
2. Analyze markets for new business opportunities in the firm
3. Develop new customers
4. Represent clients at trade shows, seminars, and industry events
5. Effectively manage a sales territory/geography as assigned
6. Provide management with detailed analyses, sales strategies, and recommendations for your territory
7. Ability to formulate and present detailed major client presentations

REQUIREMENTS

1. Preferred degree in technology, business, marketing, finance, or related field; M.B.A. a plus
2. Strong demonstrated ability in written and oral communication
3. 8+ years outside selling experience
4. A proven track record of success as compared to your peers
5. Strong computer, technology, and database skills
6. Experience in selling software solutions to upper-level management contacts (i.e., heads of marketing or sales) at Fortune 500 or 1000 companies
7. Experience negotiating contracts and agreements

There's a great deal of information in this job description about what the company is looking for in a successful candidate. Skills can be extrapolated from the posting:

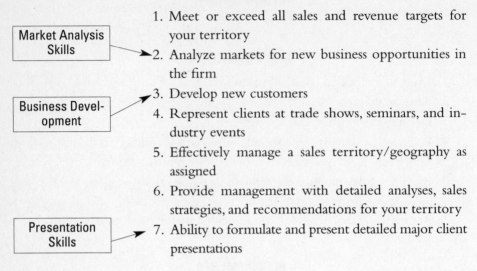

RESPONSIBILITIES

Market Analysis Skills

Business Development

Presentation Skills

1. Meet or exceed all sales and revenue targets for your territory
2. Analyze markets for new business opportunities in the firm
3. Develop new customers
4. Represent clients at trade shows, seminars, and industry events
5. Effectively manage a sales territory/geography as assigned
6. Provide management with detailed analyses, sales strategies, and recommendations for your territory
7. Ability to formulate and present detailed major client presentations

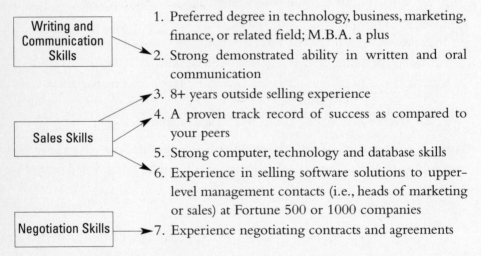

REQUIREMENTS

Writing and Communication Skills

Sales Skills

Negotiation Skills

1. Preferred degree in technology, business, marketing, finance, or related field; M.B.A. a plus
2. Strong demonstrated ability in written and oral communication
3. 8+ years outside selling experience
4. A proven track record of success as compared to your peers
5. Strong computer, technology and database skills
6. Experience in selling software solutions to upper-level management contacts (i.e., heads of marketing or sales) at Fortune 500 or 1000 companies
7. Experience negotiating contracts and agreements

Because it may seem daunting to start from scratch in making a list of your skills, look at your current job description, or descriptions of other jobs in your field as well as in previous areas in which you've worked. At this point it doesn't matter what you want to do, or even that you know you don't want to do what you're currently doing. Examining these job descriptions will only help to spur your thinking.

For an example, let's use Bill from Chapter 1. Bill studied science in school, spent a few years in a lab, then moved into sales, and is currently in marketing. Bill doesn't want to go back to working in science, and he certainly doesn't want to go back to working in sales. He likes marketing, but isn't sure he wants to stay in the healthcare industry. At this point it doesn't matter because Bill needs to take an inventory of his skills to see what he has to offer as an employee.

Good to Know:

If you're stuck on how to make a list of your skills, try these sources to help you with your list:

1) Job descriptions from your current job/previous jobs you held/jobs you are interested in;
2) Job descriptions from positions similar to ones you've held (use online job search sites to locate samples in your area of interest);
3) Old performance reviews;
4) Association Web sites in your area of interest (see Appendix A).

To get started, Bill looks through his files to find copies of old job descriptions or performance reviews so he can begin to create a list. He lists the major skills he has developed from all of the different work experiences in his career thus far.

Bill McCarrick: Skills List

1. **Sales**
2. **Science**
3. **Account management**
4. **Marketing**
5. **Presentations**
6. **Research**
7. **Data analysis**
8. **Lab experiments**

This list, however impressive it may be, is only a start. Now it's time to break down the skill areas into more specific areas of expertise.

For example, Bill starts with the first skill on his list, sales. Bill knows he is good at selling, but this can also involve prospecting, finding new customers, negotiation, or deciding with the customer what the price will be. Sales also involves account management—keeping customers happy so they will buy from you again.

Bill McCarrick: Skill Breakdown

1. **Sales Skills**
   a) **Prospecting**
   b) **Relationship development**
   c) **Customer education**
   d) **Negotiation**
   e) **Closing the deal**
   f) **Account management**

By taking one skill, sales, and breaking it down into even more specific skill areas, Bill can better communicate what, specifically, he can do. Let's say you are hiring a new salesperson for your company. One candidate says, "You should hire me because I am really good at sales." The second candidate says "I am really good at sales, specifically at prospecting and account management, which I know are both very important for this position because your company is trying to break into the market." Which candidate are you going to be more interested in?

Being specific is important because for every job opening that exists, there are many, many qualified people to fill the position. Companies have to find a way to sort through the candidates and decide who is best for the job. Shondra is the accountant who doesn't really want to be an accountant anymore. Here's what the breakdown of one of Shondra's skills looks like:

Shondra Warrington: Skill Breakdown

1. **Quantitative skills**
   a) **Financial statement preparation and evaluation**
   b) **Financial recommendations**
   c) **Data gathering**
   d) **Numerical calculations**
   e) **Journal and ledger entries**

You may find that it is difficult to break down your skills like Bill and Shondra did, and when you do, you may also find that you may not be as strong in some areas as you are at others. For example, when Bill thinks about his sales expertise, he can specify six specific skill areas. But he is most adept at prospecting and account management so he places those at the top of his list. Similarly, Shondra lists financial statement preparation and evaluation, and financial recommendations as her top skills.

Try to organize your skills and skill breakdowns by how strong they are and how much you actually want to use them. This will help you later because it will give you a good sense of the depth of your skills. It's also important to eliminate skills that you don't want to use at all. Shondra likes the quantitative part of her job but simply does *not* want to do accounting. She can make sure she doesn't fall into the trap of taking another accounting position she doesn't want by not focusing on promoting her accounting skills (journal and ledger entries).

ACTION: Break down each of your skills into specific areas, listing those that are strongest first and eliminating those that you don't want to use at all.

Now it's time to use your trusty computer. Just as you would approach a project at the office, you need to treat your job search similarly. Everyone has different organizational skills. Your office may look like a desert island, or one that's just been hit by a tornado. Either way, there is some sort of system you use to organize your papers, your files, and your thoughts. Now is the time to create a system that works with your particular organizational style to track the information you are developing about yourself and your future job.

Depending on the extent of your computer skills, you may want to use a word-processing program such as Microsoft Word or WordPerfect. If you have any familiarity with a program like Microsoft Excel, I recommend it highly because Excel allows you to list your skills in columns and then reorder and reorganize them as you go through the Career Kaleidoscope process.

ACTION: Transfer your lists of the things you value, your skills, and your skills breakdown to an electronic format.

You should go ahead and transfer your lists of values, skills, and skills breakdown to Excel or another software program. Each step in the process will have its own column. Put the things you value in one column and your skills in another. In the skill column, leave room for your skill breakdowns, too.

Bill's electronic worksheet looks like this:

Bill McCarrick: Skill Breakdown

Skill	Rank	Breakdown
Sales	1	Prospecting
		Relationship development
		Customer education
		Negotiation
		Closing the deal
		Relationship management
Account management	2	
Marketing	3	
Presentations	4	
Research	5	
Data analysis	6	

Major Area Skills (label pointing to Sales)

Skill Breakdown (label pointing to Breakdown column)

By using Excel, Bill can rank his list of skills, break them down further, or omit skills he doesn't want to include. Using Excel allows Bill to get everything down on paper, and better organize his thoughts. Whether you choose Excel or another program, the important part is that the work you are doing is now beginning to look like a project—perhaps one of the most important projects you have ever undertaken.

The list of things you value, your skills, and skills breakdown that are now in an electronic format is your working project plan that will help you create your final Career Kaleidoscope. You should use an electronic format as you work on your Career Kaleidoscope. Bill uses the electronic file as a place to store his information and can easily refine it as needed. Later he transfers his final list for each step to paper, to complete his Career Kaleidoscope. For blank Career Kaleidoscope templates you can print out, and for technology guidance, visit www.therightjobrightnow.com.

For Bill's kaleidoscope at this point, see page 25.

You've probably noticed that Bill did not include skills related to science. While he may want to return to science or healthcare in the future, he knows that for now he would like to be part of a different industry. He will focus on the strength of his other skills. Will he ignore his science and healthcare industry experience altogether? Not at all. He simply won't promote it because he doesn't want to run the risk of pigeonholing himself in that area.

His experience in science and healthcare may be valued by a company in a completely different industry, but unless he is selling himself to a company that

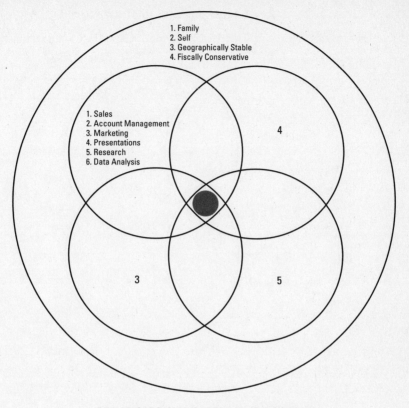

1. Family
2. Self
3. Geographically Stable
4. Fiscally Conservative

1. Sales
2. Account Management
3. Marketing
4. Presentations
5. Research
6. Data Analysis

4

3

5

BILL McCARRICK'S CAREER KALEIDOSCOPE

primarily values those skills, he shouldn't emphasize them. Think about your-self as a product and what you have to sell. We'll work on how you do it later.

Step 3: Determine Your Behaviors

Picture it: You're sitting in an interview for your dream job and the interviewer asks you that million-dollar question: "Why should we hire you?" It seems like a fair question and one which you should be able to answer quickly and easily. The reality is that while we think we know ourselves really well, when it comes to bragging most of us are not that good at it.

Not that we can't brag—we do it all the time. We brag about our last vaca-tion, a favorite sports team, or our latest electronic gadget. But it's more diffi-cult to brag about ourselves, especially when it comes to what we can do well.

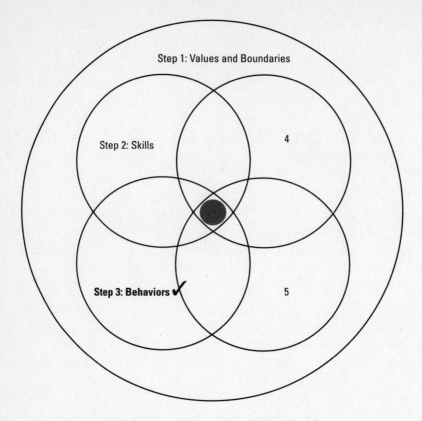

If you're at a party and everyone is bragging about how fantastic their last vacation was, the logical question to ask, to decide who really had the best vacation, is "What made your trip so great?" You're going to do the same thing with your skills and explain why you are extraordinary in that area.

So although you may be great at giving presentations, and that's something a specific job entails, you'd assume that all you have to do is say so. Not exactly. The problem is that anyone you are competing against for the job most likely will have the same skill. If you're a recruiter and every resumé you read showcases the same skills, or every candidate tells you how good they are at giving presentations, how do you decide who to invite to continue in the process, and ultimately who to hire?

The answer lies in your particular *why* (why you are good at a certain skill) and *how* (how you behave). This is the "behaviors" aspect of the Career Kaleidoscope.

Behaviors are simply the way you act—what sets you apart from others who have similar skills. If skills are the nouns, the things you can do well, behaviors are the adjectives.

Kevin is very good at presentations. So is Kim. Both have extensive public speaking experience and have been giving client presentations for years. They both have the same skill (giving presentations). You're looking to hire someone who will be responsible for giving a number of company presentations. How do you decide who would give a better presentation? You have to understand why the candidates, Kevin and Kim, are good at it.

Let's start with Kevin. He is very organized and spends a great deal of time preparing for a presentation to make sure every step is completed and that the presentation will be flawless. Kim, on the other hand, is very flexible. She comes to a presentation with a basic set of ideas, but adjusts her presentation based on her audience. She can decide mid-course to focus on a different aspect of the topic, or change the direction of the presentation if the audience so requests.

Both are good presenters but for very different reasons. Kevin is an organized presenter and Kim is a flexible presenter. When you hear Kevin and Kim provide details on why they are good at what they do, you can choose the person who will not only be able to perform the skill, but can perform it in a way that will be most successful in your company.

While it's true that people can adapt to an organization's needs, ultimately, neither they nor the company will be happy. If Kevin goes in to interview and focuses on how organized he is, and the hiring manager really wants someone who is more spontaneous and flexible, then he probably won't be hired. But if Kevin pretends to be something he is not in order to get the job, will he perform well? Will he be happy giving presentations in a manner that he is not very good at? Of course not. This is why behaviors are so important. You want to be able to use your skills, but you also want to be able to perform them in a way that is comfortable for you.

Think about your signature. If you are right-handed, and you're asked to sign your name, you use your right hand and it's really easy. In fact, you could do it with your eyes closed. But what if you were forced to sign your name with your left hand? If you're right-handed, switching to your left hand is going to be hard. You're using the same skill—signing your name—but it will take you longer, it will feel awkward, and it won't look as good. When you are forced to perform a skill in a way that isn't comfortable or in a way you aren't used to, you won't perform as well and you won't be happy. This might be your career pitfall right now, which is why it is critical to determine your behavioral strengths so you can more effectively focus on how you behave when performing a skill and why you are good at what you do.

Think about the last time you took a vacation with one or more people. Were you the person who had input into organizing or the creative part of the vacation?

Did you decide whether you were headed to the beach or mountains or whether the vacation would be relaxed or touristy? Or were you the person who planned the logistics? Did you compare prices on flights and itineraries so you would have enough time at each destination?

Regardless of your role, there were probably people involved in planning the trip who covered each aspect of it. Without the organizers, the trip might be boring. Without the planners, travelers might find themselves lost in a city or without a place to stay. Projects run more effectively when there is diversity among the behaviors of the people running them. If you know where your behavioral strengths are, you can better define why you are good at something.

ACTION: Make a list of your behaviors.

Go back to the electronic worksheet with your list of skills. You're now going to create a second column titled "behaviors" and begin to list your behaviors. Because this is harder than taking an inventory of your skills, it helps to look at your list of skills and ask yourself why you are good at each one.

Let's return to Bill and take a look at what he did. Using his skill breakdown list from Part B, he asked himself "Why am I good at this?" for each skill.

Bill McCarrick: Skills to Behaviors

Skill	Breakdown	Why?
Sales	Prospecting	I have no fear when cold calling or talking to a potential new client. I will call often and be forward where others might be uncomfortable in doing this.
	Relationship development	I am energized when I meet new people and I like getting to know them and building their trust in me.
	Customer education	I take the time to listen to a client's questions and make sure they understand the complicated technology behind a product.
	Negotiation	I can sense when a client is hesitant or when they are bluffing. I have good instincts about what the customer is thinking.
	Closing the Deal	I understand how important the bottom line is and I don't stop until a deal is closed. I don't give up and will do whatever I can to get a deal made.

Then, Bill used the answers to match a behavior to each skill. Use the sample list below Bill's to help you identify your behaviors.

Bill McCarrick: Behaviors

Skill	Breakdown	Behavior	Why?
Sales	Prospecting	**Aggressive**	I have no fear when cold calling or talking to a potential new client. I will call often and be forward where others might be uncomfortable in doing this.
	Relationship development	**Extroverted**	I am energized when I meet new people and I like getting to know them and building their trust in me.
	Customer education	**Patient**	I take the time to listen to a client's questions and make sure they understand the complicated technology behind a product.
	Negotiation	**Intuitive**	I can sense when a client is hesitant or when they are bluffing. I have good instincts about what the customer is thinking.
	Closing the Deal	**Tenacious**	I understand how important the bottom line is and I don't stop until a deal is closed. I don't give up and will do whatever I can to get a deal made.

Sample Behavioral Strengths

- Adaptive
- Aggressive
- Altruistic
- Articulate
- Attentive to detail
- Committed
- Compliant
- Conceptual
- Confident
- Driven
- Enthusiastic

- Entrepreneurial
- Ethical
- Extroverted
- Flexible
- High-energy
- Independent
- Impactful
- Influential
- Insightful
- Introverted
- Loyal

- Methodical
- Motivated
- Organized
- Patient
- Perceptive
- Perfectionist
- Persuasive
- Powerful
- Procedural
- Process-oriented
- Rational

- Reflective
- Sensitive
- Social

- Spontaneous
- Strategic
- Strong-willed

- Tenacious
- Understanding
- Visionary

Remember, this is not an exhaustive list, but it should start you thinking about how you will describe why you are good at something. It is also important to know that more than one behavior can apply to a skill. For example, you might be a good at data analysis because you are patient and attentive to detail. You make sure nothing is overlooked, and you take the time to get it right. Listing multiple behaviors for a skill is fine. Be careful not to combine too many behaviors; be specific about why you are good at a skill. By asking why you are good at a particular skill you can then define the actual behavior behind the skill.

You will find that many behaviors repeat themselves. Bill found that the reason he was good at customer education (in the breakdown of his sales skills) was that he is patient and takes the time to get things right. As he worked further on this exercise he realized that this behavioral strength applied to other skills as well.

ACTION: Rank your list of behaviors, listing the strongest first and the weakest last.

Once you have a complete list of behaviors, you need to rank them from strongest to weakest. If you have a number of repeated behaviors, eliminate any duplicates. As you look over your list, what stands out most? Think about how you behave most often, not only at work, but also in life situations in general. The idea is to get a sense of how you are most likely to behave in any given situation. Once you have your list in an electronic format, it is time to return to your Career Kaleidoscope and transfer the top five to eight behaviors in Step 3. Look at Bill's Career Kaleidoscope after this step and notice how he has ranked his behaviors from strongest to weakest.

The skills and behaviors sections of the kaleidoscope comprise what you have to offer an employer. When Bill looks at his prioritized lists he notices that his top skill is sales, but his top

Good to Know:

If you are having trouble defining your behaviors, or, are skeptical about the importance of this step, try taking a behavioral assessment like the Meyers-Briggs Type Indicator to better understand why behaviors are important and to get help defining your own behavioral strengths. Visit the Web site of the Center for Applications of Psychological Type at www.capt.org to learn more.

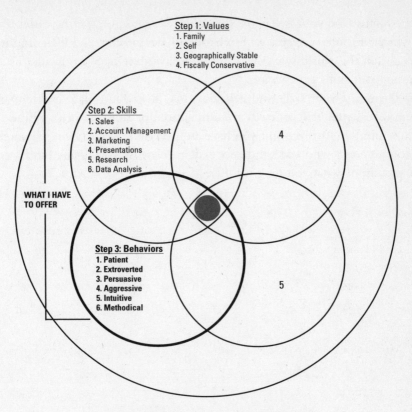

Step 1: Values
1. Family
2. Self
3. Geographically Stable
4. Fiscally Conservative

Step 2: Skills
1. Sales
2. Account Management
3. Marketing
4. Presentations
5. Research
6. Data Analysis

4

**WHAT I HAVE
TO OFFER**

Step 3: Behaviors
1. Patient
2. Extroverted
3. Persuasive
4. Aggressive
5. Intuitive
6. Methodical

5

BILL McCARRICK'S CAREER KALEIDOSCOPE

behavior is patience. While working in pharmaceutical sales, Bill was successful because he was patient with doctors (his clients), answered all their questions, but didn't give up if they didn't buy immediately. When the travel got to be over-whelming, he moved into marketing. He wasn't traveling, but he was forced to make very quick decisions and report to managers he found to be very impa-tient. Because patience is a key behavior for Bill his quick response time and im-patient managers may have been the source of his unhappiness in marketing.

Take a moment to look at the intersection of *your* skills and behaviors. You may have a light bulb go off, like Bill did. Are you using your top skills and be-haviors in your current job? If the answer is no, then you've probably found a major reason that you may be unhappy. If the answer is yes, don't give up on the quest for a job where you can be happy. We'll be exploring more issues that could be the source of your particular job distress.

Regardless of whether or not you have determined one of your career problems, now that you've taken the time to define your skills (remember, these are the nouns) and your behaviors (the adjectives), it's going to be easier to define what jobs intersect best with what you have to offer, and it's going to be easier to tell the world why this is so. You have developed a succinct list that expresses your skills as behaviors.

Determining your skills and behaviors may help you isolate problem areas, help you to better sell yourself in competition, or both. It helps refine your product mindset. At this point you have an important tool to help sell yourself, and to figure out who your audience will be, because you finally have a complete picture of what you have to offer.

3

What Do You Want in Return?

Once you have delineated your skills, the next step is to determine what matters most to you. As you look at your Career Kaleidoscope, you'll notice, on the right side, Steps 4 and 5 have yet to be filled in. The other half of the Career Kaleidoscope answers the question "What do I want in return?" In other words, what things do you expect to receive for your contribution on the job? This isn't just salary and benefits. The type of company and company culture can be an important part of what you get in return. It's up to you to determine their relative importance.

Think back to the last time you were looking for a job. Whether it was a professional position or behind the counter at your local McDonald's, there were benefits. The paychecks, the benefits, and the discounts on burgers were definite perks.

The key is to think about what you want in return for toiling away day in and day out. Whether it is the money, the opportunity to learn, the ability to take on a leadership role, or some combination of these benefits, what matters to one person might not matter to another. What mattered to you when you were younger might not matter to you now.

This may seem easy at first. After all, perks are easily identified and you know what you like. However, it pays to take a closer look. Perks are one thing, but the environment in which they are offered is quite another. Four weeks' vacation may sound great, but if you're working in an industry where vacation is rarely taken, then the benefit isn't so great, is it? It's really time to consider what you want out of the job and the context it's offered in.

First you're going to focus on Step 4 of the Kaleidoscope, the first of two parts comprising "What You Want in Return." Step 4 focuses on the type of environment and culture you want to work in. Then you'll finally get to "name your price" as Step 5 focuses on benefits and monetary rewards.

Step 4: Define Your Environmental and Cultural Factors

Caroline works in human resources (HR). She has experience in recruiting, employee benefits administration, salary planning, and labor relations. Now, about ten years into her HR career, she is the director of HR for a plant of a large automobile manufacturer where she is responsible for the needs, well-being, and development of more than 3,000 employees, and runs the entire HR function for her plant. Despite her successes, she sits at her desk completely annoyed.

For several weeks, Caroline had been receiving complaints about using vacation time from dozens of her employees. Some employees wanted more vacation while others were frustrated about the process to get approval to take vacation. She met with them, conferred with her staff, and came up with what she thought was a perfect solution: paid time-off days with a simplified notification process. But when she went to seek approval from her regional HR vice president, her idea was completely shot down: "It's against company policy, Caroline," said the VP. "If I let you do it, I have to let every director bend the rules for his or her own plant. You have to stick to the company rules."

Caroline thought that being promoted to director would finally give her the opportunity to use her creativity and come up with innovative solutions. Instead she found herself implementing whatever protocols corporate headquarters dictated. She was frustrated and wondered whether she was being too sensitive. Maybe when she got to the VP level, then she would get to be creative and innovative, but maybe not. What Caroline finally realized was that a big, corporate environment just wasn't for her. A year later, Caroline is running HR for a small consulting start-up. She got to develop their HR department from scratch. There were no corporate headquarters, no red tape, no other plants with which to contend. When she has an idea, she pitches it to the executive team and they usually support her implementing it.

As in any situation, there were drawbacks. A start-up doesn't have the stability of her old job. And there was no senior executive to mentor her, nor extensive training and development opportunities for her. Despite these differences, Caroline decided that it was the company size and the autonomy that mattered most to her.

For many people, the environment and culture in which they work are a given. They take the job for what the job is, and for what skills they might be using. But you can do the same job in several different environments and have a radically different experience.

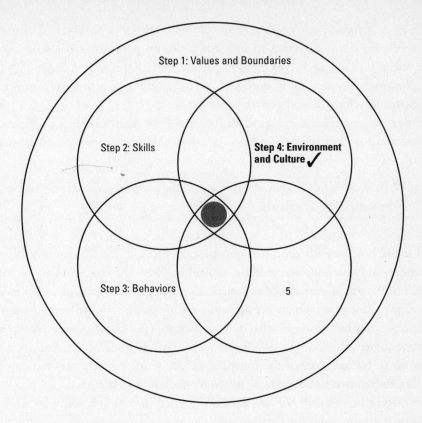

There are two major aspects to life on the job: environment and culture. You might not realize it, but you probably already have a list of preferences regarding these issues. You just may have never written them down.

Environment is the tangible aspect to your job: the physical location in which you work, the title you may carry, and where you fit in the organizational structure. For example, there are many different types of physical places you can work—an office building or a factory, on the road or out of your home. Some people like the regularity of working in a private, closed-door office every day. Others may view that same scenario as being chained to a desk, and prefer a job that has them on the road or out of the office, meeting with clients or customers. Think about what would be the ideal environment in which to work. Where are you? How long did it take you to get there? What is around you? Where are you sitting? Who is near you?

Culture refers to what life is like at a particular organization and includes everything from what your boss is like to the organization's perspective on training and developing employees. If you are working in a new field or industry, it may be very important to you that your company sends you to a certain amount of training each year. Maybe you would rather learn on the job. In this case you may care less about going to sponsored training and more about how experienced your managers or mentors are.

Together, environment and culture comprise the organizational, professional, and personal factors that matter most to you to get in return for your hard work.

> ACTION: Make a list of your environmental and cultural preferences, ranking them from most important to least important.

Go back to the electronic worksheet listing your skills and behaviors. Now it is time to add an additional column and fill in your environmental and cultural preferences, and, as you did with behaviors, rank them. If you get stuck while thinking of the aspects in an organization culture or environment that matter to you, use the list below to get started. As you create your list of environmental and cultural factors, think about how much each item matters to you. You may not care much about the size of the organization you work in, but it may be very important to you that the organization is well-known in its industry.

If you're not sure of the relative importance of a factor you may want to seek advice from friends or colleagues who are or have been in that situation. For example, let's say you are just about to start a family and plan to continue working full-time. When you didn't have children, you weren't worried about whether a company was family-friendly. Maybe now that you will soon have kids, you should care. Or maybe not. Talk to parents who have had different experiences to see what resonates with you.

Sample Environmental and Cultural Factors

Type	Factor	Questions to Ask
Organizational	Size	Is the organization a small start-up, a medium-sized company, or large corporation?
	Structure	Is the structure of the company flat (meaning there are not many layers) or hierarchical?
	Reputation	Is the organization well-known in its industry or field? Does it have a good reputation?

Type	Factor	Questions to Ask
Organizational	Politics	Is the organization political? Do you have to be careful about what you say and when you say it?
	Leadership	Who is running the company? What type of leaders are holding executive positions?
	Product or service	What does the company do? Is it something you care about or you can relate to?
	Workspace	Where do you physically sit in the company? Do you have an office, a cubicle, or no assigned space?
	Colleagues	Who are you working with? Are they social, quiet, collegial?
	Manager(s)	Who are you working for? What is his/her managerial style? How much interaction will you have? How much feedback will you receive?
Professional	Development	What is the opportunity for training and learning? Will the company pay for internal or external training? Is professional development valued by the company?
	Promotion and growth	Where can you move in the company? Is there an opportunity to be promoted? Is there a clear career path?
	Recognition	How will you be recognized at work? Is it important to you to be recognized for your work?
	Challenge	How challenged are you intellectually? Does your job regularly test your brain?
Personal	Work/life balance	How often do you have to work overtime? Do you have enough time to pursue family and personal activities?
	Schedule flexibility	How rigid is your schedule? Can you set your own hours or do you have to be at work at a certain time every day? Can you leave early or come in late if you have a personal commitment?
	Commute	How close is your job to your home? Do you walk, drive, or take public transportation? How long is the commute?
	Travel	How often do you have to travel for your job? How long are you on the road?
	Family friendly	How friendly is the company to family issues? Will they allow you to leave to deal with a family emergency? Do you have flexibility to attend events at your child's school?

Good to Know:

Try making a list of every professional job you have ever had. Make a (+) and (–) column and list every pro and con about each job's environment and culture. Then look over the list for each job and see what matters to you now.

The above list isn't exhaustive, but it will help you generate some ideas. When you think about your environmental and cultural factors, consider the work environments and cultures you have been a part of. What did you like about them? What made you frustrated? The idea is to find the right combination of factors you want on the job. Once you find the ideal combination, when your job search is in progress, you will be able to ask the right questions and make sure the job would give you what you want in return.

Bill McCarrick has thought many times about what cultural and environmental factors matter but has never been able to get the right combination. For example, his sales job was for a very prestigious company, but it required a great deal of travel. On the other hand, when he took a job that didn't require as much travel, it was for a company that wasn't as prestigious. So Bill gave up one factor to gain another. Does that matter? Only if both were high priorities on his list of factors.

Bill's list of factors and rankings appears on page 39. He had a hard time even narrowing it down to nine, since all of the items in the sample list mattered to him to some extent. So he focused on the factors he couldn't live without and what mattered most to him at this point in his career. Remember, if Bill had gone through this exercise earlier in his career, or, before he had a family, the choices and the rankings might have looked much different.

In order to compile this list, one of the first things Bill did was to revisit his list of values (Step 1 of the Kaleidoscope), in which he had listed his family and being careful with his money as important. He also thought through his career history, and what he liked most about the environment and culture of each job he has had. Bill also talked to colleagues who have been in environments he hasn't worked in. The next best thing to experiencing a particular environment is talking to someone who has done so.

You can also look to your list of behaviors for clues about what environments and cultures would best suit you. For example, working in a small company or start-up may sound appealing, but if you are the sort of person who is organized, process oriented, and likes structure, a work environment with few rules, policies, or protocol may prove to be very frustrating. Bill's Career Kaleidoscope is now finished with Step 4: Environmental and Cultural Factors added. It's time to add yours to your Career Kaleidoscope.

Bill McCarrick: Cultural and Environmental Factors

Factor	Rank	What I am looking for
Challenge	1	I have to be challenged intellectually, and I have to make sure there will be continuous challenge in the role.
Travel	2	There has to be less than 20 percent travel.
Structure	3	The organization has to be somewhat flat and not very hierarchical.
Family friendly	4	The organization has to appreciate family concerns, and it would help if my manager(s) and colleagues had families and children of their own. If an organization is family-friendly then I won't mind working longer hours.
Financial reward	5	I have to consider the total compensation package and look at roles that will financially allow me and my family to continue to enjoy the lifestyle we now have.
Size	6	The organization has to be made up of less that 3,000 people, preferably fewer.
Leadership	7	The leaders of the organization have to be passionate visionaries. I want to be able to understand and believe I can support the vision they have laid out.
Manager(s)	8	My manager should be high-energy and committed to the organization, but also be hands-off enough that I can do my job and check in with him when I need help.

When reviewing his list, Bill also realized that some of the factors have changed drastically from the time he first started working. The Career Kaleidoscope is a snapshot of where you are right now. As your life changes, and as your career goals evolve, so will your Kaleidoscope. That's the beauty of this process; it changes as you do.

Caroline is now the HR director at a start-up firm rather than running HR for one plant in a Fortune 500 company. Once Caroline realized that an environmental factor was making her unhappy, she made a drastic change in her job selection and improved her career satisfaction. Clarify where you'd like to work, and the next and perhaps easiest step is to define your ideal benefits and rewards.

Step 5: Benefits and Monetary Rewards

The headline reads STATE LOTTERY TO HIT HIGHEST PAYOFF EVER and you rush to the store to buy lottery tickets in the hope of hitting it big and living in the lap of luxury. If, like me, you've ever pooled your money with family, friends, or co-workers to buy dozens of these tickets you can admit to having the

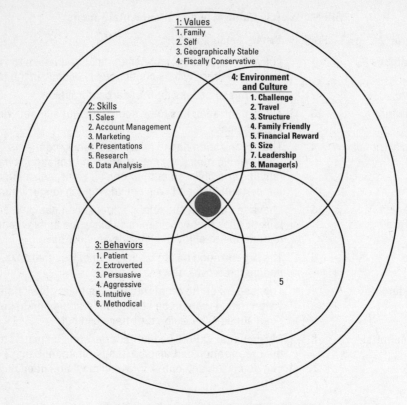

BILL McCARRICK'S CAREER KALEIDOSCOPE

world's most common pipe-dream. Because in a lottery, the odds are stacked against you, chances are that on the job, you care, at least to some extent, about what you get in return for your hard work. It's called a paycheck. It's the fuel that often keeps our fire going. At the end of a bad day you may be sick of the grunt work, but at least you know you're getting paid for it in both benefits and cash compensation.

I go into detail about compensation (salary, bonuses, and so on) in Chapters 13 and 14. For now, we are going to talk about what benefits matter most to you and establish some salary guidelines.

Let's talk about benefits first. While organizations are not required to give you benefits, most do in order to make it more enticing for people to want to work there. Benefits may include health insurance (medical, dental, and/or vision), transportation stipends, on-site childcare, a company car, or domestic-partner benefits. At this point in the process when you are searching for your

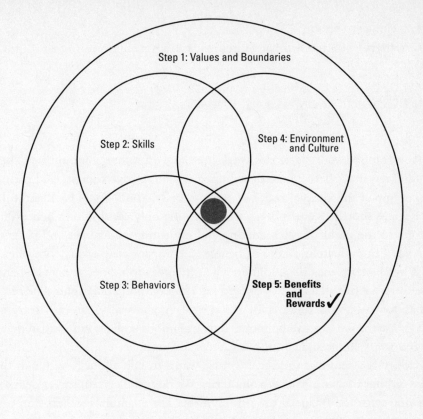

career sweet spot, a long list of tangible benefits isn't important since it won't make a crucial difference in your career. However, you may be in a situation that would require you to have certain benefits in order to take a particular job.

There aren't many absolutes when it comes to benefits. A company car might be nice, but you can always buy one, or take public transportation to work. On the other hand, suppose your spouse doesn't work and your family relies on you for medical coverage. Then, healthcare might be a "must-have" benefit. Bill Mc-Carrick is in a similar situation. His wife works for a very small company that doesn't offer health insurance. Whatever job Bill takes, he has to make sure the organization can offer healthcare coverage for himself and his family.

Other absolutes to consider:

- A medical condition that a company policy must cover
- Domestic-partner benefits

- A childcare option
- A 401(k), 403(b), or other retirement savings plan

ACTION: Determine any "must-have" benefits.

Returning to your electronic worksheet, make another column titled "benefits and rewards." If you have determined any must-have benefits, add them to the column at this time in order of their priority. You'll come back and fill in the rewards shortly. Remember, we are focusing only on absolutes here. When you get to the point of job searching and evaluating companies and potential jobs, you can evaluate the suite of benefits a company may or may not offer.

While benefits may be absolutes, when it comes to money, it may be harder to set limits. After all, no one wants to set a cap on potential, right? The reality is that, for every job, there is an average salary, and every career has average salary growth. We can't all be movie stars or famous athletes but we can decide our monetary limits and adjust our careers accordingly.

Money is a sensitive subject. No one wants to talk about how much they make or offer to take a pay cut voluntarily. We do make certain career decisions knowing what the financial reward might be. For example, teachers don't expect to make $100,000 salaries, and lawyers know that theirs has a higher earning potential than other professions. We all make choices based on what matters most to us.

Debra is a twenty-eight-year-old who has finished her M.B.A. and lives in a large city in the Northeast. She isn't a movie star, but she has just invested heavily in a graduate education. One of Debra's key reasons for attending business school was to increase her earning potential. She wants to advance her career, but she also wants to make a fair amount of money while doing it. Debra knows that in order to make a high salary she may have to work long hours. She also knows that in the city where she is job searching the cost of living is much higher than in most geographic regions. Her salary expectations are going to be higher than someone else who might not have a graduate degree or who lives in a locale where the cost of living is lower.

To refine your job requirements, you're about to set some upper and lower limits on how much salary you can and should expect for the work you do or the work you want to do. Before you set the limits, there are some ground rules:

Rule 1: No one is judging

If you want to make enough money to enable you to live a certain lifestyle, that is your choice. If making a lot of money matters to you, make sure you take that into consideration. You may have to give up other preferences in return (like a forty-hour workweek) but this process will help you determine choices and tradeoffs.

Rule 2: Be honest

If you are already living a life based on a certain income, and want to continue to do so, you can't easily move from being a lawyer to doing nonprofit work. It doesn't mean you can't, it just means there will be some sacrifices. Be honest with yourself—how much are you (and your spouse/partner/family) willing to sacrifice for your career goals?

Rule 3: Don't get ahead of yourself

You may already know how much professionals in your field or industry make at certain levels of experience. But if you're new to the workforce or are interested in making a career change you will have to research salaries for your field of interest. At this point, you're not there yet. Right now you simply want to think about what kind of salary you are willing to accept for a job you love.

Rule 4: Be realistic

We'll talk about career choices later, but be realistic about how much you can expect to make. If you're just out of school, you can't easily expect to make $80,000. If you are really committed to a career change, you might have to take a pay cut. If you can't sing, don't bet on that $1 million recording contract.

Rule 5: Consult with your spouse/partner/family

If you're banking on family support while you switch careers or go back to school, you need to have a candid conversation (if you haven't already) with your spouse/partner about expectations as a family. You want to make sure you are all on the same page about the financial situation.

You need to consider the upper and lower salary limits as well as your "goldilocks" salary—what feels just right. At this point you should think about numbers as including any and all cash compensation (i.e., salary, bonuses, anything that's cash). The three salary figures break down as follows:

Level	Description
Bottom Line	What is the absolute minimum I can earn and still maintain a lifestyle I can live with? What is the lowest I can go without sacrificing things in my life I am not willing to give up?
Acceptable	What is a salary that is "just right"? One that wouldn't be at the high end for those with my experience and skills, but one that I would be satisfied with.
Best Case	What is a salary that would make me excessively happy, but is also realistic for my level of education, skills, and behaviors. What is the most I could logically expect at this point in my career?

When you get to the nuts and bolts of the job search you'll focus on breaking down compensation into multiple components. For now, you just want to get an idea of the ballpark levels of total compensation you wish to achieve.

ACTION: Determine your three salary levels—a bottom line, a happy medium, and a best-case scenario.

Once you have established your three levels add them to your electronic worksheet. Bill added his to the list after careful consideration about how low he was willing to go for the perfect career. With a wife and family to support, he cannot afford to start from scratch with a new career, but he can go a bit below his current salary of $79,000 if he has to, for the right position.

Bill McCarrick: Benefits and Rewards

Benefit/Reward	Detail
Must-have Benefit	Healthcare
Bottom-line Salary	$75,000
Acceptable Salary	$82,000
Ideal Salary	$95,000

Now, having completed Benefits and Monetary Rewards (Step 5), Bill can add the final piece to the base of his Career Kaleidoscope. You, too, should be able to add the final piece of your Career Kaleidoscope, so that it looks something like Bill's.

For Bill, it wasn't just the listing part that was hard, but also ranking his skills, behaviors, and environmental and cultural factors. It is hard to be forced

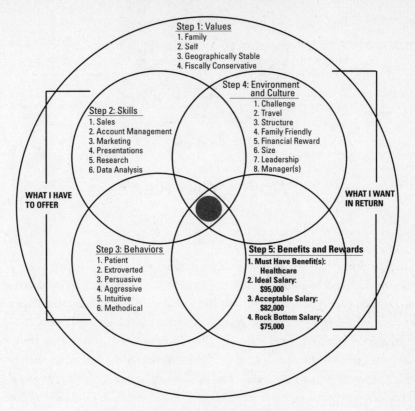

BILL McCARRICK'S CAREER KALEIDOSCOPE

to make choices when you really want it all. It's possible that any career mistakes you have made so far were caused when you tried to correct something wrong in your current job. In doing so, you may have given up something else. Why keep giving up one thing to get another? Bill had the same question. Now his Career Kaleidoscope has narrowed down his preferences so he is more aware of what he is willing to give up and what he has to retain in order for him to truly be satisfied with his career.

As you know, career preferences change over time, but you don't want to sit back and wait to see what happens. You have to think ahead as best you can to try and take the right steps forward. Will your career path be a straight line to CEO? Maybe. Maybe not. The last part of your Career Kaleidoscope will help you begin to think about what lies ahead, whether the years left in your career number four or forty.

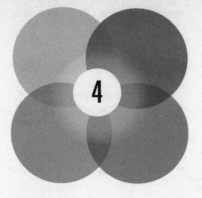

4

What's Your Plan?

While you don't have to know at this moment the exact job you want in ten years, you do need to make sure that the next step you take is one leading toward a general destination. Will you be a leader? A subject matter expert? To determine where you are going you've got to set some general goals.

Kathleen, a business consultant, dreaded interviews. It wasn't that they made her nervous, or that she didn't prepare well enough. She cringed in anticipation of that question you've probably had to answer more times than you'd like: "Where do you want to be in five years?" Kathleen had a college degree and knew that she would still be working in five years but she was always afraid to get any more specific. If she mentioned starting a family, she thought companies would be too afraid to take a chance on her. If she mentioned her desire to climb the corporate ladder, she thought companies might peg her as overeager.

The "where will you be" or "where do you want to go" questions are frightening for most people. Whether it's a fear of being locked into a specific career path or the apprehension of not knowing where you'll be in five weeks (let alone in five years), we put off thinking about our career futures for many reasons. Yet it's possible to look ahead without getting locked into anything.

The sixth part of the Career Kaleidoscope involves determining your career vision, which is a kind of happy compromise between "I know every detail of where I will be and what I will be doing in five years" and "I'll cross that bridge when I come to it." You don't have to plan or decide every element of where your career is headed. However, you do have to think about your general direction.

Think about your career as if it were a vacation. You don't have to decide every stop along the way, or how you will spend each day. After all, the weather could change at a moment's notice and your scuba trip could be sidelined.

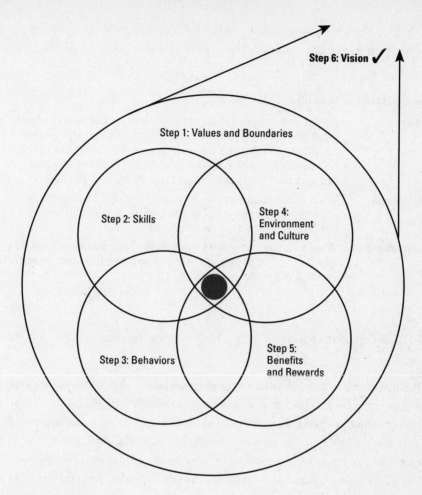

However, you do have to have a general idea of what you want to do and how you might accomplish this.

The same goes for your vision. In Step 6, you're going to define your vision—a general idea of where you want to head. The beauty of it, like the rest of the Career Kaleidoscope, is that it is based on where you are now, and can be changed as your life changes. More important, it will help you make good decisions now, so you stay on track in the future.

There are three factors to defining your vision and each addresses one burning question about your career future. Remember, you do not have to get excessively specific here. The goal is to think about a general direction for each factor: focus, importance, and environment.

For each of the vision factors, you need to think about how you would answer the questions in the chart above. This will clarify the elements of your vision.

Vision Factor	Questions To Consider
Focus	Do you see yourself rising through the ranks of management, gradually taking on more responsibility and managing more people? Or do you see yourself as an expert in a field, relied on for your skills or knowledge, but not in charge of broad responsibility and managing a large number of people?
Importance	What role will career play in your life? Will it be of primary importance? Or will it fall second, third, or fourth to family, hobbies, or other aspects of your life?
Environment	Where do you see yourself physically? Are you surrounded by a large number of people? Are you working from your home? Are you at a client site or working in the field?

ACTION: Complete your vision factors for five years from now.

Return one last time to your electronic worksheet and add two columns for your five-year vision. The first one will list your vision factors of your vision. *Focus* reflects what kind of role you aspire to; *importance* is how your career ranks in comparison to other things in your life (family, hobbies, etc.); environment the type of company you see yourself in. The second column will be left blank for you to fill in your choices for each factor. As you consider these factors, you will start to formulate ideas about your own personal vision. Then you can complete your vision factors by narrowing down your thoughts into a classification.

As you narrow down your classifications for a five-year vision, take a look at how they fit together. Did you put your career importance as third but your focus as CEO-bound? Let's be real here. It's unlikely you can rise to the level of CEO and not have your career rank first or second in your life. This is not necessarily an absolute, but now is the time to take a long hard look about how you want to live your life and the legacy you want to leave.

Keep in mind that no one is judging you. If you rank your career above your family, that is your choice. Plenty of people make that choice. You have to be honest with yourself, while at the same time being realistic about what you'd like to achieve.

Once you have determined the classifications you are comfortable with, take

Vision Factor	Classification Examples
Focus	• CEO-bound
	• Management team
	• Subject matter expert (SME)
	• Team leader
	• Consultant
	• Individual contributor
Importance	• First (above all else)
	• Second (only to family)
	• Third
	• Fourth . . . etc.
Environment	• Large, corporate
	• Traveling from client to client
	• High-growth
	• Small organization
	• Start-up business
	• Home-based business/consultant

it to the next level. Depending on your age and how many years you have left in your career, try classifications for a ten-year or a twenty-year vision. These are just long-term projections. Thinking about the future will help you make better decisions now. If it pains you to think beyond five years, then stop for now. You can always come back to it later.

ACTION: Complete your vision factors for ten, and if applicable, twenty, years from now.

Bill has struggled with where he wants to go next. So how could he possibly plan out his vision? Bill does have a general sense of how he wants his career to fit in with the rest of his life, so completing his vision factors was easier than he had anticipated.

Bill McCarrick: Five-Year Vision

Vision Factor	Detail
Focus	Team leader
Importance	Second
Environment	High-growth firm

You'll notice that five years from now Bill would still like to be a team leader. He isn't sure he is ready or wants to ascend to management yet, and in a high-growth company, he thinks he can make a bigger impact (and make more money) lending his subject matter expertise while perhaps managing a few people.

Bill also completed a ten-year vision for his Career Kaleidoscope. He's decided not to think beyond that for now, but knows he can always add a 15- or 20-year vision to the Kaleidoscope at a later date.

Bill McCarrick: Ten-Year Vision

Vision Factor	Detail
Focus	Management
Importance	Second
Environment	High-growth firm/large firm

You'll notice that his importance factor stayed the same for his ten-year vision, but the focus and environment factors changed somewhat. Bill feels that, in ten years, he wants to be in line for a management role, but he still wants to make his family a priority. He'd like to remain with the same firm (he prefers stability to job hopping) but in ten years the high-growth firm he now desires to be a part of will likely have grown into a large firm.

Again, these are Bill's general guidelines, and you should think of your vision factors similarly. Just as Bill will pay special attention to how any career possible decisions fit in with his vision, so will you with your vision.

Look at the electronic worksheet that Bill used throughout the process, and will continue to use as he embarks on a job search, as well as his Career Kaleidoscope.

Reflections from Bill:

Throughout the process I answered many of the questions asked of me, reflected in my Career Kaleidoscope. While I kept all of the notes and details (such as the skill breakdown), I was also instructed to create a second version, which is a high-level version of my electronic worksheet. I used this second

Bill McCarrick: Electronic Career Kaleidoscope Worksheet

Rank	Skill	Rank	Behavior	Rank	Environment/ Cultural Factor	Benefit/ Reward	Detail	Vision Factor	Five-Year Classification	Ten-Year Classification
1	Sales	1	Patient	1	Challenge	Must-have benefit	Healthcare	Focus	Team Leader	Management
2	Account management	2	Extroverted	2	Travel	Rock-bottom Salary	$75,000	Importance	Second	Second
3	Marketing	3	Persuasive	3	Structure	Acceptable Salary	$82,000	Environment	High-growth	High-growth/ Large Company
4	Presentations	4	Aggressive	4	Family Friendly	Ideal Salary	$95,000			
5	Research	5	Intuitive	5	Financial Reward					
6	Data Analysis	6	Methodical	6	Size					
				7	Leadership					
				8	Manager(s)					

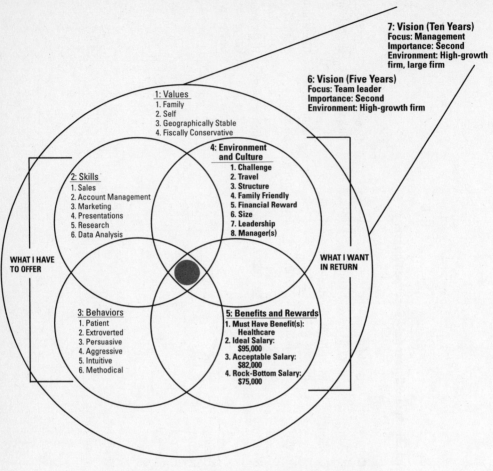

7: Vision (Ten Years)
Focus: Management
Importance: Second
Environment: High-growth
firm, large firm

6: Vision (Five Years)
Focus: Team leader
Importance: Second
Environment: High-growth firm

1: Values
1. Family
2. Self
3. Geographically Stable
4. Fiscally Conservative

4: Environment and Culture
1. Challenge
2. Travel
3. Structure
4. Family Friendly
5. Financial Reward
6. Size
7. Leadership
8. Manager(s)

2: Skills
1. Sales
2. Account Management
3. Marketing
4. Presentations
5. Research
6. Data Analysis

WHAT I HAVE TO OFFER

WHAT I WANT IN RETURN

3: Behaviors
1. Patient
2. Extroverted
3. Persuasive
4. Aggressive
5. Intuitive
6. Methodical

5: Benefits and Rewards
1. Must Have Benefit(s): Healthcare
2. Ideal Salary: $95,000
3. Acceptable Salary: $82,000
4. Rock-Bottom Salary: $75,000

BILL McCARRICK'S COMPLETED CAREER KALEIDOSCOPE

worksheet as the major tool for my job search while keeping a copy of the actual Kaleidoscope above my desk for inspiration.

At this point, your electronic worksheet should be complete, and you should have a Career Kaleidoscope that looks like Bill's above (with your own entries, of course). If you are still struggling, don't worry. This process takes time. Debra's example of her final electronic worksheet and Career Kaleidoscope is on page 53.

Notice the line on Debra's worksheet. Making choices is often the hardest part of this exercise. So the line helps Debra differentiate between what is a "must-have" and what is a "nice to have." All of her entries above the gray line are her "must-haves." It is the "must-haves" that make up Debra's Career sweet spot.

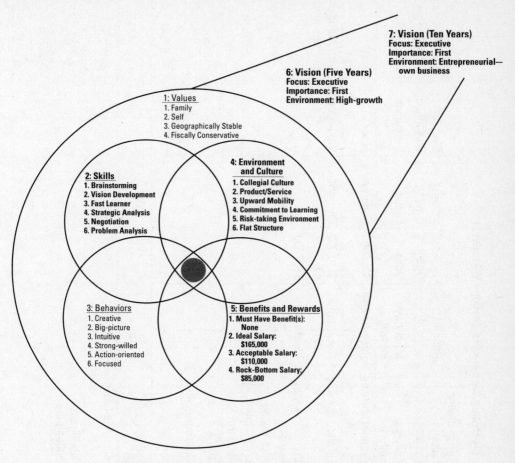

7: Vision (Ten Years)
Focus: Executive
Importance: First
Environment: Entrepreneurial—
own business

6: Vision (Five Years)
Focus: Executive
Importance: First
Environment: High-growth

1: Values
1. Family
2. Self
3. Geographically Stable
4. Fiscally Conservative

**4: Environment
and Culture**
1. Collegial Culture
2. Product/Service
3. Upward Mobility
4. Commitment to Learning
5. Risk-taking Environment
6. Flat Structure

2: Skills
1. Brainstorming
2. Vision Development
3. Fast Learner
4. Strategic Analysis
5. Negotiation
6. Problem Analysis

3: Behaviors
1. Creative
2. Big-picture
3. Intuitive
4. Strong-willed
5. Action-oriented
6. Focused

5: Benefits and Rewards
1. Must Have Benefit(s):
   None
2. Ideal Salary:
   $165,000
3. Acceptable Salary:
   $110,000
4. Rock-Bottom Salary:
   $85,000

DEBRA CARSON'S COMPLETED CAREER KALEIDOSCOPE

The Career Sweet Spot:

Your Career Sweet Spot is the combination of all the things that matter to you most. It is the job and the organization where you can find your "must-haves." They are the top two to four items in each section of your Kaleidoscope. As you continue through *The Right Job, Right Now*, you'll learn more about how to find these "must-haves" and make sure you find your own Career Sweet Spot as you embark on a job search and deal with other career development and management issues.

Take a moment to look at how different Bill and Debra's Career Kaleidoscopes are. They reflect the differences in what each person wants from his respective career.

Debra Carson: Electronic Career Kaleidoscope Worksheet

Rank	Skill	Rank	Behavior	Rank	Environment/ Cultural Factor	Benefit/ Reward	Detail	Vision Factor	Five-Year Classification	Ten-Year Classification
1	Brainstorming	1	Creative	1	Collegial culture	Must-have benefit	None	Focus	Executive	Executive
2	Vision development	2	Big picture/ visionary	2	Product/service	Rock-bottom salary	$85,000	Importance	First	First
3	Fast learner	3	Intuitive	3	Upward mobility	Acceptable salary	$110,000	Environment	High-growth	Entrepreneurial/ own business
4	Strategic analysis	4	Strong-willed	4	Commitment to learning	Ideal salary	$165,000			
5	Negotiation	5	Action-oriented	5	Risk-taking environment					
6	Problem analysis	6	Focused	6	Flat structure					
MUST-HAVES ABOVE ↑ and "NICE TO HAVES" BELOW ↓										
7	Brand and development management	7	Passionate	7	Collaborative					
8	Product development	8	Understanding	8	Politics					
9	Large team management	9	Motivated	9	Work/life balance					
10	Research	10	Dedicated	10	Intelligent colleagues					

Rank	Skill	Rank	Behavior	Rank	Environment/ Cultural Factor	Benefit/ Reward	Detail	Vision Factor	Five-Year Classification	Ten-Year Classification
11	Staff development and mentoring	11	Perceptive	11	Quick-moving					
12	Cross cultural/ international mgt	12	Confident	12	Competitive in industry					
13	Technology fluency (PowerPoint, spreadsheets)	13	Committed	13	Respected in industry					
14	Business development	14	Honest	14	Commitment to women					
15	Client management	15	Tolerant	15	International focus					

You'll also notice that certain areas are more specific than others. Bill's skills seem to be better defined and focused, while Debra's are more general. This is not surprising because Bill has had a narrower career path than Debra. However, Debra's vision is more constant than Bill's. Debra's long-term goal has always been to run her own business, so she is developing as many skills and experiences as she can to help her attain this goal.

How does the Career Kaleidoscope actually impact these choices? As Debra says: "If I hadn't gone through the exercise of creating my Career Kaleidoscope, I would not have had the immediate insight to determine what I needed and how I could get it. I used the framework to make better decisions about what I could give a firm and make sure I got what I needed."

And for the long term? "Since I completed the Career Kaleidoscope for the first time," says Debra, "I have been in two jobs, and am now running my own business. But I still use the Kaleidoscope as a benchmark to determine whether my career situation still meets my needs and if I still have something to offer in my current opportunity. It is a good tool to continue to evaluate where my career is headed."

Doing the Career Kaleidoscope can point you in the right direction *and* can help you make changes as needed. As Debra points out: "The Kaleidoscope helped me to determine my best next steps. After completing the research on myself, I did an extensive amount of research on potential positions and firms. In my case, conversations with my eventual employer led me to believe the organization was a strong fit. However, the organization's strategy changed a few months into the job. Completing the Career Kaleidoscope helped me realize the potential issues with this early on, and when I made the choice to leave, I used the Kaleidoscope again to find my next best step. Sometimes you can't help what changes with a company. But if you are in control of your own career you can control what happens to you."

5

Are You Ready?

It's time to take the pattern you've created and determine your personal strategy. First, you have to do a surprise check. Some of what you see in your Career Kaleidoscope won't come as a shock. But some will, and you need to come to terms with what you've discovered. Second, you have to do a reality check. There's nothing worse than searching for a job when you don't know what it is you want, or finding a job that you can't take because your family can't move. Once you've understood your needs and what's actually possible, then you can make the right next move.

Surprise Check

First, you want to consider any surprises you have encountered in each part of your Career Kaleidoscope. You have put a great deal of energy into creating it; now is the time to step back and look at it in its entirety. Specifically, you want to look at your Career Sweet Spot. The "must-haves" (from each section of your Career Kaleidoscope) comprise your Career Sweet Spot. This is what you'll be aiming for as you move forward. Before you make a move, make sure you are fully comfortable with the target. The chart on page 58 provides questions to consider as you do a surprise check for each part for your Career Kaleidoscope.

ACTION: Do your own surprise check.

In doing your own surprise check, the goal is to become comfortable with all of the elements of your Career Kaleidoscope. This may be tough—you may be making

Career Kaleidoscope	Surprise Check
Values	Are you surprised by how much your values affect your career? Based on your values, are there any next steps that you can immediately eliminate?
Skills	Are there any skills you have been using that you have decided you don't want to use anymore? Does that eliminate your current job, even your current field, from your next steps?
Behaviors	Are you getting to use any of these behaviors in your current job search? Are any of them missing, which you never noticed until now?
Environment and Culture	Has this been a sticking point for you? Are you doing what you want to do but in the wrong place? Or are there just certain factors you know have to be present?
Benefits and Rewards	Does your salary matter more or less than you thought it would? Did you have a surprising conversation with your spouse/partner/family about how rewards and benefits affect your life?
Vision	Is this something you have put thought into before? Or is it a completely new exercise? Are you still wary about where you are headed, or do you have a solid idea about where you want to go?

some hard choices for the first time. And if you are still skeptical or not comfortable with your choices, answering the questions above will help you get there. Think about it this way: if you are not completely confident with what you have to offer and what you want in return, how will a company be confident in you?

To make sure he is ready to move forward, Bill has done his own surprise check:

Career Kaleidoscope	Bill's Surprise Check
Values	I always knew family was important, but after talking with my wife, I realized we have to make it a priority together. This means I have to be committed to less travel and be sure to involve her in career decisions, and she has committed to do the same.
Skills	I was always so good at science and liked it when I was younger, so it was hard to admit that this has changed. It isn't that I don't like it anymore, but I don't want the skills in this area to be my primary focus. I have to keep reminding myself of that or it will be easy to get sucked back into that field again.
Behaviors	I need to find a job that can combine my extroversion and my patience. I am always missing one or the other. In science I was patient but not extroverted; in marketing I

Career Kaleidoscope	Bill's Surprise Check
	get to be extroverted but not patient. This shouldn't be a surprise but it is. I had almost forgotten how patient I was because I haven't had a chance to be.
Environment and Culture	I knew I would always need to be challenged in my job, but I hadn't paid much attention to travel.
Benefits and Rewards	My wife and I made the decision that I am the one responsible for healthcare. I was surprised that she was so nervous I would consider something otherwise.
Vision	I had not put much thought into my vision before and had only focused on the next job I would get. But I realized that if I do want to rise in the ranks and take on a management role in the next ten years, I need to bear this in mind.

Reality Check

Commitment-phobes beware. Now you are really getting ready to make a commitment to what comes next. The reality check gives you an opportunity to take one last look back. Are you ready to make decisions? Have you really been honest with yourself? Wavering or extreme hesitation will only hurt your progress. It's time to get serious. The chart on page 60 provides questions you can answer to make sure you are being realistic and ready to move forward.

ACTION: Do your own reality check.

As you do your reality check, pretend there is no turning back. If you found a job that hit each one of the "must-haves" in your Career Sweet Spot, would it be the perfect position for you at this point in time in your life and career?

As you can see, Bill is being honest with himself. He's made (along with his family) some specific choices and he needs to remind himself what these are, and then focus on opportunities that fit.

Going outside of these boundaries (for you and for Bill) is dangerous. Not only is it a waste of time, but to ignore the choices you have made or to stray beyond your Career Sweet Spot will bring you back right where you started. It's not worth being tempted by one great aspect of a job or opportunity, only to be disappointed in the long run.

In Part Two, you're going to learn how to use all of this information to your advantage. The Career Kaleidoscope and Career Sweet Spot have brought to light the strengths you have to offer and what you want most in return. You still need to learn how to use the results of your Career Kaleidoscope.

Career Kaleidoscope	Reality Check
Values	Are you ready to make decisions based on your core values? If you listed your family or a specific location as a value or boundary, are you ready to commit?
Skills	Does your list of skills include the ones you really want to use? Can you commit to a new field or career if you really don't want to use skills valued in your current field?
Behaviors	Are you confident in your behavioral strengths? Can you give examples of them to demonstrate why they are strengths?
Environment and Culture	Can you eliminate organizations or types of organizations that don't match the type of environment and culture you want to be in?
Benefits and Rewards	Are you comfortable working within the salary levels you have created? Can you commit to focusing on a job within the level of benefits and rewards you've identified?
Vision	Have you shared your vision with the people in your life that should have a say? Are you being honest about where you're headed, based on other life choices you also want to make?

Career Kaleidoscope	Bill's Reality Check
Values	I've decided to make family my priority with my career secondary. I know this might mean that a few positions won't be options for me but I have made my decision.
Skills	If I involve science at all in my next position it can really only be if the company is in a healthcare or science field. I have made this decision and will not pursue jobs that have scientific or lab work as a major skill area.
Behaviors	I have to get out of marketing. The marketing role I have now is about making quick decisions and moving quickly. No wonder I am not happy. I am much more comfortable when I can take my time and do things right rather than be forced to always move forward when I feel like we aren't ready.
Environment and Culture	I need to make sure any job I even remotely consider has a low level of travel (less than 20 percent) or that the travel is local.
Benefits and Rewards	I cannot consider jobs or opportunities that don't have healthcare. It's as simple as that.
Vision	If I really want to climb to a management role I have to focus on trying to find a company I can really grow and stay with. I also must see a long-term path for myself there.

PART TWO

Career Action: Getting Your Butt in Gear

You've taken a good, long look at yourself, now it's time to use the results of the Kaleidoscope Career Model™ *and put thought into action* with a realistic look at what it takes to get *the right job, right now*.

Here's the deal with your career thus far. If your career isn't working, it's probably because you're either handling it poorly or not at all. Most career problems can usually be attributed to continuing to do the wrong thing, or spending way too much time making excuses. Why waste any more time? Take a long, hard look at what you have been doing (or maybe the *lack* of what you've been doing). It's time to take action and make something happen.

You have spent a great deal of time thinking about what you have to offer from a career perspective and what you want in return. You imagined your career five to ten years from now, and even focused on where your trouble spots might be as you proceed. Now it's time to put all that effort into action.

Getting Focused

Now it's time to take a deep breath, take your newly created strategy from Part One, and get moving. You'll learn how to determine whether you're ready to take action, and if you're not, how to complete the research you need to get ready. You've got the insight and you've got the confidence.

To be sure, you did a great deal of work in Part One to determine what you have to offer and what you want in return. Remember, you're only armed with information at this point (and good information, at that.) Now you have to figure out how and where you are going to use it.

Our first order of action is to decide where you stand, from a career perspective. Did your Career Kaleidoscope make clear where you have gone wrong or do you need to revisit the contents? Are you financially and tempermentally able to start a job search right now? Either way you have to know where you stand and what you're capable of before you proceed.

Once you figure out where you are, you need to figure out where you are going. What is your ultimate goal with this process? Are you in the planning stages or are you ready to start a job search? When will it begin? How much time do you have?

Where Are You?

Your completed Career Kaleidoscope in Part One may have illuminated for you that you like your career but simply need to do your job in a different environment that is a better fit with your behaviors. Or you may not be getting what you want in return for what you do and have to move to a new industry to realize the benefits and rewards that are most important you. You may already know where you are—ready to make a change.

Before you can jump headfirst into a job search, you need to figure out when you want to leave your old job and how much time you have to find a new one. Even if you completed your Career Kaleidoscope in Part One and still don't where you are, that doesn't mean you should throw your hands up in disgust. It just means that while you have the information you need, you're not sure how to use it. And in order to figure out how to use that information, you're going to have to do some research. But this time, instead of researching what you have to offer and what you want in return, you've got to research what's out there to find the fit with your Career Sweet Spot.

Your Career Kaleidoscope helped define you as a product and guided you to figure out what qualities you can "sell." Now you have to figure out not only to whom you want to sell "the product," but who would actually buy it. In a perfect world, you would be able to research the answers to each of these questions, looking at all of the fields that fit your needs in depth, but taking the time to do extensive research isn't an option for everyone.

For example, if you have been laid off, or are in a situation where you can't be unemployed for long, you may not have time to make a complete career change. If you are supporting a partner, spouse, or family member(s) you also may have only limited time. It's important to get a sense of timing before you start to research your options. Is it a better idea to take your time and do it right? Of course. But not everyone has the same amount of time and you want to make sure you leave enough time to spend on an effective job search.

Once you have a sense of how much time you can put into researching your options, then you can get down to business. Remember, you don't have to quit the job you have now in order to think about what you want to do next. If it makes more sense (from a financial-security standpoint) to research your options while working, then do it. As you probably realized when completing your Career Kaleidoscope, you have to do what works best for you in your current situation.

To get a sense of where you are, you want first to look back at your surprise check and reality check from Chapter 5. It should bring issues to the surface from your current situation or current job. What was important to you in what you have to offer? Were there certain skills or behaviors that you have to make sure you use? What was important in what you want in return and your vision?

The goal here is to get a good sense of where you are. Do you have the ability to make a complete career change or do you want to use the results of your Career Kaleidoscope to find a new environment? Perhaps you're not in a position where you can take action right now but want to be prepared when you are ready. Which of these best describes your current situation?

Location	Description
Window-shopping	You're beginning to think about how you can make your career more satisfying for the long term, but aren't ready to take action just yet.
Taking My Time	You want to make a change, but you're currently in a situation where you can take your time doing so. You may have financial stability on your side, or may be in a bearable or even likable job situation. Either way, you have the time to move somewhat slowly and carefully.
Need to Move Fast	You may be in a career situation that is unbearable or you may have been just laid off. You need to make a change quickly but don't want to accept the first job that comes along. You want to take some time, even if it's brief, to try to find the best situation.

ACTION: Determine where you are.

Having a strong sense of where you are will help you make better use of the time you're about to invest in the rest of the process. How long will it all take, you wonder. Like many other career questions, there is no one right answer. Some career experts will tell you that a job search will take one month for every $10,000 you want to make. Others will say it depends on what level of position you are looking for or how much work you put into the search.

In reality, it varies. By completing your Career Kaleidoscope you may have already put in days' or weeks' worth of time. Nonetheless, it's better to overestimate the time you need.

Where Are You Going?

Now that you have a sense of where you are, it's time now to focus on your ultimate goal. Are you the window-shopper or do you need to move quickly? Once you have a sense of timing, you have to figure out what you want to get out of this process. Is your goal to find a job? Or maybe you just want to figure out what type of career or environment would make you the happiest. Think about why you started reading *The Right Job, Right Now* and where you hope to be by the time you finish the book.

ACTION: Determine what your end goal is from this process.

With your goal in mind, it's time to take another step ahead. You've got to create your path to get there. Whether you have a few ideas in mind, or are starting fresh with the results of your Career Kaleidoscope, you now have to use the information you have to see what careers, jobs, and environments are a best fit for you.

You do not have to figure out the exact position you want to proceed to. But you *do* have to have a good idea of either the field or industry you want to be in. If you don't have a good idea of who your audience is, it's hard to sell the product well. If you're selling a certain type of car, you need to know who would be most likely to buy the car, so that you can structure your message to attract those types of buyers.

One of the biggest mistakes that many job seekers make is to try to sell what they have to everyone. This isn't an effective strategy because you have to know your audience to effectively sell your product (yourself).

From a job-seeking perspective, the audience is either the field or the industry. The field is the actual type of job you might hold: accountant, salesperson, marketing manager, investment banker, or human resources generalist. The industry refers to the type of company or organization for which you work and what they do to make money, such as manufacturing, consulting, consumer products, technology, education, or healthcare. It is very important to understand the distinction between field and industry because the choices you make in either area can hugely affect your job search and your career satisfaction.

The type of job you hold might vary by industry. A human resources generalist in a manufacturing industry has to have a good understanding of union and labor regulations, while the same role in a consulting firm isn't concerned with labor law, as there are no union workers in those firms. Additionally, the environmental and cultural preferences from your Career Kaleidoscope might rule in, or out, certain industries based on your preferences.

You might also be more interested in an industry than a specific field. For example, you might be very interested in technology firms and open to serving multiple roles at such an organization as opposed to wanting a specific role but being open to multiple industries.

You don't have to choose an exact field or industry, but you do need to narrow down your preferences if you want to begin a fruitful job search. You've got to be able to define your audience in one or both ways (field and/or industry) in order to see results. We'll talk more about how you'll market yourself effectively to your audience in Chapter 8. Before you can find a fit with what you have to offer and what you want in return, you've got to revisit what matters.

If certain elements of "what you have to offer" are very well defined or specific, it may be easier to narrow down specific fields. Bill McCarrick had some elements to his "what you want in return" list that he knew he could find in a number of industries. But the skills he wants to use in combination (sales, account management, marketing) would, he knew, limit his focus to a few specific fields. If your Career Sweet Spot focuses on your marketing, communication, or public relations skills, you can focus on potential career paths that may combine several skill areas (marketing communications manager), or just one (all types of careers in public relations).

On the other hand, Debra Carlson had some skills and behaviors that could be applicable to many fields. But on her "what you want in return" list there were some environmental and cultural factors that were more specific. These helped her narrow down her focus from an industry perspective. Because one of the things that mattered most to her was the product or service the company was engaged in, it was easy for her to focus on specific industries.

Let's say you are very interested in sports and recreation and want to work in that area. You may be able to narrow your industry focus to firms that sell related types of products (sports apparel or equipment) or provide services in this area (sports marketing, sports leagues, sports broadcasting) and are open to applying your skills to various fields in this industry.

Finally, and perhaps most important, look at the elements of your Career Sweet Spot. As you do your research and have conversations with professionals in fields and industries you are interested in, always keep your Career Sweet Spot in mind. After all, the elements in your Sweet Spot are what you defined as most important to you—things you are unwilling to sacrifice when it comes to your career. If you're interested in a certain field or industry, and after talking to experts and professionals in that field or industry, you realize it won't allow you to use all the elements in your Sweet Spot, why pursue it further?

To understand how this works, let's get back to Bill and look at the highest ranked elements of each section of his Career Kaleidoscope that make up his Career Sweet Spot:

- *Skills:* Sales, Account Management, Marketing, Presentations
- *Behaviors:* Extroverted, Patient, Persuasive, Aggressive
- *Cultural and Environmental Factors:* Challenge, Travel, Structure
- *Benefits and Rewards:* Healthcare, Acceptable Salary of $82,000

Looking at his Sweet Spot, Bill can make some immediate decisions about fields and industries. For example, Bill has always had an interest in working for a nonprofit organization. After all, it would be great to work for an organization that has purpose and meaning. But Bill also made the decision (along with his wife) about what an acceptable (and rock-bottom) salary would be. For example, Bill was able to rule out the nonprofit industry when he realized he would never be able to make his target salary (at his current level) in that world. Why waste time talking to people in that industry and researching opportunities? You'll learn more in Chapter 8 about how to research career options so you can compare them to your Sweet Spot and make good decisions about what will work and what won't.

This may sound severe, but it's not. Bill made a personal decision that salary was important and he needs to follow through with that for his career search. If he wastes time exploring opportunities that don't fit with his preferences—the elements of his Career Sweet Spot—he will only find himself trying to make tough decisions, becoming frustrated that there is no good solution and wasting precious time.

You can figure out what's worth pursuing and what's not by looking at your Sweet Spot to determine if you can already define field or industry preferences. By using your Career Kaleidoscope, you should have a list of preferences in each area. Your list may be well defined in both industry and field or in one or the other. On the other hand, you may have a few ideas in each area but are far from being well defined. Either way, it's time to do some research.

> **ACTION: Make a list of your preferred industries and your preferred fields.**

At this point, you want to make a list of your preferred industries and preferred fields. Go back to your electronic worksheet and create another page. If you're using Excel (or a similar spreadsheet program), create a new page in the Excel workbook. At the bottom of the screen, you will see tabs—each tab is one sheet. The first sheet contains the columns that you used to list and rank the elements that went into your Career Kaleidoscope. You can make Industry and Field Research the second tab.

If you're using a word processing program, just create another page for your industry and field research. Your lists may be somewhat long at this point, and that's okay. You'll learn how to narrow them down.

If you aren't sure where your skills would fit, or what industries would be most appealing, focus on fields first. Start with a broad understanding of how businesses work and what major fields comprise most organizations:

- **Sales:** giving the customer an opportunity to buy a product. It may be building relationships one-on-one with potential customers, or mass selling

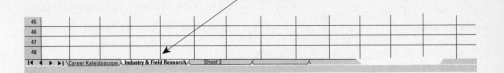

45												
46												
47												
48												

I◄ ◄ ► ►I \Career Kaleidoscope \ **Industry & Field Research** \ Sheet 3

to many customers at one time. Either way, sales roles focus on trying to get your customers to buy your product or service.

- *Marketing:* making customers or buyers aware of the product or service being offered. This may include everything from creating advertisements and doing research on potential customers to keeping track of how well your product is selling in the marketplace.
- *Finance and accounting:* tracks the past and forecasts the future financial performance of an organization. Finance and accounting roles may focus on creating financial reports for the government, creating budgets and allocating resources for different departments or functions, or helping a company plan for financial success.
- *Operations:* how a product or service is put together and how it physically gets to the customer. Product manufacturing, assembly, and facilities management may all be a part of operations.
- *Human resources:* focuses on the people in the workplace. This may include recruiting new workers, training and developing the workforce, or dealing with benefits and compensation.
- *Information technology:* automates the workplace through the use of technology. This may include networking systems, or helping other departments use technology to perform better.

If any of these areas pique your interest, great. (These are very, very basic definitions of the major functions of a firm, designed to point you in a general direction.) Maybe you don't want to work in business. That's okay, but don't go any further unless you have some items on your field and industry lists.

If you're feeling particularly unfocused, start by listing some fields and industries of interest. To jumpstart your thoughts, recall the products or services you use on a regular basis. Or think about your hobbies and interests. If you really enjoy home projects, you might start by researching the construction industry or focusing on firms that cater to this interest. You don't have to work in an area that coincides with one of your hobbies but it is a good place to start researching.

> **Good to Know:**
>
> Start with industry research only if you are really focused on getting in one specific industry like fashion or entertainment. It's much easier to find a field that fits first and an industry second rather than trying to fit yourself in multiple fields in one industry.

No matter how well defined your target audience (industry, field, or both), be sure you go into the job search process as well informed as possible. This includes not only researching fields and industries of interest but also talking to people who work in those areas. If your lists are either too long or not adequately defined, it should be obvious that you may have to do more research.

Remember, if you don't know enough about what you have to offer and what you want in return, you can't sell yourself effectively. And if you don't do enough research to know where you would be a good fit and know enough about that field or industry, you'll waste more time on an unproductive job search or find yourself in a job you didn't really want in the first place. Put the time in now, and save yourself years of frustration later.

There are two parts to the research process: learning on your own (Level 1 research) and learning from others (Level 2 research). It's important to undertake them in that order. If you're interested in human resources and you know someone who works in that field, it may be tempting to immediately pick up the phone and ask your contact all about his or her career. Imagine if you only get one phone call and that call is only fifteen minutes long. Do you want to spend that time asking about what human resources is, or do you want to spend that time focused on questions about why your contact likes his job, what his specific challenges are, and what his career path looks like?

People are usually willing to help you, but they are also busy. Make the best use of their time (and yours) and do research on your own first. This way, if after you read about what human resources is really like, and you find it won't be a good fit, you can spend time on contacts in fields that are of genuine interest.

For Level 1 research, if you have items on both your field and industry lists, start by focusing on the fields that interest you most. You want to understand what people in that field actually do, and what types of jobs you might get in that field.

Whether you are focusing on field or industry, there are a number of different ways to go about Level 1 research. Simply running a Web search on your field or industry of interest can be helpful but there are numerous additional ways to learn about fields and industries:

- *Field and industry guides:* There are hundreds of published guides that will give you an overview of the field or industry you're researching and what to expect from a career there. These guides can be found in your local bookstore or from career Web sites like www.vault.com or www.wetfeet.com.

- *Association Web sites:* Almost every major field and industry has its own association—use the list of resources in Appendix A as a start or do a web search (for example: "marketing association"). Many association Web sites also have "competency models" or lists of skills required for success in the field. These models and lists can jumpstart your research process as well as introduce you to the language of the field or industry.

- *Field and industry magazines and journals:* Most fields and industries also have magazines or journals with relevant articles about trends and news in that field or industry. Check your local bookstore—magazines are usually arranged by subject. A college or local library is also a great place to start, as libraries are likely to have the best selection.

- *Company position descriptions:* Looking at job descriptions in specific fields or industries will also give you insight into what that firm or field might be like.

- *Salary Web sites:* Basic reports from Web sites like Salary.com can provide information on the range of salary you might expect. (This is just to give you a baseline so you know if a particular position is worth pursuing—you'll do more in-depth salary research much later in the process.)

- *Job Web sites:* Web sites like www.simplyhired.com, jobster.com, www.careerbuilder.com, and www.monster.com also have sections on field and industry research. If you are using these sites at this point, be careful not to jump ahead and start reviewing job descriptions or applying for jobs. You're only in the research phase and not ready to move ahead.

Start by researching one field or industry at a time, and comparing it to your Career Kaleidoscope and your Career Sweet Spot. Would the field or industry allow you to use the skills and behaviors you most want to use? Does the industry or field match your environmental and cultural factors? This step may take some time but by comparing fields and industries of interest to each element of your Career Kaleidoscope, you should be able to decide whether it is worth it to continue researching or pursuing certain fields and industries.

Level 1 research will ensure that you are educated about the fields and industries that you want to continue pursuing. This lays the groundwork for talking to professionals and getting the most out of your Level 2 research.

ACTION: Use your Level 1 research to eliminate fields and industries that aren't
a fit and to learn the basics about the ones that are.

At the very least, you should know the following for each field and industry
you are interested in pursuing before moving on to Level 2 research:

Level 1 *Field* Research Questions:

- What does the field encompass?
- What skills and behaviors are most prevalent?
- What types of jobs are most common in this field?
- What type of education is needed/valued in this field?

Level 1 *Industry* Research Questions:

- What are the different parts of the industry? (i.e., in technology, there is
  software, hardware, technology consulting, etc.)
- How have changes in the economy affected the industry?
- What is the latest news or the latest trends in the industry?
- What is the future of the industry?

Use your electronic field/industry worksheet to track the data and information
you find.

Once you have done your Level 1 research, you should have narrowed down
your field and industry list. If for now you are focusing on one or the other
(fields versus industries), that's fine. There will also be some fields, such as investment banking or advertising, that are industry-limited. For example, if you
want to work in advertising, you can work in the professional services industry
for a firm that contracts with companies to do their advertising. Or you can
work in-house for a company that can afford such staff or needs to have in-
house advertising staff, such as in the retail or consumer products industries.

Either way, you want to be able to focus on one or two fields (in several industries), or one industry and several fields before you move into Level 2 research.

Level 2 research is where you will talk to people in your desired field or industry. Commonly called informational interviewing, Level 2 research is the
best way to fill in the blanks about the fields and industries you are considering
and determine where your focus will be for a job search.

STOP Talking to others is an essential part of the job search process. At this point your goal is to make connections in order to learn about the fields and industries that interest you. You are not trying to find a job (you're just not ready!). Will you make contacts you can use later? Absolutely. Chapter 8 focuses on networking and how to use those contacts once you start your job search. Try not to get ahead of yourself while doing Level 2 research.

In Level 2, your goal with informational interviews is to get information first, and make contacts second. By gathering your information in Level 2, there are a few things you want to keep close at hand. First, your list of potential fields and industries will help you determine who to talk to. Second is your Career Kaleidoscope. As you are talking to contacts, what they say will either resonate with your Career Sweet Spot or it won't. If they are describing their field and it doesn't match closely with the skills you want to use or the environment you want to work in, take note because this field or industry may not be right for you.

To get started, you have to find your contacts. For each field or industry you are interested in you should speak with at least two contacts in two places. For example, if you are researching the technology industry, make sure each contact you talk to has a different type of job in the industry. If you are researching investment banking, each contact you talk to should work in different industries. The idea is to get different perspectives and not rely on only one person's opinion.

ACTION: Begin your Level 2 research by finding contacts in your field and industry areas of interest.

There are a number of different ways to find contacts, and in Chapter 9, you learn more about finding the contacts who can lead you to job opportunities. For now, you're finding the contacts who are willing to talk. As you look at your electronic workbook, and your narrowed-down list of fields and industries, start to think about the people you can find and how you'll find them. Here are some ways to get started:

- *Family and friends:* Everyone knows someone. Ask friends and family if they know anyone who works in the industry or field you are interested in.
- *Local business organizations:* Rotary Clubs, local chapters of business fraternities, and local Chambers of Commerce are just a few of the many local organizations that have lists of business contacts and local business leaders.

- *Affinity/membership groups:* Were you a member of a fraternity or sorority in college? Are you affiliated with religious, volunteer, or social groups? Ask around—you're bound to find contacts in your field or industry of interest among these groups.
- *College/university connections:* The career services office of your undergraduate or graduate institution is another great place to start. Most career services offices have massive electronic databases of alumni and their employment data.
- *Cold requests:* If you're dying to work for a certain company or leader, try contacting that person directly. While the chance of response might be lower than most, there is still a chance. What do you have to lose?
- *Current employer:* If you are currently employed, you have an entire organization of people you can potentially talk to in order to learn about other fields or jobs within the organization. Tread carefully here. You don't want your boss to think you are leaving, but you don't want to ignore what might be your greatest (and most accessible) source of information.

If you are having trouble locating contacts, or you live in an area where networking opportunities are limited, try an online contact database such as www.linkedin.com or www.ryze.com. Online sites can be very helpful, but don't rely solely on online contacts.

STOP In Chapter 8, we'll go into these sources in more depth and discuss how you might use each source most effectively.

After you compile your list of people you'd like to contact, it's time to start making requests. Before you pick up the phone or start pounding out e-mails, there are a few things to keep in mind.

1. Do background research

If someone referred you to a contact, ask him what he knows about the contact's work habits, the best way to reach the contact, and any other important background information. Search your contact's name on the Web. Take note of their industry and if it's a busy time for their business.

2. Don't expect immediate replies

Your contacts are busy. They likely will want to help you but can't always respond immediately. Give them time. If you make a call or send an e-mail, wait at least ten days until you try again. When you do, be sensitive to the fact that you already contacted them once.

3. Cater to your contacts

Make your schedule amenable to theirs. Cater to their availability. Ask what days or times work best for a conversation and plan around their schedule. After all, they are doing you a favor. Don't schedule hour-long calls. Instead, aim for fifteen- or twenty-minute conversations. You should be able to get all the information you need in that time.

4. Prepare, prepare, prepare

In order to make the best use of the fifteen-to-twenty-minute conversation, you have to be well prepared. Put together a list of questions you want to ask about the contact's field or industry. Good questions to ask, that will help you decide if the focus area is a good fit for you, are pretty simple:

- What do you like most about your job?
- What do you like least?
- What's the hardest part about working in your industry?
- What is the future of your field or industry? Where do you see it headed?
- What has been your career path in this field or industry?
- What is your daily schedule like? What is a typical day or what kind of meetings do you attend?
- What is the culture like in your industry/at your organization?
- What qualities does a professional have to possess to be successful in your field/industry?

If your contact is very busy, or you can't find a time that works, try sending your questions in an e-mail and ask for short replies.

5. Own the conversation

If you have questions and are prepared, this part should be easy. Remember, you are the one who scheduled the conversation. Thus, you're responsible for initiating the call, starting up the conversation, knowing when it's time to move on to the next question, and ending the call. If the meeting is in person and involves food and/or beverage, you're responsible for picking up the tab. (This applies to you even if you are a poor college or graduate student.)

6. Obey the 90/10 rule

You initiated the conversation to learn from your contact, not to drone on about your own career aspirations. Therefore, 90 percent of the conversation should be the contact sharing information with you. You should be talking only about 10 percent of the time. And that 10 percent should mostly be a short introduction about yourself, your pre-prepared questions, and your ending the conversation and thanking the contact.

7. Mind the time

Watch the clock. If you scheduled fifteen minutes, take only fifteen minutes. As time winds down, say something like, "I want to be respectful of your time, are you able to answer one more question?"

8. Be grateful and show it

The contact is doing you a favor. Be sure to thank them at the beginning and at the end of the conversation. Then, follow up with an e-mail or a personal, handwritten note thanking them as well. A little gratitude goes a long way. This step is extremely important.

Remember, you are in information-gathering mode during this conversation. Don't try to sell yourself now. You're simply not ready. And you need to make that clear. Here's how:

"Hi, John, this is Laura Collins, a former co-worker [friend, daughter, hairdresser, whatever] of Marlon Warner's. I am doing some career research right now on the consumer products industry [or specific field] and Marlon suggested I talk to you since you have extensive experience in the industry. Would you have about fifteen minutes to spare? I just have a few questions about your experiences as I think about where I might head next."

In this case, John, the contact, might be willing to talk to Laura immediately, so she needs to have her questions ready. More likely, John will want to schedule a conversation so Laura should also have her calendar open and at hand.

> ACTION: Get in touch with your contacts so you can narrow down your focus areas and proceed with a job search if necessary.

As you are having your conversations, you should not only be taking really great notes (you'll need them later!) but you should also be tracking information about your contact including how to reach him, background information, and status of the connection. Let's see how Bill is doing it.

Bill, who you know is unhappy in his marketing role, has been thinking about consulting as an option. But while he knows generally what consultants do, he has never compared it to what he wants to do. So he's found four contacts, each of whom hold different roles in different types of consulting firms. First, Bill tracks the contacts in this section of his eletronic workbook:

Organization	Industry	Contact	Connection	Status	To Do	Notes
Alston Consulting	Consulting	Steven Garmuth, (201) 555-1675, sgarmuth@alston.com	Friend of my brother's	Conversation about the consulting industry scheduled for March at 2:30 p.m. I am to call him.	Send e-mail on March 3 confirming call.	Steven is a managing director and has been with Alston, a small firm, for three years. Was previously at Accenture for five years. Has M.B.A. and started as an accountant before getting into consulting.

In addition to tracking your contacts, you should also be tracking the answers to each question you ask. You can take the answers and compare them to your Career Kaleidoscope after you've gathered all of your data. For example, one of Bill's top environmental and cultural factors is travel—he doesn't want to have to leave town on a regular basis. If, when talking to a professional in the consulting industry, Bill learns that travel is extensive in the industry, he can compare that answer to his Career Sweet Spot and see immediately that the industry isn't a fit. It will also help you see where there are patterns between certain types of roles and industries.

Here is the template Bill will use to track his answers:

Consulting Industry Contacts

Question	Steven Garmuth	Alison Laquell	Justin Shapiro	Lisa Clavishell
What do you like most about your job?				
What do you like least?				
What's the hardest part about working in your industry?				

(*continued*)

(*Table Continued*)

Question	Steven Garmuth	Alison Laquell	Justin Shapiro	Lisa Clavishell
What is the future of your field or industry? Where do you see it headed?				
What has been your career path in this field or industry?				
What is your daily schedule like? What is a typical day or what kind of meetings do you attend?				
What is the culture like in your industry/at your organization?				
What qualities does a professional have to possess to be successful in your field/industry?				

You don't have to write down every word your contact says, simply get the main themes and highlights. You will need to refer to these later.

Once you have had your conversations, you should feel ready to make some decisions about where you are headed. Your Career Kaleidoscope makes clear what you want to do in a job and what you want from that job. Your conversations should fill in the missing pieces so you can see whether a certain field or industry is a fit. Don't be disappointed if a field or industry you had your heart set on doesn't seem as glamorous after you've had your conversations as it did before your research. Sometimes a job isn't all it's cracked up to be. It's better to know that sooner, rather than learning the hard way after one miserable month on the job.

ACTION: Decide on your focus.

At this point, you should either be focusing on one field (i.e., sales) or one industry (i.e., technology). Remember, the broader your focus, the harder it will be to market yourself during the job search process. If you can narrow your focus to specific roles in a field or industry, that's best. (Just don't get so focused that you think there is only one position in the entire world that fits.)

As you decide where your focus lies, it's time to decide on a direction and move forward. If you can't make a decision, this means there are still unanswered questions. You have to go back and find the answers either through industry and field research or through conversations with your contacts. It should be *information* that is pushing you forward and not your gut (or your mother).

You've done all the necessary work to arrive at a decision and you should feel confident. If you're hesitant, it probably means you were pushed in a certain direction because you think it will please someone else, or it's what you're "supposed" to do, or you don't have enough information. The goal is not to find the perfect career. It's to find the perfect career for you. It may help to think about your Career Kaleidoscope as your home base. When in doubt, when confused, return to your home base to remind yourself of the skills and behaviors you really want to use, and what you want in return from a career. Any time you question a field or industry, ask yourself: Does this focus match my top factors in each area? Does it match my Career Sweet Spot?

STOP GPS Check—Are you at any of these positions right now?

- If you are hesitant or apathetic, turn around and go back. If you're not confident and excited about the focus you are about to pursue, you're going to have a hard time making any progress. Employers can tell when you're not excited about a position. So can networking contacts. So can you. Unless you are energized about your focus, your job search is going to be a very lonely process.

- If you still aren't sure where you are headed or need to do a significant amount of research on your options for action, make sure you take the time to do so (that is, if you have the time). The next chapters focus on actions that require you be fairly confident about where you are headed and the type of job you are looking for.

- If you've made significant progress and have a good focus area but aren't ready to proceed for other reasons, stop for now. You may be in a position that doesn't allow you to immediately undertake a job search. Perhaps you need to save some more money, or want to get one more promotion before you move on. That's fine. Just don't use it as an excuse to stay stuck. The longer you wait to take action, the more complacent you'll get.

By now you should be pretty confident about the type of job you are seeking. While you don't have to know the exact title, industry, and company name, you should have a general idea of the audience you're going to sell yourself to. The more you know about the audience, the better you can tailor the product—you!

Starting a Search

At this point, sending out resumés and waiting for results is sure to result in failure because you have to prepare before you jump in. There are several ways to launch, organize, and time a real, proactive job search. Also, you'll learn how advanced technology affects your search and how to play with the big boys (and girls).

> **STOP** You should be ready to start a job search. If you don't know where you are headed, it's time to look at or revisit Part One of *The Right Job, Right Now* to figure that out. One of the worst things you can do is to jump into a job search without having a good idea of what you want.

If you are ready to forge ahead, it's time to get organized. Don't worry; the steps in Chapter 7 will help you develop a more effective, timely, and results-oriented job search. You can adapt these steps to whatever method works for you.

Before you can think about getting your hands dirty, you've got to make sure you are in the right mindset. Be prepared: It often gets bad before it gets good. If you've ever planned for a wedding or any large event you know what I mean. The months of planning, wrestling with budgets and decisions, and deciding who to invite, can be overwhelming, tiring, and frustrating. There are even times when you wonder if you should proceed. Deep down, you know that what waits at the end of the process is worth it all in the end. It's going to be the same here.

Just make absolutely sure you're ready. Put up copies of your Career Kaleidoscope everywhere—at your desk, on your bathroom mirror, and on your refrigerator. It's time to get into project management mode. You have to think about your job search like a project and treat it just like you would any other. Imagine if you were assigned a project at the office, and you worked on it whenever you felt like it, with no deadlines and no timelines. Do you think it would ever get done? And if it did, would it be done well?

> **Good to Know:**
> Schedule job search time in large blocks, at least two hours at a time. This way you are more likely to get more accomplished, and ensure you have time to track your work in you electronic workbook. If you're still employed full-time, this might be hard during the week, but that doesn't mean you can't block chunks of time on the weekends.

Imagine the results if you send out resumés when you find positions of interest and merely wait to see what happens. Maybe you used this approach in the past and that's why previous job searches weren't successful. It may be why friends or colleagues complain about trying to find new jobs. They haven't approached a job search like a project.

Project Management

Managing a project requires multiple steps: assessing time, creating a timeline, setting goals and milestones, and having deadlines and accountability for the process. It's not as hard as you think.

1. Assessing Time

If asked, you could probably put percentages on time spent on each of the tasks you do at work. Ten percent of your day is spent on one project, 25 percent on another. You should think about your job search in the same way. In the past, career experts always said you should spend as much time looking for a job as you do in a job. Not true. You need to spend a fair amount of time, but it needs to be quality time. And if you do the search right, it shouldn't take over your life. Should it take precedent? Yes, you do need to shift priorities a bit. Before you can determine how long your search will take, you have to assess how much time you can put into it. Making time for a job search means that something else has got to go. It might be TV time, it might be family time, it might be personal time. It will be your choice—but you have to decide before you begin the search.

Determine realistically how much time you can devote to a search and block the time out on your calendar. If you resort to working on the search only when you have free time, it will never become a priority. You also need to make sure you have uninterrupted time. Whether you have to lock your bedroom or office door, turn off the phone, unplug the TV, or hire a babysitter, do whatever it takes. You can even go to the local library or bookstore if you're tempted by distractions at home. Also, don't let anything trump the time if you can help it. If you receive an invitation to go shopping, play basketball, or watch your favorite television reruns, just say no. You've got a job to find and there are no excuses allowed.

2. Timeline

When do you want to have your new job? Next month? Next year? You need to have a timeline in place to determine how long you are actually willing to devote to this process. Can you have a new job in less than a week? Probably not. Can you find one in less than a year? Absolutely. You want to take your time and find the right fit for your Sweet Spot. However, if you're currently unemployed, or, you're currently employed and have just about had it with your current job, you've got to set an end goal.

There are a million rules of thumb for how long a job search should take. One month for every $10,000 you want to make. Six months in a good economy, over a year in a bad one. Keep in mind that these rules are averages. They include people who have no idea how to do a productive job search and people who are job-search rock stars (soon to be you, of course). So set a time goal for yourself and trust the process. The bottom line is that the more quality time you can spend on the search now, the more quickly you will find the quality position.

3. Goals and Milestones

What's a project without goals? If you've ever been a consultant or been in a job where they begged you to "think outside the box," you know what I mean. You can't plow forward without knowing where you are headed. What will your goals be along the way? If you set a timeline of finding a new job in six months, then try breaking that time out monthly. What will you accomplish each week, each month? As you continue to read *The Right Job, Right Now*, you'll be given more tools and guidance on progressing through the search. Remember that as you read each chapter, you have to set goals for when you'll complete each action. If you don't, how can you reach your ultimate end goal of finding your perfect career?

4. Deadlines and Accountability

Many people hire career counselors or coaches because they need to be accountable to someone. Between family obligations, current jobs, keeping up with friends and the distractions of daily life, who has time to waste?

Can you hire a professional? Sure. Do you have to? Not at all. If you're the self-motivating kind, setting goals and milestones should be enough to keep you on track. If you're like the rest of us normal people, you might just need a regular dose of accountability. You can also find a former colleague, mentor, or boss and ask them to be your career advisor. It's not a big job, just someone who is willing to call you once every few weeks and get a progress report. Make sure that this person isn't a close personal friend or significant other. So you can ensure objectivity.

The Magic of Organization

Organization may be your strong suit or the bane of your existence but, either way, you've got to find the Goldilocks position—somewhere right in the middle. If you proceed without any plan for organization you'll find yourself frantically looking for information or being ill prepared at the wrong time. Over-organize or -engineer your search and you'll spend more time labeling file folders than making networking contacts.

Some method of organization is necessary. You're probably going to have to stretch out of your normal "modus operandi" a little bit. If you're usually the queen of organization, you might want to loosen the reins and spend more time on content than spreadsheets. But if you're a go-with-the-flow kind of guy, it's time to step up the organization a notch.

One way to keep yourself on track is to use your electronic workbook to manage your entire search. Have a tab in the workbook for each aspect of the search and make it easy to track resumés submitted, contacts made, and a job search to-do list. See page 84 for an example of what the tabs of your workbook might look like.

You can also do this in a word-processing program if that's more your speed. But an Excel workbook works best if you have access to such a program.

> **Good to Know:**
> Trying to find a job in a different area than the one in which you currently live? If you can, get yourself a mailing address in that general area so companies don't have to be concerned about your willingness to move or the expense of your relocation. Try using a friend or family member's address, or a P.O. box. After all, most recruiters won't contact you by snail mail anyway. Another strategy is to get a cell phone with your target location's area code.

It's okay if you have your information set up differently; just be sure that you have ready access to all the information you have compiled so far, and that your organizational system can adapt to the addition of new information.

Understanding Recruiting from the Company Perspective

When you are embarking on a job search, it's important to "think like a recruiter." Unless you have an idea what is happening when you apply for a job and how the process works from the company's perspective, you're going to be miles behind your competitors. If you are commonly frustrated with human resources (HR) people or think that because you've hired people before in previous jobs you know the routine, you're wrong. Understanding the process from HR's perspective, whether you like them or not, may be the difference between a productive job search and a futile one.

It's important to understand that many (if not most) medium-to-large companies are now using recruiting management systems (RMS) or applicant tracking systems (ATS). In addition to the benefit of being able to find more candidates this way, these systems help companies comply with the law. According to the government, if a company is a certain size, it has to keep records of every candidate who applies to the company. Managing candidates and applications electronically makes life (and protection from lawsuits) much easier for companies. In most if not all cases, you will have to apply online at some point—we'll talk about exactly when and how in the next chapter.

In addition to making life easier for companies, use of an RMS or an ATS also makes life easier for candidates. Imagine if you had to actually print and mail resumés like job seekers had to do years ago? Some companies still accept hard copy resumé submissions but it's becoming very rare. However, although online submission may seem easier, unless you understand how these systems work, you may be hurting your chances without knowing it.

When you submit your resumé online, the system "captures" or "scans" the resume and cover letter (if one is submitted). What that means is that it copies the text and converts it into the format specified by the system. Then, the re-sumés are cataloged by the system based on the position to which you applied. Each resumé also has an associated code so recruiters and human resources managers can track the number of resumés submitted for each position and other statistics, such as how long it takes to fill certain positions.

Once your resumé is in the system, a recruiter is usually assigned to that position or job requisition. In a typical process, the recruiter responsible for filling that job is the first line of defense. Some frontline recruiters are purely administrative, making sure the resumé is readable, and organizing the resumés as they come in the system. More likely, recruiters review the resumés in batches and make immediate decisions on whether or not the candidate will continue in the process. If the resumé seems like a match, the recruiter will "migrate it" or move it to the interview queue. The recruiter might also add comments to an electronic notes section at the bottom of the candidate's electronic file jus-tifying why the candidate should be interviewed or expressing any concerns. If the resumé is not a fit, it will be immediately archived in the system, and no one else will ever see it unless the archives are searched (which doesn't happen very often).

Note: While recruiters most often manage the line or queue, in some com-panies recruiters may only assume an administrative role, passing all resumés to a hiring manager or staff member for a go or no-go decision on an interview. This is more common in small or more traditional companies.

Depending on the company, once moved to the interview queue, other re-cruiters or hiring managers may have access to the system and the resumé. The electronic file is then moved through the system as the candidate progresses through the interview process or archived when the candidate is rejected. The systems even have the ability (if the company chooses to use it) to generate pre-written rejection letters, which can be automatically composed and sent out when a candidate is electronically moved to the rejection queue.

This may sound robotic, and it can be, but what's most important, it has huge implications for your job search that are crucial to understand before you move forward:

- The style and structure of your resumé may actually hurt your chances. A simple format matters if you want to actually make it through the system.
- You can't bypass these systems altogether. But you can "game" the system in some cases by making sure your resumé is in a format that the system can easily read, or include keywords in your resumé that you know a recruiter might use to search incoming resumés.

- Cover letters are often scanned in the system after the resumé. So you can't assume your cover letter will always be read. If the resumé isn't a strong fit, the recruiter will archive you immediately and not get to the cover letter.
- Recruiters have power. A recruiter may be the first (and often only) person who looks at your resumé. So you have to make it easy for the recruiter to see you are a fit for the job.
- Recruiters have to justify their decisions. No one wants a hiring manager to come back to HR and say "why the hell am I interviewing this person?" If you make it easy for a recruiter to plead your case, you're one step ahead.
- Recruiters have their performance evaluated, too. Often it is based on how quickly they find or source candidates, how good those candidates are, and how satisfied hiring managers are with the process. If you make a recruiter's job easier, your chances increase for getting further along in the process.

These issues are just the tip of the recruiting iceberg, but you can see now why you can't begin a job search blindly, and how in just a matter of a few years (and some hotshot technology) job searching has changed for the candidate and for the company. If you understand the business of recruiting and try to step into a recruiter or hiring manager's shoes to really get a sense of how your candidacy is evaluated, you will have an advantage over others applying for the same job.

STOP *The Right Job, Right Now* assumes you have the legal right to work in the country you are living in. With changes in world security in the recent years, countries are much more strict about granting citizenship. In the United States, many companies require citizenship for employment, because if you don't have a green card or the legal right to work in the United States, sponsorship can be very expensive (and take a very long time) and companies often don't want to foot the bill. Not all companies ascribe to this school of thought so if you aren't a citizen of the country you want to work in, be upfront and honest with potential employers. That way, you don't waste your time or theirs.

Recruiting from Your Perspective (Commonly Called Job Searching)

You're looking for jobs, trying to find options, and seeing what's out there. You need to review your options and decide what you're interested in pursuing further. With your Career Kaleidoscope in hand, and your chosen field and/or industry clearly defined, finding the perfect match shouldn't be too difficult. You just have to know where to look and determine who's in the market to buy what you have to sell. You should start with this question: What are your job-search options?

Five to ten years ago, all job searches began in the classifieds. You might have poured a cup of coffee, opened up your local newspaper, and put your red pen to work circling the ads that made the most sense. Things have changed. Those trusty newspaper ads are still holding strong, but they now compete with online job boards, company Web sites, job aggregators, career fairs, and other resources.

With so many options, and so many of them online, how can you possibly navigate them all? Every source has its pros and cons. Recruiters spend hours trying to decide and justify which source to use, and while you don't have to choose one right now, you do need to make sure you know what's available.

A Final Note About Technology and Job Searching

The way you are job searching today may look different from the way you job search next year. Technology has a great deal to do with this. For example, as recently as 2004, there were few publicized worries about how a person's online presence would affect his/her job candidacy. But today, article after article warns of job offers being denied or employees being fired for unlawful or unbecoming behavior online. Pre-2000 you probably never thought about showcasing your job credentials on a blog or personal Web site. Now, that behavior is commonplace.

Because technology changes so rapidly, it's hard to recommend the exact formula for using technology in your job search. However, ignoring the benefits and risks of technology is not an option.

1) Personal Web presence

What you do on your own time should be your own business. But increasingly, in the world of work, it's not. Recruiters may search Web sites like MySpace.com or Facebook.com for more detail on a job candidate's behaviors. If your site or page is tame, you may be okay. But if it showcases inappropriate or unlawful behavior, it might prevent you from getting a job or even worse, having a job offer rescinded. This is not to say you shouldn't use the Web to comment on blogs, participate in online discussions or even have a family Web site. But you should ask yourself before

Job Search Options

Source*	What It Is	Examples*	Pros	Cons	When to Use
Newspapers	A traditional job search method, many newspapers have weekly or daily job postings both in the paper copy of the newspaper and on the newspaper's Web site.	The newspaper and associated online site of any major daily or weekly newspaper; usually found in papers	• Easy to access • Most jobs are geographically focused	• Losing popularity to other posting options • Can be expensive for companies to post • No specificity—will include jobs of all types and levels	If you're set on staying in a certain region, it can't hurt to rely on the local newspaper as a resource. But don't waste time checking it every day. Most newspapers have searchable online postings. Set up a search and have relevant postings e-mailed to your inbox each day instead.
Career Fairs	A live version of job searching, career fairs events with booths are for employers set up openings with job.	Major newspapers, associations, and colleges often host fairs with companies sometimes interviewing on the spot.	• They are a great way to deliver your marketing message and submit a resumé at the same time • They are a good way to practice your job search skills and networking	Employers often meet hundreds of people in one day and you can get lost in the shuffle	Career fairs are good as a supplement to your job search. They are most effective when the search is targeted to a specific group (ex-military, minority or gender specific, field or industry specific) and are limited to a certain number of attendees.
Online Aggregators	Fairly new to the job search process, online aggregators are Web sites that don't post job	• www.indeed.com • www.simplyhired.com	• Huge time saver; you don't have to visit multiple Web sites	• You can't apply online directly at the aggregator but instead have to go to each site	If you're running a broad search, set an online search and have relevant postings e-mailed to your

Source*	What It Is	Examples*	Pros	Cons	When to Use
	openings but aggregate, or bring together openings from other sites. You run one search on an aggregator and it searches multiple sites for job openings. When you click on a job opening of interest, you leave the aggregator and go to the site where the job is posted.		• You find postings from sources you might have otherwise ignored	of each job you're interested in • The quality of job postings is only as good as the sites the aggregator includes in its search	inbox each day. Evaluate the quality of the position listings and sources you receive to determine whether to continue using.
General Online Job Sites	General job sites are almost commonplace now. For a fee, these sites will post almost any job from a legitimate company on their searchable Web site.	• www.CareerBuilder.com • www.Craigslist.org • www.Monster.com	• Great way to get familiar with what's out there • Broad range of positions • Ability to post your resume and invite responses	• May not feature specialty positions or popular jobs that don't need advertising • More difficult to sift through the volume of jobs to find specific positions of interest	Find one or two sites you really trust, set up an online search and have relevant postings e-mailed to your inbox each day from and evaluate the quality of the position listings and sources you receive to determine whether to continue using.
Specialty Online Job Sites	Often connected with a specialty publication, specialty online job sites post jobs for a fee, but limit their postings to a specialty industry or field.	• DICE (IT jobs) • Jobs In the Money (Finance Jobs) • Chronicle of Higher Education (education jobs)	• Good to find jobs in your specific field • Jobs posted are often highly specific or technical	• Often ignored by some companies because posting fees are high • May miss out on jobs in similar fields	If you're set on a specialty area, or have a very specific interest, specialty Web sites may be one of the best ways to find relevant positions.

Source*	What It Is	Examples*	Pros	Cons	When to Use
Association Web sites	Almost every profession has a nonprofit organization that governs and educates. As an added service to professionals, the associations often maintain job postings.	• Association of International CPAs (AICPA) • Society for Human Resource Mgt. (SHRM)	• Good to find jobs in your specific field • Jobs often screened by staff to ensure legitimacy and relevancy	• May only include jobs from association members • May miss out on jobs in similar fields or at competing associations	Like specialty sites, if you're set on a specialty field/industry, or active in a professional association, these Web sites are a good way to find relevant positions.
College and University Sites	Career centers at colleges and universities often maintain job posting Web sites managed by outside vendors (see examples) that post jobs directed at the university's students or alumni.	• Experience • Job Trak	• The college may have a relationship with the posting employer, giving you an easy in • Jobs are posted because of a specific interest in the associated school	• Jobs are usually posted for multiple schools, increasing your direct competition • Jobs may be posted only if the school has a program in that area, so you might not find direct matches	Evaluate first to determine the quality and level of the postings. If there are postings of interest, have a search set up with results sent regularly to your inbox.
Company Sites	Almost every company has a Careers section on its Web site with job postings and information on life at the company, benefits, and even potential career paths. Companies may also have special site access and listings for alumni of the firm.	The Careers or Job Postings section of any company Web site	• Usually updated by a company's recruiting system so postings are often very timely • Jobs searchable by function and office location	• You're obviously limited to just this one company • You might not have access to all company openings since some may be filled internally or the posting is only put up briefly to meet legal requirements	Visit and apply directly to a company Web site only if you're specifically interested in a certain firm. (Note: If you know someone at the firm, you may want to have them submit your resumé instead for better results—see referrals below).

Source*	What It Is	Examples*	Pros	Cons	When to Use
Affinity Group Web sites	Religious, community, or social groups often exist to serve the needs of their members, which may include job postings of interest.	• NetImpact (for corporate responsibility) • 85 Broads (for women in business) • 40Plus Clubs	• Postings are typically tailored directly to the needs of members • Postings may come from another member and provide you a direct networking connection as well	• Postings may be limited or not updated regularly • Postings may not be searchable or well organized	If you have a very specific or narrow interest or geography, these sites are a good way to locate openings you might not have found otherwise.
Networking Sites	Since more than 50 percent of jobs are found through networking contacts it only makes sense that these sites are increasing in popularity. These sites help you set up an online library of contacts so you can use your contacts to find more contacts, and so on.	• Jobster • Linked In • Ryze	• Most contact systems are searchable so you can search for contacts in a certain field or firm • You can do excellent due diligence on a company and/or a position before an interview	• Connections don't always work out, and can often take a great deal of time • There may or not be an associated job postings site.	If you work in a field where networking is key, then the use of these sites should be a no-brainer. But since they rely on your contacts' willingness to use the site, if your friends and contacts aren't active on the site, they don't always work as well. Either way, you should still investigate at least one of these sites because networking is such a powerful part of the job search.
Referrals	Another strong source of candidates for recruiters, it is esti-	• Company alumni • Friends, family, or former colleagues	• You can get in-depth information about the position and the	You can't bank on the reputation of your referrer—he or she may	Once you know what your focus area is, you should always let the people in

(continued)

(*Table Continued*)

Source*	What It Is	Examples*	Pros	Cons	When to Use
	mated that more than 30 percent of hires come through referrals of people who already work (or have previously worked) at the company. Companies often reward their employees (an alumni) for referring candidates who are eventually hired.		company from the referrer • The referrer can check on the status of your candidacy • The referrer may receive compensation if you're hired	or may not be well respected in the company or have enough clout to make an impact	your Rolodex know so you can be alerted to potential opportunities to be referred. If you are interested in specific companies, proactively approach contacts at those companies to see if there is a referral program.
Executive Recruiters or Head-hunters**	Common at the executive level, executive recruiters or headhunters work on hard-to-fill positions for companies, either on retainer (a flat fee to work on one position until it is filled) or on contingency (paid by the company to the headhunter who actually fills the position).	• Management Recruiters Int'l • Korn/Ferry • Heidrick and Struggles	• Good for manager or executive-level candidates • If you're a good match, the headhunter will do all it can to rally on your behalf	Headhunters are usually working on behalf of the company rather than the candidate, so don't expect exceptional customer service unless you are a good match for the position.	If you are at the executive or managerial level, it may make sense to at least investigate potential headhunters that specialize in your field or industry focus. Use Appendices A & C to learn about and research a few and then contact one or two of interest. (Note: You should never rely solely on a headhunter for your search, or, pay a headhunter *any* money.)

*The sources listed here (and more) can be found in Appendices A & B.
**Appendix C provides a complete overview on using executive recruiters.

any posting: "Would a potential employer find this to be inappropriate?" While you may have control over your own personal Web site, anything you post to another site or blog could be stuck in the Internet forever.

2) Professional Web presence

Many professionals are creating their own Web sites in order to maintain a professional online presence. This may be a career Web site where you showcase your resumé, work experience, or even work samples. Or, it may be a site that demonstrates your subject matter expertise where you write articles about specific topics or provide advice. Either way, it's a great way to appear in more Web searches and get more attention if a recruiter or employer searches your name on the Web. If you're just going to post your resumé and/or experience, you may want to stick to using a site like LinkedIn.com that allows you to post that information and feed it to the Web. However, if you have expertise or more information to showcase, a professional Web site that showcases your experience and expertise is a great idea. Just be sure whatever you post is extremely professional. If found by a recruiter or employer, they will assume it's the same quality of a work product you might provide for them.

3) Blogs

Weblogs, commonly called "blogs" are essentially online diaries. Like a journal or newsletter, they track personal musings, thoughts, and insights for general public consumption online. Many blogs allow readers to comment on what the author has posted and can provide personal insights about specific experiences. In the work world, blogs are very popular. Some may focus on life at work, specific industries or fields, and of course, on job searching and advice. If you're interested in a company, do a Web search to see if the company has a blog—they can be invaluable sources of information. Microsoft (http://blogs.msdn.com/jobsblog/) and T-Mobile (http://recruitersdumpingground.blogspot.com/) are both well-known for their career blogs that are managed by company recruiters. The best way to use blogs is for information purposes. They can augment conversations you have with contacts and give you information and insights you never knew existed.

4) RSS Feeds and Wikis

You may have never heard of the term "RSS feed" or "wiki." But in the simplest terms, they are ways to get information. A wiki is an online resource of information about a particular topic that allows users to read, edit, and add in content they know about that topic. RSS, which stands for "Really Simple Syndication" or "Rich Site Summary" is a technology that allows a user's computer to go and find specific news and information on a certain topic, and have it "fed" to the computer on a regular basis. Both RSS feeds and Wikis are really just ways to get more information about companies, industries, and jobs. Wikis are great for researching areas you don't know much about while RSS feeds ensure you have the latest news and headlines in your field or industry of interest.

5) Online assessments and gatekeepers

Job seekers may also find themselves stumped by technology in the job search. Companies like Sears and The Home Depot may require you to take an online test before they will even evaluate your experience. Other companies may have technical solutions in place to keep you from applying to a job multiple times or limit you from contacting individual recruiters. Even if it's frustrating, it's important to know that recruiting is becoming more and more digitized every day. That's why technology is important in your search, but shouldn't be your only tool.

Finally, don't forget to stay on top of changing technology trends. They change the way companies do business regardless of what business they're in. And, they'll change the way you work *and* job search.

Overload Alert

If you haven't searched for a job in a while, you may be overwhelmed by the sheer number of resources. Don't worry. You're not going to use them all—you're going to choose the ones that work best for you and create a strategy for yourself.

You also have your electronic workbook—your best organizational friend. As you target jobs and send out resumés, you should be tracking your submissions. It makes keeping on top of your search that much more manageable and helps you to track and follow-up every move.

Most important, you've got your Career Kaleidoscope. You're going to use your Career Sweet Spot to carefully choose positions to apply to that are a fit with your Sweet Spot.

STOP Much of what comes next will entail some hard work. Only you know your time constraints and patience-threshold level. How much work can you actually commit to? The more you do, the more successful your job search will be. Do you have to do it all? Not necessarily. Pick and choose what works best for you, or do it all to really set yourself up for success.

Job applications and resumés are sometimes received in a rolling process. Candidates are evaluated as they are interviewed and when a hire is made, the company stops accepting resumés. Other positions are kept open for a period of time, and after the application closing date, the company reviews all of the resumés and decides who to call in for an interview, and makes a hiring decision from that pool. More often than not, especially with the introduction of technology into recruiting, you're going to find yourself in a rolling process.

Does this mean you have to be the first person to apply for a position? Not necessarily. The earlier you apply, the more likely you will be considered. Companies often measure recruiters on what's called "time-to-fill" or how quickly a recruiter can fill a position. So recruiters and hiring managers are going to try to find good candidates fast. On the flip side, if you see a position that's been posted for a long time, it may mean the company is having a hard time finding a good candidate. So if you are a really good fit for the role, don't be discouraged by how long the posting has been up. Apply immediately. Most companies won't keep positions posted unless they want to hire someone.

Now you know what you want, what your focus is, and which companies and industries are in the market to buy what you have to sell. But you've got some competition. Are you ready to learn how to come out on top? In the next several chapters, you are actually going to begin your search. We'll start with getting in that product mindset and creating a marketing plan so you can out-sell your competitors. You'll then get out there and test out your "commercials" and slogans, nail down interviews, and navigate job offers.

8

Selling the Product (That's *You*, Genius!)

Now that you're ready to put yourself on the market and search, it's time to think about yourself like a product and understand the tools you have to promote yourself. These include: a personal introduction, resumés, cover letters, a portfolio, and, possibly, proactive work samples. You don't have to use all of them but you should know what your options are.

Before we get started, think about a time when you watched an infomercial and thought "I should have thought of that" or "I had that idea first." For every product out there, a million other people had the same idea but not everyone had the energy to do something about it. Of those that had the energy, only a few had the know-how to engineer the product and get it to market. There may be many qualified candidates for a job but if you put the energy and focus into presenting yourself in the best light you can succeed above the rest.

Let's take another look at your Career Kaleidoscope. Your Career Sweet Spot, the top elements from each section of the Kaleidoscope, are in the center. They represent the confluence of things that matter to you most, your "must-haves," and the elements that make you unique as a professional—your product attributes. Because there are many qualified people for every job, you need to learn how to position yourself as a product in the best way possible.

Getting in a Product Mindset

The first step toward selling a good product is defining its attributes. Professionals who work in marketing focus on what makes one product better than another. That's why the Career Kaleidoscope is so important. Imagine what a marketer would do if he didn't know what attributes of a product made it so great? How could he possibly sell the product? The same goes for you. The work you did to define your Career Sweet Spot and the rest of the factors in each section of your Career Kaleidoscope are now going to come into play.

You know your attributes, but what about your customers (recruiters, potential employers)? It's not enough for marketers to know their product really well, they also have to know their audience. All of the products you see on your grocery store shelf got there only after the company that made them did a significant amount of market research through focus groups, product testing, or interviews, to learn what the customer wants.

Now you need to revisit your field and/or industry focus to become familiar with what matters to them. Just as a company pitches its advertisements and marketing to its target audience, you need to target your focus areas. Only then will you be ready to create your marketing tools. Companies define their product, do their market research, and then create their advertisements. That's why you created your Career Kaleidoscope and defined your focus areas before you attempt to create your resumé.

When a company launches a new product, it often creates several advertisements that emphasize different attributes targeted to different audiences. For example, a pizza commercial on a sports channel might showcase how the "jumbo-size pizza feeds all the guys for the big game." The same pizza might be advertised on a children's show emphasizing "free cartoon toy with every pizza ordered." Customers consider the pizza because it has the qualities of the food they are looking for (fast, easy, tasty), but they choose one brand of pizza over another based on the unique qualities a particular brand offers.

It may be difficult to think of yourself as a pizza. But *you* are the product that you are pitching and selling to a targeted audience. When you defined your focus area, you may have chosen one field or multiple industries. You are the same person but when you sell yourself to each of these focus areas, you're going to emphasize different qualities based on your audience.

Bill has experience and interest in both marketing and sales. But he has been frustrated in his attempts to find the right job and the right fit for his skills and needs. After completing his Career Kaleidoscope and finally understanding his Sweet Spot, Bill decided to pursue an industry that might be a better fit for him. One of the areas he is focusing on is the consulting industry.

When Bill did his research, he did both Level 1 and Level 2 research. You will recall that Level 1 research ensures that you are educated about the fields and industries you want to continue pursuing. During his Level 1 research, Bill discovered that consulting was a good fit with his Career Sweet Spot. It would make good use of his sales and account-management skills, and his patient, extroverted, and persuasive tendencies would be highly valued. Level 1 research raised the issue of travel. Bill had always heard that consulting required extensive travel. It was important for Bill to find out if this is true, because a limited amount of travel was part of his Sweet Spot.

Level 2 research, as you remember, is where you talk to people in your desired field or industry. During his Level 2 research, as he was deepening his familiarity with the industry, the matter of travel was given top consideration. Bill also asked about typical career paths, levels of education, and other roles in the industry besides those of consultants themselves. After four different conversations and his own research, Bill was able to isolate a specific field within the consulting industry that seemed appealing to him. Not only was travel less of a factor, the job was also a better fit with Bill's skills and behaviors.

He learned that it might be harder to move into a large consulting firm at a mid-level without having had specific consulting experience that included managing the financials (budgets and billing on a project.) But he confirmed that his skills and behaviors would be very applicable and several contacts mentioned an area that consulting firms use to bring in new clients: business development. Business development seems like a great focus for Bill, and he is ready to begin creating his marketing tools based on the audience.

ACTION: Further define your focus area or areas.

The first step in the marketing process is to break your chosen focus areas into target markets and to determine which market you want to pursue initially. Like Bill you may have several targets, but each should be well defined, such as "business development roles in the consulting industry." You don't have to pursue one at a time, but you do have to start somewhere. Once you learn how to promote yourself to one market, changing the message for other markets will be a breeze. Examples of well-defined targets include:

- Plant Manager: manufacturing or retail
- Financial Analyst: technology, healthcare, or pharmaceutical
- Staff Attorney: corporate or business law
- Human Resources Generalist: government or consulting
- Marketing Manager: consumer products or retail
- Manager: information security
- Civil Engineer: construction or commercial
- Investment Banker: financial services or mergers and acquisitions

If you are focused on one field, say sales (though you're willing to work in a number of different industries), try focusing on one or two industries to start. Sales as a field requires negotiation, cold calling, and/or relationship management, but a technology employer looking for a sales professional may value different skills and behaviors than a pharmaceutical employer looking for a sales professional.

Regardless of your industry or interests, it is important that you determine what your target market values in its employees. There are a number of different ways to do this. You can use online job descriptions to track industry and position needs, revisit some of the research sources from Chapter 6 to learn even more about your target industries or fields.

If you don't want to get specific and prefer to focus on a field or industry only, you will have to customize your "commercials" (resumés, cover letters, and so forth) for this broader target audience.

Once his focus area was defined, Bill referred back to the details of his research conversations for that focus area to his Career Kaleidoscope, to confirm there would be a fit. He then came up with Sweet Spot questions—the top questions he would ask himself about each opportunity.

Sweet Spot Questions

1. *Skills:* Does the position require my marketing and creativity skills as well as my organizational and account-management skills?
2. *Behaviors:* Will the successful candidate be both patient and aggressive?
3. *Environment and Culture:* What amount of travel is required? How much will I be challenged intellectually?
4. *Benefits and Rewards:* Is healthcare a given? Can I get a sense if the position is in my salary range?

A yes to all questions meant it was an opportunity worth pursuing. As Bill began to look at opportunities, he could immediately rule in or out certain opportunities to target. For the ones that matched positively with his Sweet Spot questions, and as he researched the position or firm and began to go through the interview process, Bill could use his Career Kaleidoscope to ascertain if the position was a fit.

Keep in mind that these Sweet Spot questions are specific to Bill. After he researched fields and industries, and talked to professionals to narrow his focus, he compared the results to his Sweet Spot and asked questions focused on his specific attributes and needs. After you do your research, you can compare the

results to your own Sweet Spot and ask yourself whether a certain field or industry you want to pursue will make use of what you have to offer and give
you what you most want in return.

> ACTION: Based on your Career Sweet Spot and the research you have done on
> your field and/or industry focus areas, create a list of Sweet Spot questions to
> help you immediately rule in or out opportunities as you find them.

Marketing Tools: How to Craft Your Message

Picture it: you're in the grocery store and looking for a box of cereal. You scan
the shelves up and down, trying to decide which one to pick up. You pick up a
few, examining the labels, the product's claims, and its ingredients before set-
tling on one and throwing it in your cart. You've made the decision to give it a
try. Only later, after you've tasted it, will you decide if you're hooked. You
can't make that decision in the middle of the store.

Job searching is the same way. At this point, I want you to think about getting the recruiter or hiring manager (your customer) to "pick up and notice"
your product. This is where your resumé, cover letter, and other marketing
tools will come into play. Later, you may be called in for an interview, for the
prospective employer to decide whether *you're* worth it, and we'll talk about
interviews in Chapter 10. For now, you want to get selected.

You've probably got some sort of resumé. Let me guess—it's a historical
document that lists where you went to school and where you've worked, right?
It might be a short history of responsibilities, or a long chronicle of successes.
Either way, you're not going to use it anymore. The standard "tell-all" historic
version just won't work. Just imagine if all that box of cereal had on it was a list
of ingredients and a bulleted description of how it was made. Would you be
even tempted to pick it up? Probably not.

I'm not suggesting that you come up with some catchy commercial jingle.
You are a professional, after all. But you can't rely on whoever reads your resumé to put the pieces together and decide that you're worth it. You have to
make it painfully obvious.

You're going to make a few things crystal clear. You're going to tell anyone
who will listen who you are, what you bring to the table, and what you're
looking for. This is why defining your focus areas is so important. You have to
go through the following seven-step process for every focus area.

Step 1: Create your marketing message. You will use this message to introduce yourself to contacts, answer the "tell me about yourself"
question and start your resumé.

Step 2: Create a resumé template that conforms to business expectations
and works with the technology many organizations now use.

Step 3: Create a content library of resumé bullets that demonstrate "what
you have to offer."

Step 4: Choose specific bullets from the content library and complete your
base resumé.

Step 5: Create a cover letter shell that conforms to business expectations
and recruiting technology.

Step 6: Choose additional content bullets and complete your base cover
letter.

Step 7: Determine which additional marketing tools make the most sense
for you.

Step 1: Creating Your Marketing Message

Remember when iPods and MP-3 players first started selling? No one knew
what they were or what those funny terms meant. But Apple and other companies started using succinct marketing messages to let potential customers know
they could "carry an entire library of music in their pockets." Had that message
been confusing, too technical, or too long, the product might not have gotten
off to such a successful start.

You're not about to create a jingle or funny slogan, but you are about to
start the process by creating your own message. The point of creating your
message is so that everyone you talk to in your search knows what you want to
do and why you'd be good at it. Without the right message, you'll have a really
hard time getting in any doors.

There are three aspects of the marketing message: who you are, what you
bring to the table, and what you are looking for.

- *Who You Are*: What kind of professional are you? This isn't the time to be
  general. How would you define yourself in just a few words?
- *What You Bring to the Table*: This includes the skills and behaviors section
  of your Career Kaleidoscope, the "what you have to offer."
- *What You Are Looking For*: What is it that you want? Make clear the position you are looking for in terms as specific as possible.

To put your message together, try taking it one part at a time. Here's how Bill did it:

Dimension	Detail
Who You Are	Marketing and business development professional
What You Bring to The Table	Marketing, sales, and account management experience. Over nine years in marketing and sales. Patience necessary for finding new clients but also aggressive. Persuasive. Good at presentations and at analyzing sales data.
What You're Looking For	Business development position in a management consulting firm.

ACTION: Pull together the components of your message: who you are, what you bring to the table, and what you're looking for.

Essentially, Bill's marketing message pulls together the factors from the skills and behaviors parts of his Career Kaleidoscope. Now he's got the information, he needs to tailor it to his audience. In many cases, honing his message means speaking the language of the target market.

For example, from his research, Bill learned that in consulting, the term "account" isn't used but rather client. He wouldn't be managing or finding accounts, but instead, client relationships. He also knows that he wouldn't be analyzing sales data, but forecasting potential client deals. Finally, he won't use the term "sales," as that word isn't used very often in consulting, either. Instead, he'll focus on "developing new business." It's the same concept but different terminology. With that in mind, Bill creates his initial marketing message:

"I am a marketing and business development professional with more than nine years of experience in successfully finding and growing business opportunities. I am particularly aggressive in pursuing new leads while being patient enough in order to make sure the deal gets done. My expertise also extends to powerful marketing and business development presentations as well as forecasting the potential financial impact of the business I grow. As my career is progressing, I am looking for a mid-level business development position for a management consulting firm that would focus on growing a local market in conjunction with company strategy."

Now, Bill's got a strong message designed to immediately pique the interest of his audience: business development recruiters and hiring managers.

ACTION: Create your marketing message aimed specifically at your first target audience.

Once you have your marketing message, you can adjust it to your specific needs depending on your situation, who you are talking to, or where you are in your search.

Step 2: Creating Your Resumé Shell

Bill's marketing message is the essence of what he wants to do. It serves as the base of his resumé. The next step in the marketing process is to create the shell of your resumé. The shell or format of the resumé is the easiest part, so let's get that out of the way first and then you can focus on content.

Before we dive into the resumé itself, and how you'll use your newly created marketing message to get started, I have to clear up a few things for you. There are a million recommended resumé formats. There are resumé templates in word-processing programs you can use. Don't. The format you're about to learn should become your best friend because it works in business. It's simple, gets your information across, and conforms to business expectations and the recruiting technology that's used today.

STOP Some experts recommend skills-based resumés where the format doesn't list your skills and results by job but by skill. I don't. They're hard to read, and the reader is easily confused by what skill or what result came from which job. Resumés are read counterclockwise. The reader scans down the left-hand side to see where you have worked and up the right-hand side to get a sense of timing. Enable your reader and make it easy!

We'll start with format, and then we'll get to content. There are two sample formats included in this chapter: One sells your work experience first and the other sells your education first. The idea is to start with your strongest selling points. If you are going to land your next job because of a degree you have just attained, then your education should come first. But if your work experience is what the employer will be more interested in, then that goes before education. Either way, each format contains the following sections:

- **Header:** your name and contact information
- **Profile:** a shortened version of your marketing message

- **Professional Experience:** details of the work experience you have had relevant to the position to which you're applying
- **Education:** details of the formal education you have had leading to a degree or as part of a degree program
- **Professional Development:** a summary of how you have continued to develop yourself professionally, including details on your training, certifications, technology skills, volunteer work, and language skills

When you look at the format recommendations beginning on page 108, you will notice that they are in a simple font, and have no elaborate graphics, lines, or italics. Because many organizations are now using computerized Resumé Management Systems, it is important that your resumé be "scannable." This means when your resumé is received, it is scanned immediately into an electronic database before it is read by anyone. These systems can't read fancy fonts, graphics, or other aesthetic features. They also often left-justify (line up on the left-hand side of the page) every line, so simplicity will ensure that when your resumé is scanned into the system and printed, it will appear the way you intend. Bill's original resumé had his headers in the left margin followed by the text.

Bill's Original Resumé

It looks nice when it's printed out, but here's how a recruiter will likely see it when Bill applies for a position online:

Bill McCarrick
37 Marston Circle | Atlanta, GA 12345
(410) 555-7789 | billmccarrick@emailaddress.com

EDUCATION VIRGINIA TECH Blacksburg, VA
Bachelor of Science, 1995
• Major: Biology; Minor: Health Sciences
EXPERIENCE ALLIED HEALTH COMPANY Atlanta, GA
2002–present Allied Health is an $8-billion pharmaceutical firm specializing in medicine and health solutions for

See how everything runs together? The boldface type and the lines disappeared as did any sense of formatting. Not only does this make the resumé hard for the recruiter or hiring manager to read, but even if they get past your headache of a resumé, when you come in for your interview your interviewers are going to have this terribly formatted version of your resumé in front of them. In any case, it's not exactly the impression you're going for. Recruiters usually print resumés for use directly from the system, or, in some cases, they simply route the electronic version (as it appears above) directly to the interviewer. Even if you bring a copy with you they will have already seen the one given to them in advance of the interview.

This doesn't mean you have to have a plain resumé, or that you can't use lines or boldface type, but you want to make sure that the format you use will work in any situation. After all, you might be attaching your resumé to an e-mail to a networking contact, submitting your resume as RTF (rich text format) on an online job board such as Monster or CareerBuilder, or passing a paper copy along to a friend. It's also important to keep in mind that you want your format to reflect your skills and experience well and you may want to combine pieces of both format options. Whichever format you choose, work on your format first. Content comes next.

In each of the recommended

Good to Know:

If you are applying for a government position or a position in a non-American company, a different format may be recommended or required. For example, government submissions often require a specific resumé format and associated application, and international companies (and academic institutions) may request your photo and/or an academic resume often called a curriculum vitae or CV). If you are in this situation, be sure to consult the organization for specific formatting instructions.

formats, you'll notice that they start with a profile that is a shortened version of your marketing message. You probably will also have specific questions about the format in each section. For example, why are the dates right-justified? Since resumés are read counterclockwise, it's important for the dates to stand out. When formatted electronically, the dates may shift over to the left again, but they won't hurt the formatting. Small tricks like these will help ensure that your resumé works *with* the system, not against it. A complete formatting guide follows on page 108.

Selling Your Work Experience First

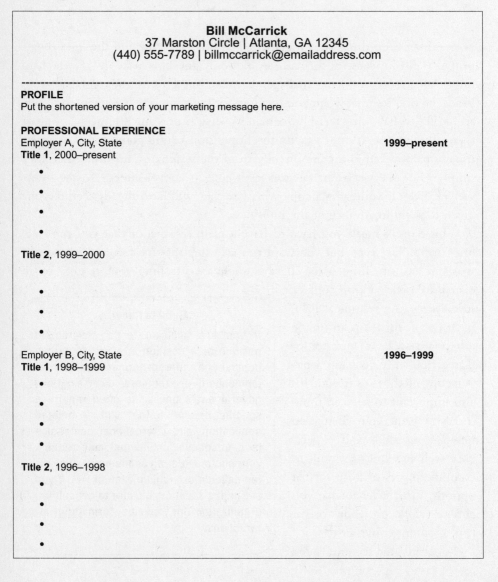

Bill McCarrick
37 Marston Circle | Atlanta, GA 12345
(440) 555-7789 | billmccarrick@emailaddress.com

PROFILE
Put the shortened version of your marketing message here.

PROFESSIONAL EXPERIENCE
Employer A, City, State   **1999–present**
Title 1, 2000–present

-
-
-
-

Title 2, 1999–2000

-
-
-
-

Employer B, City, State   **1996–1999**
Title 1, 1998–1999

-
-
-
-

Title 2, 1996–1998

-
-
-
-

EDUCATION
BS, Biology   **1995**
Minor: Health Sciences
Virginia Tech, Blacksburg, VA
Honors and Achievements: Erwin T. Dowds scholarship for academic excellence

PROFESSIONAL DEVELOPMENT
Technology skills: Microsoft Word, Microsoft Excel, Microsoft PowerPoint, Bloomberg,
                           Lexis-Nexis
Training: Leadership for the Next Century, Advanced Facilitation
Languages: Fluent in French, proficient in German
Volunteer: Reading tutor, Hendley Elementary, Atlanta, GA

Selling Your Education First

Stephanie Marstelle
111 King Street, #402 | Chicago, IL 12345
(248) 555-0952 | marstelles@domainname.com

PROFILE
Put the shortened version of your marketing message here.

EDUCATION
MBA Finance, GPA: 3.6/4.0   Expected May 2006
Graduate University, Chicago, IL
Finance Projects: List projects completed, client/company names if applicable. Include any projects
done in conjunction with coursework.
Finance coursework: Advanced Financial Accounting, Corporate Financial Theory, Derivative
Securities, Financial Statement Analysis, U.S. Federal Income Tax, Investment Analysis and Portfolio
Management

BS Economics, GPA: 3.2/4.0
Minor: Political Science   May 1995
State University, Somewhere, PA
Study Abroad: International Economics, University of Spain, Madrid, Fall 1998
Honors and Achievements: State University scholarship for academic excellence, Treasurer—Delta
Sigma Pi professional business fraternity, self-financed 100% of education

PROFESSIONAL EXPERIENCE
Title   2000–2004
Employer A, City, State

-
-
-
-

Title
Internship A, City, State   Fall 1999

-
-
-

Title
Internship B, City, State   Summers 1998, 1999

-
-
-

PROFESSIONAL DEVELOPMENT
Technology skills: Microsoft Office (specify specific programs if advanced), Crystal Reports 9.0, BizBench 2003, HarrisData Financial Management
Training: Advanced Microsoft Excel (June 2002), Effective Presentations (December 2002)
Certification: Certified Financial Analyst (CFA), completed Part I (March 2003)
Languages: Fluent in Spanish, proficient in French
Volunteer: Habitat for Humanity (2004–2006), Locks for Love (2003)

ACTION: Create your resume shell

Let's get the shell of your resumé together so you're ready to get serious about marketing.

Overall

As you set up your document, keep in mind that while the resumé shell will likely be one page, when you add in your content, you may go to two pages. As long as you have at least five years of work experience, two pages is fine. No matter how long you have been working—even you big, bad executive types out there—never go over two pages. You also want to make sure you use a simple font (Arial or Times New Roman are the best) and you have margins of about one inch. You can get away with less than one inch but don't go below one-half inch. Finally, don't think about using one of those pre-designed resumé templates that some software programs offer. They may seem to make your life easier now, but will only cause huge formatting and uploading problems later.

You also may want to consider adding a line or two under each company name to describe the company. This is entirely optional, but some job seekers like to include what the company does, how much it is worth, and even its stock symbol so the reader knows about the kind of environment you worked in.

Header

Your header contains your name and contact information so that organizations can identify and contact you. When completing this section, bear in mind:

- Don't confuse the header on your resumé with the header (or footer) function in your word-processing program. If you use the header function for your resumé header it may not make it through the resumé scanners. Imagine—a great resumé and no way for a company to contact you. Not so helpful in finding a new job.
- Center the header—and make sure it is the only thing that is centered. It balances out the page and will read fine even when scanning systems force it to be left-justified.
- Be sure your name stands out, and if you have a nickname you normally go by in your professional life, include it in parentheses.
- Include one or two phone numbers where you can be easily reached (home and cell are best) and be entirely sure that the contact information is correct; the outgoing messages on those voicemail numbers should be professional and simple. Even if you love the smooth jazz playing in the background of your voicemail or the voice of your cute eight-year-old leaving the message, you're going to need a professional voicemail to pinch hit for the duration of your search.
- Use an e-mail address that reads professionally instead of an informal one that relates to a family nickname, favorite sports team, or hobby; neither ScrapbookingQueen@domain.com or EaglesRock@email.com is what you're going for here.
- If you're currently working, don't use your work e-mail address or phone number. Otherwise it may seem as though you're job searching at work—which you don't want to showcase (even if you are).
- Include certifications or degrees if common to do so in your field (i.e., including J.D. after your name is common if you have a law degree, but including M.A. or M.B.A. is not).

Example Header:
Elizabeth (Beth) R. Johnson, C.P.A.
1215 Dogwood Trail | Denver, CO 11111
(303) 555-1111 (h) | (303) 555-2222 (c)
beth_johnson@domainname.com

Profile

Your profile is a shortened version of your marketing message that appears at the top of your resumé. It should draw the reader in and make clear to him what you want to do. However, unlike your marketing message, it should not be conversational, long, or in the first person. When completing this section keep in mind:

- It should be three to five lines at the top of your resumé. If you have only a few years of work experience, stick with two or three lines. If you're a manager or an executive, four or five is acceptable.
- It should not be phrased in either the first person ("I") or third person ("Ms. Johnson").
- It should not sell anything you can't demonstrate from your work experience. Your profile tempts the reader into wanting to read further. You must be able to back up your claims in your content (we'll get to that shortly).
- You can include a degree if the job requires it, or if you're about to finish a degree program (i.e., "M.B.A. candidate with six years of . . .").

Example Profile:

Technical marketing manager with successful track record at entrepreneurial start-ups and strong project management skills. Keen ability to motivate and manage people, and strong, hands-on technical skills in Web-based marketing. Highly motivated and organized professional seeking a marketing management position in a for-profit company.

If you are struggling with the profile for now, you're in good company. Kyle, a marketing manager in the media industry, wants to translate his experience into a project management or product development role. Here's his initial try at creating a profile:

Profile: Take 1

Project manager with eight years of experience. Have developed a lot of programs and have marketing experience. Am detail-oriented and focused on business strategy while maintaining timelines and budgets. Proven negotiator looking to continue success by forging new relationships with internal corporate clients as well as outside vendors.

This is a good start but it is somewhat hard to follow. Here are some suggestions to make it even stronger:

1. Don't use first-person tense. Kyle's use of "Am detail-oriented" reads as written in the first person.
2. Is his first sentence as strong as it could be? Because it is the first thing a reader will read when picking up Kyle's resumé, he needs a stronger opening.
3. Is he selling the skills that matter to his audience? Negotiation may be important in a number of roles, but is it one of the things he should sell to his audience? Not necessarily.
4. What is he looking for? Putting only skills and strengths in a profile leaves the reader to guess about where you want your career to go. Don't leave it up to the reader. Tell them what you are looking for.

Check out how much stronger Kyle's revised profile is:

Profile: Take 2

Motivated and highly organized project manager with more than eight years of experience successfully developing and implementing marketing and partnership programs. Background in trade show and special promotion planning and execution with success in forging strong relationships with both internal corporate clients and outside vendors. Detail-oriented professional looking to leverage strengths in marketing and partnerships in a Product Development Manager role.

The revised version is strong, not too long, and showcases the things that will matter most to the person making the hiring decision. When we get to the content of your resumé, we will revisit your profile and ensure that its content backs up what you have in your profile.

Professional Experience

The Professional Experience section is designed to showcase elements of your work history that are the most relevant to the audience receiving your resumé. Remember, you are not putting in content (sentences next to your bullets) right now. We'll soon focus on the content of this section. For now, just get the formatting right and include a few bullets for each position. When formatting this section, there are a few things to think about:

- For each employer, be sure you list each position beginning with the most recent first—it shows progression and promotion—and make sure you put bullets under each position. If you list all your positions first and then put one set of bullets underneath, you can't show how your responsibilities increased and improved as you moved up in the organization.

- Don't trade bullets for paragraphs. There's a reason good advertisements are concise—they get your attention.
- Position the date for the entire time you worked at the company almost to the far right (but not all the way over—if someone opens your document and their margins are set bigger than the ones you have, your date will fall to the next line and interrupt your format.)
- If you had multiple positions at one company, put dates you worked at each position after the position title (see below).
- List company name first, but use capital letters for what will matter more to your audience: the company name or your title.
- List titles in terms your audience will understand. Don't ever (and I mean *ever*) lie on a resumé. But if your title is Budget Associate IV, will a reader know what that means? Substitute a generic title (Budget Manager in this case) that makes more sense. If your old boss would agree that your role was that of a Budget Manager, then you should feel comfortable adjusting the title on your resumé.

Example listing in Professional Experience:

Discovery Communications, Bethesda, MD   **2000–2003**

HUMAN RESOURCES MANAGER, 2002–2003
- Bullet 1
- Bullet 2

HUMAN RESOURCES GENERALIST, 2000–2002
- Bullet 1
- Bullet 2

Education

The Education section is designed to showcase degrees or coursework you have completed at degree-granting institutions. When completing this section, keep in mind:

- Be formal—don't write sentences (i.e., BS, Business and not "received BS in business").
- List the degrees first—they are always more important than where you got them, even if you did go to Harvard. However, be sure to list the name of university or college below the degree, as it should be included.

- Include major, thesis, and/or specific coursework if these are important to the audience reading your resumé.

- If you are at the managerial or executive level, you shouldn't waste space on additional information such as coursework or university honors and awards unless they are crucial to your field, or you completed a degree very recently.

- If you choose to include the school's city and state, be sure to list it after the institution.

- If you are currently in school, put your projected graduation date if degree completion is more than a semester away (i.e., "Expected May 2005").

- Tab over graduation dates almost to the far right, as explained above.

- Include Grade Point Average (GPA) only if you are in school or about to finish a degree, or, if you have less than three years of work experience and an exceptional GPA (3.5 or above). If you are in school, or about to graduate, include graduate GPA if over 3.6 and include undergraduate GPA if over 3.0. Keep in mind that some companies, regardless of how much work experience you have or how long you have been out of school, may request GPAs and test scores. Have this information ready just in case.

Professional Development

The Professional Development section is designed to showcase the additional work and effort you have undertaken to develop yourself professionally. When completing this section, keep in mind:

- Use formal titles of software and be sure to spell them correctly and use correct capitalization.

- Be sure to include leadership roles if you have them (i.e., Vice President, Baltimore Chamber of Commerce).

- Volunteer activity is optional; include it if it shows community involvement or is relevant to your area of expertise (i.e., finance analyst who is also treasurer of a local community group).

- Interests (though not included below) are also optional. If you choose to include interests, do so only if unique or outstanding (i.e., triathlete, licensed pilot). Don't list interests that are common (love to travel) or are too personal (married, three children). After all, this is a business document.

Example listing in Professional Experience:	
Technology Skills:	Formal training in: XHML, HTML, ASP, JavaScript, SQL, Dreamweaver, Flash, and Photoshop; proficient in all Microsoft Office programs, advanced training courses in PowerPoint and Excel
Awards:	ABC, Inc., Customer Service Excellence Award, 2001 and 2003; "Best Navigation" (2004) received as lead designer of ThisWebsite.com
Associations:	American Marketing Association, Public Relations
Volunteer:	Webmaster, Boy Scout Troop #535 of Eastern Maryland

Now that you have a resumé shell created, take a minute to go back over the format using the checklist below.

Resumé Formatting Checklist

☐ **Overall:** Your resume should *never* be more than two pages (unless it is a CV for an academic job or a government application); do not use a resumé template from a program such as Microsoft Word.

☐ **Style:** Don't go any smaller than 10-point font (10–12 point is desirable depending on the font you use); don't make margins any smaller than .5 (1.0 is desirable); don't use different fonts, fancy fonts, or graphics and don't overdo the use of capitals, bold, or other stylistic tools (if you are in a very creative field such as graphic design, check with peers to see what's customary).

☐ **Readability:** Use font size, caps, and boldface to make resumé readable (these can usually be picked up by electronic systems that scan resumés); ensure that dates, positions, and titles stand out when visually scanned.

☐ **Tense:** Use correct tense throughout your resume—never, never, never use first ("I") or third person ("Ms. Johnson worked in . . .") on a resumé.

☐ **Justification:** Don't use the tool that allows you to end-to-end justify your text (this is where paragraphs are even on either side and spacing is different in between words); tab dates to the right, and left-justify everything else.

☐ **Underlining:** Don't use underscore or lines—resumé management systems and scanners won't read them, instead use boldface, caps, and different font sizes to make resumé more readable and streamlined.

☐ **Consistency:** Make sure your spacing and formatting are consistent. If you indent the job title in one section, make sure you indent all job titles; if you capitalize headers, make sure you capitalize all headers, and so forth.

☐ **Capitalization:** Make sure you *only* capitalize formal titles—functional areas such as education or marketing don't need to be capitalized unless they are part of a course title, publication title, or other formal title.

☐ **Jargon:** Watch jargon—make sure you spell out names and then put the corresponding acronym in parentheses the first time you use it: i.e., Social Security Administration (SSA).

☐ **State:** Use postal abbreviations and no periods (i.e., PA, TN, or DC).

☐ **Citizenship:** Don't include this on a resumé unless you a new citizen of the country.

☐ **References:** Don't include them or indicate they are available, as you *should* always have them available. (We'll cover how to handle references later in the chapter).

☐ **Read and review:** Fix even the smallest errors—read and reread your resumé dozens of times including out loud and backward to catch punctuation or misspellings that the spell-check function ignores (i.e., form instead of from).

☐ **Test your resumé:** Send to several friends via e-mail and also test your resumé out on company Web sites to see if formatting remains intact—post the resumé on the site and see what happens when it is electronically formatted.

You should now have a shell of a resumé that's easy to read, technology friendly, and is ready for your content.

Step 3: Creating Your Content Library

You've got a strong resumé shell, but now you have to fill in the blanks and tell the reader what you did at each job. You'll hear numerous opinions about what to write on a resumé, and what recruiters, hiring managers, and professionals want to see. If you take away anything from *The Right Job, Right Now*, let it be this:

Your resumé is your personal commercial. It should not only showcase what you did, but how you did it better or differently than someone else with similar experience. Simply put: it sells you.

Think about it this way. Two financial managers are applying for the same job, and have similar experience. One of the managers has the following bullet on his resumé:

- Managed budgets for all departments

And the other manager (who also has the same responsibility at his job) has this bullet:

- Managed overall budget of $1.1 million; created innovated Access database to manage all budget activities, including expense tracking, vendor payments, and spending patterns, resulting in director's approval of new budget allocations and a savings of more than $20,000.

Which candidate do you think will get called in for an interview? Does this mean you have to write long paragraphs and share excessive detail? No. The goal is to whet the appetite of the reader and get them excited about what you could do if you were hired.

Before we move any further, let me dispel a few myths for you:

MYTH #1: A resumé should list job descriptions or what you were responsible for at each job.

A job description should list what you were responsible for. A resumé should list what you actually did. It shouldn't list everything. A resumé is a collection of highlights. You will choose highlights that will matter most to your audience and describe the actions you took and results that followed.

MYTH #2: Each bullet on a resumé should be only one line.

By limiting yourself to one line for each bullet, you severely limit the ability to put any detail in your resumé that separates you from other candidates. The goal is to find the balance between selling yourself by well-chosen descriptions and being concise at the same time.

MYTH #3: You should list every job you have ever had on your resumé.

As a general rule, if you are a business professional, you should not list anything before college (no need to know where you got your high school diploma) or any jobs that aren't related to your career. For example, if you worked at McDonald's while you were in high school, it probably won't matter to your audience—unless you're applying to work at McDonald's corporate headquarters. In that case, the recruiter might be impressed that you understand how their business works, and have actually been behind the counter. On the other hand, if you're a manager or executive, you may be tempted to omit jobs that you think aren't relevant. If you're tight on space you can simply list jobs at the beginning of your career (without any content). Be careful about leaving out jobs in the middle of your career. Gaps on your resumé can be problematic (though they can be managed). You don't want to give the impression that you weren't working for a period of time unless you really weren't.

MYTH #4: You don't need a profile on your resumé.

This might be one of the most hotly contested myths. If you want to be a strong competitor, you need a profile. Without a profile, you run the very big risk of letting the reader decide whether you are a fit for the position in question. It's like selling a product with no advertising. The product may be good, but sometimes you have to reel the audience in so they get to see it. I say it time and time again: The resumé gets you in the door, and the interview gets you the job. Right now, you just want to get picked. Additionally, the profile sets up the content of your resumé. It makes the reader perk up and say "hmmm, interesting, I want to read more." Then the content of the resumé gives examples and verifies the claims you made in the profile. It's a perfect piece of marketing.

You reach perfection by creating a content library to use for your search. A content library is essentially a collection of resumé bullets. Every time you send out a resumé, you choose the bullets that will matter most to your audience. You have already done the work determining what you have to offer with your Career Kaleidoscope. Now you need to come up with examples. Essentially, for each skill you have listed on your Kaleidoscope, you want to have an example of how you used that skill in one or more of your jobs. Bill, who at this point had decided on business development roles in the consulting industry, has created his resumé shell. Now he needs to create his content. He returns to his electronic workbook and creates a third tab: his content library. Bill's library is essentially empty now, but each blank space is a potential resume bullet. Here's how it works. For each skill he wants to sell, Bill goes back to the original breakdowns he created when he developed his Career Kaleidoscope. As you'll see below, he's broken down his sales skills as an example. Then for each of the jobs he has held so far, he thinks about whether he has an example from that job to potentially showcase on a resumé.

For example, he didn't use most of his sales skills as a staff scientist, so he doesn't have any examples there. But he does have examples of research and data analysis from his time as a staff scientist. Bill goes through his whole chart and puts an X where he can't demonstrate skills/behaviors and a ✓ where he does have an example. Now Bill needs to fill in powerful content in his resumé.

Once Bill creates his content, all he has to do is determine which content to cut and paste into his resumé for a given job. Your background should match at least 75 to 80 percent of what the job description is looking for, if you consider

Jobs Held

Rank	Skill	Canton Pharmaceuticals: Staff Scientist	Canton Pharmaceuticals: Sales Representative	Canton Pharmaceuticals: Marketing Manager	Allied Health: Marketing Manager
1	Sales	✗	✗	✗	✗
	Prospecting	✗	✓	✗	✗
	Relationship development	✗	✓	✓	✓
	Customer education	✓	✓	✓	✓
	Negotiation	✗	✓	✓	✓
	Closing the deal	✗	✓	✗	✗
	Relationship management	✗	✓	✓	✓
2	Account management	✗	✗	✓	✓
3	Marketing	✗	✗	✓	✓
4	Presentations	✗	✗	✓	✓
5	Research	✓	✗	✓	✗
6	Data analysis	✓	✗	✓	✓
Rank	**Behavior**				
1	Patient	✓	✓	✗	✗
2	Extroverted	✗	✗	✓	✓
3	Persuasive	✗	✗	✓	✓
4	Aggressive	✗	✓	✗	✗
5	Intuitive	✗	✗	✓	✓
6	Methodical	✓	✓	✗	✗

applying. Otherwise, honestly, it's just a waste of your time. Job descriptions are meant to give an overview of the basic requirements for the job. Why would they invite a candidate in for an interview who didn't meet at least a majority of the requirements? Applying for a small number of jobs that are a strong match with what you have to offer and what you want in return will yield many more results than simply mailing your resumé to every position that's a vague match.

For example, if Bill found a job description for a business development manager in the consulting industry by reviewing the description below, he highlights the major skills they are looking for. This not only tells him that the job is a good fit, but that now his resumé will match what they are looking for.

Once Bill has highlighted the job description, he goes to his resumé shell and lists the skills and behaviors from the job description that he knows he can showcase in each job. Remember, while he can showcase his data analysis and research skills during his days as a staff scientist, he can't showcase sales skills.

JOB OPENING: Suburban Atlanta office

Management Solutions is currently seeking a Business Development Manager for our suburban Atlanta office. This unique and exciting opportunity requires a savvy business development professional with experience in consultative or services-oriented sales. This is an amazing opportunity to make a huge impact by taking the company to a higher level. This position offers a tremendous amount of responsibility, autonomy, and the opportunity to build a new office from the ground up. Management Solutions offers a generous compensation package with an attractive incentive bonus plan, and an outstanding benefits package.

Responsibilities include:

- Developing and building existing business accounts
- Developing new business relationships
- Developing and building a pipeline of opportunities
- Meeting with and leveraging partner relationships
- Delivering presentations
- Supervising teams delivering projects

The right candidate will have:

- Eight-plus business experience and at least 5 years in business development/delivery capacity
- Proven track record in implementing account penetration strategies
- Proven experience developing senior-level relationships, and achieving revenue goals
- Exceptional interpersonal skills and ability to build lasting client relationships
- Excellent presentation, communication, and negotiation skills
- Expertise in team selling, consultative selling, and relationship management
- Willingness to travel minimally: travel requirements: 10–15 percent

---

If research skills aren't important to his audience, as in this case, then, under his role as a staff scientist, Bill can eliminate any content about research and instead put content that focuses on data analysis and other skills/behaviors that are more applicable. Once Bill has made his choices based on the job description, his resumé now looks like this:

Bill McCarrick
37 Marston Circle | Atlanta, GA 12345
(440) 555-7789 | billmccarrick@emailaddress.com

PROFILE
Marketing and business development professional with more than nine years of success finding and growing business opportunities. Aggressive in lead pursuit while maintaining patience and professionalism during negotiation. Strong presentation and financial forecasting abilities. Seeking a mid-level, local-market business development position within a management consulting firm.

PROFESSIONAL EXPERIENCE

ALLIED HEALTH, Atlanta, GA   **2004–present**
Title 1, 2004–present
   • Marketing
   • Presentations
   • Extroversion
   • Sales (business development)

CANTON PHARMACEUTICALS, Alpharetta, GA   **1996–2004**
Marketing Manager, 2003–2004
   • Marketing
   • Presentations
   • Data Analysis
   • Sales (business development)

Sales Representative, 1998–2003
   • Aggression
   • Sales (business development)
   • Patience
   • Presentations

Staff Scientist, 1996–1998
   • Data Analysis
   • Customer Education
   • Methodical

EDUCATION
BS, Biology   **1996**
Minor: Health Sciences
Virginia Tech, Blacksburg, VA

PROFESSIONAL DEVELOPMENT
Technology skills: Microsoft Word, Microsoft Excel, Microsoft PowerPoint, Lexis-Nexis
Training: Strategies for Superior Selling (1999), Advanced Facilitation (2003)
Languages: Fluent in French, elementary Spanish
Volunteer: Reading tutor, Hendley Elementary, Atlanta, GA

You can see he has keywords listed by each bullet. Now he needs to go back to his content library and make his selections based on keyword.

STOP If you feel like you are really short on time, or just don't have the energy to create a content library, at least use the keyword trick above. Doing so will ensure that your resumé really markets you to your target audience. And if you can make time to create a content library later, great. If you start sending out more than a few resumes, you'll see just how valuable it is.

Of course before Bill can pull his bullet points for his resumé from his content library he has to create it first. And so do you. The best way to start is to go through and try to create the content on your own. Use your job description, old performance evaluations, and any notes you have kept on your successes to create a bullet point for each box of your content library where you have a ✓. If you don't like using a chart, try compiling your content in a word-processing document and breaking it out by job or by skill.

ACTION: Create your own content library.

Right now, you are starting with a base resumé for your first target audience. You will want to do a base resumé for each of your targets. If you have to send a resumé to a contact and not necessarily for a specific position opening, you'll choose the base resumé that's the best fit for the contact. *You should also customize your resumé every time you send it.* Just as marketers do when selling a product, your content should sell what matters most to the audience who will read it.

Regardless of how you choose to manage your content, as you begin to create your content, it is important to remember several crucial things:

1. **Don't simply list a job responsibility.** You have to help the reader to understand not only what you did but *how* you did it better than someone else with the same job description.

2. **Use metrics or numbers whenever possible.** Quantify—include the amount of the budget you managed, the number of people you supervised, the percentage increase in sales, the number of client accounts you managed, etc. Metrics are not just for finance professionals—look through your resumé to determine where a bullet point can become more detailed when it is quantified or when you add scope.

3. **Lead your bullets with action words.** This format allows you to indicate what you did first, and then end with the result. Be sure to use the present tense for a job you still hold (Manage ten . . .) and past tense for jobs in the past (Developed a comprehensive . . .).

4. **Eliminate vague words.** Using words like "some" or "various" or "many" doesn't give the reader an idea of exactly what you're referring to.

5. **Don't use the words "responsible for."** It can leave the reader wondering, "Well, he was responsible for that but did he actually do it? And how?"

When you do your first draft of your content library, you should start with job responsibilities, but never end there. To help you create powerful content, try the six dimensions of the Resumé Bullet Creation framework: Who-what-where-when-why-how →WOW!

The idea is to use a combination of the first six (who, what, where, when, why, how) and end with a WOW (the result of what you did). This method not only makes your content powerful, but helps you manage your work history and career success and long-term achievements. Later in your search it also will make preparing for interviews a walk in the park.

To use this Resumé Bullet Creation framework, ask yourself the series of questions below about each job responsibility. Once you have answered all of the questions, you can combine all or some of the components with the WOW.

This is how the financial manager from our earlier example did it:

Resumé Bullet Creation Worksheet

RESPONSIBILITY: Manage budget		
Who	Who did you do it for?	Managed budget for 15-person human resources department serving 400 people in the office
What	What exactly did you do?	Allocated $1.1 million in funds and expenses for department, approved spending, tracked expenses, ensured vendors were paid, and alerted manager of overages
Where	Where was the work performed?	"Compiled data in an Access database I created"
When	When was the work done?	Have done this for two years, work on it every week, monthly reports send to HR Director

(continued)

(*Table Continued*)

RESPONSIBILITY: Manage budget		
Why	Why did you do it?	Want to eventually manage large HR projects and Director thought having budget experience would help
How	How did you do it?	Used one day a week as way to manage budget and still do other tasks. People knew what day was the "budget day."
WOW!	What was the result?	Using the Access database I created, I found where money was being spent excessively and maderecommendations to Director on where to cut so we could afford HRIS upgrade for department.
RESULT	• Managed budget of $1.1 million; created innovated Access data base to manage all budget activities, including expense tracking, vendor payments and spending patterns, resulting in Director's approval of new budget allocations to allow for much-needed department software upgrade.	
NOTES	This individual didn't include every dimension in the resulting bullet above, but instead chose the items she thought would be most important to her audience. Further, she can use this chart to help address interview questions about this particular responsibility.	

Review some of these other content examples to help you become more efficient in crafting results-oriented and accomplishments-focused content for your resumé:

- *Finance professional:* Utilized primary research, advanced financial analysis, and forecast modeling techniques to provide competitive market assessments, policy analysis, and market forecasts used to evaluate emerging trends and developments in the telecommunications industry.

- *Marketing professional:* Dramatically increased search engine rankings by researching and implementing the latest techniques (e.g., Web page optimization) to generate high search engine rankings on desired keywords that resulted in reaching and maintaining a top ten position on Google, AltaVista, AskJeeves, and AlltheWeb.

- *Real estate professional:* Managed government-assisted and conventional multifamily residential properties in New Jersey, New York, and Maryland; maintained occupancy rates between 95 and 100 percent; prepared monthly status reports on seven properties; worked closely with local and state housing authorities; conducted monthly site visits to out-of-state properties; was involved in advertising and marketing decision-making process.

- *International or Non-Governmental Organization (NGO) professional:* Supervised six internal staff members and oversaw an annual budget greater than $500,000; negotiated and resolved budget and staff issues with local and overseas staff and teams of domestic and foreign specialists in Russia, Turkmenistan, Kazakhstan, Azerbajan, and Uzbekistan.
- *HR professional:* Designed and delivered more than a thousand hours of training for executives, managers, and employees on risk prevention, wellness, and the work/life topics that have an impact on more than 300 corporations, institutions, and community organizations; received ratings of "excellent" from over 94 percent of participants.
- *Sales professional:* Served as operational leader of supplier of learning toys and games, educational materials, and classroom resources to schools, childcare centers, parents, and teachers, with seven retail locations, two catalogs, and 70+ employees.
- *Management professional:* Developed start-up business and financial strategy acquiring necessary financing, developing sales and marketing leads, and creating company technical databases, while emphasizing team building among a six-person staff.
- *Healthcare professional:* Performed an assessment and gap analysis for a process redesign implementation pertaining to staffing, facilities, referral management, and operations for the Guthrie Healthcare Clinic.
- *Sales Professional:* Increased sales 171 percent due to acquisitions and new store openings while experiencing two years of more than 100 percent profit increases thanks to expense stability and increased distribution.

Step 4: Complete Your Base Resumé for Your Target Market

Career Kaleidoscope? Done. Resumé shell? Done. Content library? Done. You should be feeling pretty accomplished by now. You are completely comfortable with what you have to offer and what you want in return, and you've got a good sense of your message. Now it's time to pull it all together.

With your content library complete, you're ready to finally put together

your first piece of marketing material, your first commercial—your resumé. You should be able to cut and paste at this point, inserting content into your resumé to create the base resumé for your first target market.

The base resumé is just that—a starting point. For Bill, it is the starting point to apply for every position that plays a business development role in the consulting industry. Now every time he wants to apply for such a job, he pulls out the base resumé for this target market, compares it to the job description, and makes any changes he thinks are necessary to further customize the resumé to the company. Essentially, he's followed this path shown in Figure 18.

Now, you need to finish your base resumé.

ACTION: Finish your base resumé for your first target market. Then put it aside for a day or two.

Once the base resumé is done, it's time to step back for a day or two to let your mind clear. Then you come back to your resumé to review the content. What does the progression look like? Kyle, whom we met earlier in the chapter, is a marketing manager who is now interested in project management or product development. As Kyle has also gone through this process, it's important to see how vastly different his resumé is now, and how much better it is.

When Kyle first started, his resumé was a historical document that was not only long-winded but didn't give the reader any idea what he brought to the table and what he was looking to do. His resumé looked like this:

KYLE JORGENSTEIN
227 W. Columbus Avenue, #301, New York, NY 11010
(212) 555-1475 – kyle_jorgenstein@emailaddress.com

Work Experience	**MEDIAWAY Inc.,** New York, NY *3/98–present*

Marketing Manager, Ad Group
Client & Corporate Communications Liaison & Advertising Acct Executive

- Client & Corporate Communications Liaison for the Ad Group; in-house advertising agency for MEDIAWAY Inc. Communicate with MEDIAWAY Inc. magazines, other properties (including TV Networks), legal departments, production teams, and media vendors to promote inter-company cross-promotional opportunities. Plan, present, and execute event and radio promotions. Organize promotion objective, develop prize or gift, negotiate costs, write promotion "talk-sheets," oversee operations and follow-up with all parties to ensure success of the campaign. Create pre-sentations, promotional material, event displays and collateral material that clearly represent the marketing objective. Oversee program setup and special events.

- Account Executive managing print and out-of-home advertising campaigns (consumer and industry marketing efforts) for MEDIAWAY Inc. magazines. Develop creative brief, direct and/or consult with creative team, coordinate media schedule, negotiate rates and ad placement with national and local media vendors. Acquire all legal clearance from photographers and Time Inc. Legal Department. Coordinate creative and production teams. Develop and maintain clients' budgets.

Related Honors:
- MEDIAWAY Inc. Consumer Marketing Achievement Award for the launch of *Life Today* magazine
- US Ad Review 2000 for the "Find Yourself in Life" consumer advertising campaign
- 2 Time Inc. "INCITE" Awards: 1 for Event Promotion 1 for Vida en Espanol radio promotion

Kraft and Ryan Advertising, New York, NY *1/97–3/98*
Media Planning, MegaMart Accounts and New Business Pitches
- Created and presented media plan options to client and account groups
- Prepared and implemented annual print, television, and radio advertising campaigns

Colgate University Office of Admissions, Colgate, NY *5/96–12/96*
Lead Undergraduate Recruiter, Northeast Region
- Presented information sessions at high schools and college fairs, orga-nized open houses, hosted events, and assessed prospective candidates for admission
- Cultivated university relations with other universities and high schools guidance counselors

Education	**Colgate University,** Colgate, NY *8/92–5/96*

Bachelor of Arts, May 1996, from College of Communication Studies
Concentrations: Public Relations & Journalism with a minor in
    Business

Related Skills	Proficient in Microsoft Excel, Word, Powerpoint, and Internet research tools

Now that you're an expert in self-marketing and resumé creation, you can probably see immediately why Kyle's search wasn't successful when he was using this resumé. There are obviously a number of formatting issues that Kyle can fix to ease his search process, and make it more likely that his resumé will actually be read.

More important, Kyle's resumé isn't a marketing tool. It details his experience but in long, general paragraphs. He covers job responsibilities without focusing on what he did differently or how he improved the task or issue at hand. He lists awards, but doesn't connect them to his work experience or make clear what the most important aspect of his resumé is.

Finally, Kyle makes it hard for the reader to believe he can make the transition from media and advertising work to marketing project management and product development. There is no profile to draw the reader in or to highlight relevant skills, and the content focuses only on where he has been. It doesn't connect with where he wants to go.

In Kyle's case, he didn't have time to create his content library, so he decided to get his format fixed first and simplify his content. Once he had the shell in

---

KYLE JORGENSTEIN
227 W. Columbus Ave., #301, New York, NY 11010 – (212) 555-1475
kyle_jorgenstein@emailaddress.com

PROFESSIONAL PROFILE

Motivated and highly organized project manager with more than eight years of experience successfully developing and implementing marketing and partnership programs. Background in trade show and special promotion planning and execution with success in forging strong relationships with both internal corporate clients and outside vendors. Detail-oriented professional focused on maintaining timelines and budgets, looking to leverage strengths in a Product Development Manager role.

PROFESSIONAL EXPERIENCE

MEDIAWAY Inc., New York, NY   **1998–2000**
Senior Marketing Manager, 2004–present
- Determine client needs, negotiate partnership deals, and supervise asset allocation with corporate partners
- Manage international client advertising and direct marketing campaigns with oversees vendors
- Develop, communicate, and enforce policies for multiple corporate partners and 20 internal clients

Marketing Manager, 2002–2004
- Managed the implementation of business protocol designed to promote and manage clients' print media assets
- Grew new business source to $30 million in 4 years
- MEDIAWAY Inc. Consumer Marketing Achievement Award and President's Award for new brand launch

Associate Marketing Manager, 2000–2002
- Created and implemented program to leverage internal corporate assets for magazines
- *US Ad Review 2000* for consumer advertising campaign

Assistant Marketing Manager, 1998–2000
- Launched new brand via creative "grassroots" marketing opportunities
- Time Inc. "INCITE" Awards: event promotion and radio promotion

KRAFT AND RYAN ADVERTISING, New York, NY   **1997–1998**
Media Planner
- Researched and presented media plan options to client and account groups
- Prepared and executed annual print, television, and radio advertising campaigns

COLGATE UNIVERSITY, Colgate, NY   **1996**
Undergraduate Recruiter
- Presented information, organized open houses, hosted events, and assessed prospective candidates for admission
- Cultivated university relations with other universities and high school guidance counselors

EDUCATION

BA Communications, May 1996
Minor: Business Marketing
Colgate University, Colgate, NY

PROFESSIONAL DEVELOPMENT

Technology Skills: Microsoft Word, Microsoft Excel, Microsoft PowerPoint, Bloomberg, ABC/MRI
Training: Business Writing Seminar, Effective Management Seminar, Professional Presentation Clinic
Certification: New Jersey Licensed Realtor
Languages: Proficient in French, basic knowledge of Italian & American Sign Language

---

place and his content started, he could then focus on making his content even stronger.

The second version is much improved. The format is much easier to read and navigate and Kyle's career progression is promoted instead of obscured, as it was in the previous version. He also uses the jargon of his target audience—marketing—instead of focusing too much on advertising and media planning. Did he lie or alter what he did? No, he just focuses more on the aspects of his experience that will be most important to his audience.

Kyle still has some work to do on his content. While he now knows what he wants to sell in each bullet, he needs to expand in terms of scope, detail, and results. On the next page, you can check out some of the suggestions (in italics) I gave Kyle on taking his content to the next level. You'll notice that the suggestions are mostly questions that the reader might be thinking while reading

PROFESSIONAL EXPERIENCE

MEDIAWAY, INC. New York, NY   **1998–2000**
Senior Marketing Manager, 2004–present
* Determine client needs *(How? Who are the clients?)* negotiate partnership and trade deals *(How many and how much?)* and supervise asset allocation with corporate partners *(such as?)*
* Manage international client advertising and direct marketing campaigns with overseas vendors *(How many? Where?)*
* Develop, communicate, and enforce policies *(What kind?)* for multiple *(How many?)* corporate partners and 20 internal advertising clients *(Why? To ensure national brand consistency?)*

Marketing Manager, 2002–2004
* Managed implementation of business protocol designed to promote and manage clients' print media assets *(But did it really do it? How?)*
* Grew new business source *(Which was?)* to $30 million in four years *(How does this compare to other years?)*
* MEDIAWAY Inc. Consumer Marketing Achievement Award and President's Award for new brand launch *(Lead with activity first and indicate "resulting in")*

Associate Marketing Manager, 2000–2002
* Created and implemented program to leverage internal corporate assets for magazines *(Such as? How did this work?)*
* *US Ad Review 2000 (Is this an award? Will people outside of ad industry know it?)* for consumer advertising campaign (*tell me more about campaign or scope of reach*)

Assistant Marketing Manager, 1998–2000
* Launched new brand via creative "grassroots" marketing opportunities *(Such as? What happened? Any results?)*
* MEDIAWAY Inc. "INCITE" Awards: event promotion and radio promotion *(Don't just list award. Describe event and indicate that it resulted in a certain award for . . .)*

KRAFT AND RYAN ADVERTISING, New York, NY   **1997–1998**
Media Planner
* Researched and presented media plan options to client and account groups *(Such as? Can you describe them? Can you put any metrics in about size of options ($4 million media plan) or talk about the percentage that became deals?)*
* Prepared and executed *(How many?)* annual print, television, and radio advertising campaigns. *(Including? This reads like a job responsibility. Needs more metrics or detail, scope of responsibility)*

COLGATE UNIVERSITY, Colgate, NY   **1996–1997**
Undergraduate Recruiter
* Presented course information, organized open houses, hosted events, and assessed prospective candidates for admission *(Can you provide any metrics about number of students reached?)*
* Cultivated university relations with other universities and high schools guidance counselors *(For what reason? How did relationships help school?)*

Kyle's resumé. Many of the suggestions and questions can be addressed if Kyle uses the Resumé Bullet Creation framework on page 122 to make his content more detailed and results-oriented.

After Kyle reviewed these questions and suggestions, his final version of his base resumé is strong in both format and content. It markets to his target audience, and makes him stand out when compared to peers with similar experience.

KYLE'S FINAL VERSION

KYLE JORGENSTEIN
227 W. Columbus Ave., #301, New York, NY 11010 — (212) 555-1475
kyle_jorgenstein@emailaddress.com

PROFILE

Motivated, highly organized project manager with more than eight years of experience successfully developing and implementing marketing and partnership programs. Background in trade show and special promotion planning and execution. Proven success in forging relationships with both internal corporate clients and outside vendors. Detail-oriented and focused on managing timelines and budgets. Looking to leverage strengths as a Product Development Manager.

PROFESSIONAL EXPERIENCE

MEDIAWAY INC. **New York, NY**   **1998–present**
Senior Marketing Manager, 2004–present
- Determine partnership programs for publications such as *People, Fortune, People en Espanol,* and *InStyle,* through market research and over 40 partnership negotiations and trade deals worth upwards of $20 million
- Supervise asset allocation with corporate partners such as AOL, New Line Cinema, and the Turner Networks
- Develop, communicate, and enforce corporate accounting and legal policies to over a dozen corporate partners and over 20 internal advertising clients to ensure Time Inc. brand integrity and consistency

Marketing Manager, 2002–2004
- Managed successful implementation of a new business protocol designed to control and protect clients' print media assets when trading ad space with other companies and magazines
- Developed first organization and utilization plan for internal ad space as a branding source, growing to $30 million in four years; as a result, assigned to fully manage this high-value resource and serve as an internal design consultant for clients hoping to maximize their ad campaign's placement in other publications

Associate Marketing Manager, 2000–2002
- Created and implemented program to leverage internal corporate assets for magazines by developing a communication network with over 30 magazines to keep abreast and utilize their last-minute remnant ad space to other clients' no-cost branding advantage
- Managed placement of free national ad space to highlight *People*'s "Real People" branding campaign, valued at $2 million, to ensure campaign's free ad placement; resulted in a team *US Ad Review 2000* from *AdAge* magazine

Assistant Marketing Manager, 1998–2000
- Launched two new Time Inc. brands via creative "grassroots" marketing opportunities for *People en Espanol* and *REALSIMPLE* magazines through trade shows, on-air radio contests, and parade floats to increase talk value and buzz with little to no budgets, resulting in an *"INCITE" Award*

KRAFT AND RYAN ADVERTISING, New York, NY   **1997–1998**
Media Planner
- Researched and presented media plan options to client and account groups for Kraft Products, including Country Time lemonade and Maxwell House coffee as well as new business pitches to national restaurant chains resulting in a seasonal, daily-executed campaign for Country Time lemonade and the win of new national accounts

COLGATE UNIVERSITY, Colgate NY   **1996–1997**
Undergraduate Recruiter
- Presented course information, organized open houses, and assessed over 5,000 candidates for admission
- Cultivated university relations with other universities and high school guidance counselors

EDUCATION

BA, Communication Studies   **1996**
Minor: Business Marketing
Colgate University, Colgate, NY

PROFESSIONAL DEVELOPMENT

Technology Skills: Microsoft Word, Microsoft Excel, Microsoft PowerPoint, Bloomberg, ABC & MRI
                           research tools
Training: Business Writing Seminar, Effective Management Seminar, Professional Pre-
                           sentation Clinic
Languages: Proficient in French, basic knowledge of Italian & American Sign
                           Language
Volunteer: Group Therapy Facilitator/Grant Recipient, Juvenile Psychiatric Unit, St. Mary
                           Hospital, Hoboken, NJ

Step 5: Create a Cover Letter Shell

Although the resumé is done, it is but one of the marketing tools you have to have ready for your job search. Next comes the cover letter. Years ago, formal, written letters of introduction were used to introduce friends, family, and colleagues, in what was a more genteel world. We're not so old-fashioned anymore, but the cover letter, essentially the modern form of a letter of introduction, is still alive and well in the job search.

Are cover letters necessary? Yes and no. Cover letters aren't required unless the job posting specifically asks for one. If the posting doesn't ask for a cover letter, it's your call. Some experts see the cover letter as a must, but as the job search process continues to evolve with technology, there may be a time when they disappear completely. Right now they are still commonplace and offer you an additional opportunity to market yourself.

As you did with your resumé, you will get your cover letter format together first and then customize the content based on audience. You also want to make sure your cover letter conforms to business expectations and re-cruiting technology.

> **Good to Know:**
>
> Since your cover letter often appears after your resumé in the Resumé Management and Applicant Tracking Systems used by companies, don't assume your cover letter will always be read. Many job seekers make the mistake of putting crucial information in the cover letter that should go in the resumé.

So let's talk about format. When you apply for a job, your cover letter will be scanned in along with your resumé. In most Resumé Management or Applicant Tracking Systems, the reader will see the resumé first, followed by the cover letter. You want to make sure that your cover letter complements your resumé. You don't want it simply to repeat what's on your resumé, or have it refer to skills or experiences that aren't mentioned anywhere on your resumé.

With that in mind, there are eight parts to a cover letter:

- **Header:** Like your header from your resumé, the cover letter header contains your contact information. In fact, it should match your resumé exactly so if they are printed out, there won't be any doubt that the documents belong together.

- **The "To" Address:** As with a formal business letter, you also want to make sure you have the name and address of the person to whom the letter is addressed in the top left-hand corner. Be sure to confirm the spelling of the name and address, too.

- **Salutation:** Always address the letter formally (Dear Ms. or Mr.) and always to someone specific (not "to whom it may concern"). If you don't have a name, find one by looking in the phone book, online, or by calling the front desk of the company and asking for one.

- **Introductory Paragraph:** This paragraph is a creative version of your marketing message. It grabs the reader's attention, tells the reader what kind of professional you are and details the name of the position you are applying for as well as how you heard about the position (recruiters always want to know how well their advertising worked!).

- **Marketing Paragraph 1:** List one skill/behavior/experience you want to showcase and put it as a placeholder for paragraph 1.

- **Marketing Paragraph 2:** Choose a second skill/behavior/experience you want to showcase and put it as a placeholder for paragraph 2.

- **Closing Paragraph:** In the last paragraph of the letter, you want to reiterate the key points from your marketing message and close with a call to action—what do you want to happen next? Are you taking the action or asking the reader to?

- **Sign-off:** Close the letter formally and leave space to sign your name. Even if submitting electronically, leave space between the "Best Regards," and your name. Make sure your name reads exactly as it does in the header. You don't want any confusion about what you prefer to be called.

Bill used a job description as his guide to write his base cover letter. As a result, your cover letter shell might look something like Bill's:

Bill McCarrick
37 Marston Circle | Atlanta, GA 12345
(440) 555-7789 | billmccarrick@emailaddress.com

September 21, 2006

Sharon R. Thompson, Lead Recruiter
Marmand Corporation
1150 Ponce de Leon Ave., Suite 6000
Atlanta, GA 44010

Dear Ms. Thompson,

Are you looking for an aggressive marketing and business development professional? Paul Thompson, a financial analyst with Marmand and a former colleague of mine, drew my attention to the open business development manager position (#2019). With over nine years of success finding and growing business opportunities and an already strong list of connections here in the local market you are looking to develop, I am eager and interested in sharing more details with you about what I can bring to Marmand in this role.

Marketing Paragraph 1: Allied Health: Marketing presentations

Marketing Paragraph 2: Canton Pharmaceuticals: sales and negotiation

These experiences, in combination with my persuasive and outgoing demeanor, equal and exceed the majority of the requirements for the position. In addition, I understand the importance of bottom-line focus at a public consulting firm such as Marmand and would commit to doing everything I can to reach Marmand's strategic, growth, and financial goals. I would like to further detail this commitment to you and your colleagues directly in an interview. I look forward to hearing from you.

Best regards,

Bill McCormick

You'll notice that Bill wrote the bulk of his letter using placeholders for the marketing paragraphs. This is now a shell he can use for other cover letters that are directed at similar positions. Be sure you sufficiently customize each letter (and change the company name!) so it isn't pegged as a form/copied letter.

Step 6: Add Details to Your Marketing Paragraphs and Complete Your Base Cover Letter

In addition to making certain that your cover letter doesn't come across as a form letter, you don't want to forget that it is a marketing tool. Your two marketing paragraphs are a great opportunity to sell yourself to the company based on the company's needs. Now it's time to finish the cover letter by completing the marketing paragraphs.

> ACTION: Complete the marketing paragraphs and finish your base cover letter.

Because this is a base cover letter you want to use examples for your marketing paragraphs that are going to be applicable to various audiences in your focus field. In Bill's case, he chose the job description he used to design his marketing message to help him complete the marketing paragraphs in his base cover letter.

Based on the job description, Bill created his marketing paragraphs and ended up with a complete base cover letter:

Bill McCarrick
37 Marston Circle | Atlanta, GA 12345
(440) 555-7789 | billmccarrick@emailaddress.com

September 21, 2006

Sharon R. Thompson, Lead Recruiter
Marmand Corporation
1150 Ponce de Leon Ave., Suite 6000
Atlanta, GA 44010

Dear Ms. Thompson,

Are you looking for an aggressive marketing and business development professional? Paul Thompson, a financial analyst with Marmand and a former colleague of mine, drew my attention to the open business development manager position (#2019). With over nine years of success finding and growing business opportunities and an already strong list of connections here in the local market you are looking to develop, I am eager and interested in sharing more details with you about what I can bring to Marmand in this role.

Currently, while managing the marketing of new ventures at Allied Health, I create marketing concepts specifically to interest large-scale investors. I design and deliver marketing presentations at the executive level to demonstrate both immediate and long-term return on investment. As a result, I have exceeded my new business revenue goals by 35 percent, have created a training plan for junior managers to mirror my marketing strategy, and received individual praise from the CEO for my creativity and tenacity.

Prior to that, in my sales role at Canton Pharmaceuticals, I managed my own sales territory and assessed the viability of new business territories. Specifically, I developed and launched a pilot market assessment analysis program, which involved assessing business potential in a new territory through weekly financial comparisons with currently successful markets. This analysis has since been adopted company-wide and enabled the senior management team to raise the success rate of new market penetration from 45 percent to 89 percent in only two years time through the use of data modeling and forecasting.

These experiences, in combination with my persuasive and outgoing demeanor, equal and exceed the majority of the requirements for the position. In addition, I understand the importance of bottom-line focus at a public consulting firm such as Marmand and would commit to doing everything I can to reach Marmand's strategic, growth, and financial goals. I would like to further detail this commitment to you and your colleagues directly in an interview. I look forward to hearing from you.

Best regards,

Bill McCormick

You should always pay close attention to the job description when writing the marketing paragraphs in your cover letter. Even after you've completed your base cover letter, be sure to customize it further for each job to which you apply. Think marketing. The more specifically you target your audience, the more likely they are to "pick you" as the product (in other words, call you for an interview).

You can get creative with your cover letter. This doesn't mean colored paper and clip art (by all means, don't even think about such things). But it does mean you can let someone else help sell you. Try opening your letter with a powerful quote that epitomizes your work ethic or highlights one of your key strengths. Another option is to include a quote from a colleague or manager about the results of your hard work on a particular project? For example, you might try something like this:

- The success of the project was cited by the division vice president: "Janice's creativity and commitment to this launch were overwhelming. This was the most successful launch in the firm thus far, due particularly to her attention to detail and her incredible foresight."
- In fact, my most recent performance evaluation highlighted my ability to stay calm under pressure: "Phil has an outstanding ability to maintain grace and stability during the most stressful of times. Whether it is the end of the quarter or the end of the year, he remains focused on exceeding his target numbers, and he always hits his goal."

Quotes are always a powerful option. Just make sure you don't forget to detail the action and result that led to the commendation. You want to make sure the reader knows how you earned all that glowing praise.

Your cover letter doesn't have to be long (it should never go over a page) but it does have to be powerful. You also want to make sure it is well-written, as it is the first writing sample your future employer will see. Here's a final checklist to follow to make sure you're on the right track:

Cover Letter Checklist

- ☐ **Overall:** Your cover letter should be no more than one page—period. Be sure the header matches the header on your resumé.
- ☐ **Style:** Use the same font, font size, and margin size as you do on your resumé. Be judicious with the use of boldface type and capitals.
- ☐ **Readability:** Follow the eight-step format and make sure your paragraphs are not excessively long. If you prefer, use bullets when detailing your experience in the marketing paragraphs if you know your reader will only be glancing at your cover letter quickly.
- ☐ **Tense:** Use the correct tense throughout your cover letter, using the present tense when talking about a job you are currently in and the past tense when talking about a previous job.
- ☐ **Justification:** Don't use the tool that allows you to justify your text. Left-justify all text (except your header, which should be centered the same way it is on your resumé).
- ☐ **Grammar and spelling:** It's easy to miss grammar and spelling errors in a cover letter, so try reading your letter backward and out loud to catch

any errors. Have a friend (or two) proofread your letter to check for grammatical errors and to confirm that the document sells your candidacy well.

☐ **Risks:** Unless the job calls for it, this is not a time for humor or excessive egos. You are marketing yourself but you don't want to come across as too boastful or immature.

☐ **Jargon:** Stay away from technical jargon and abbreviations.

☐ **Customization:** The cover letter you have just created is a basis to start from. You must customize the letter for each job opportunity. By all means, don't merely change the company name. If you try to make one letter fit all jobs it will either sound generic or detail skills that aren't applicable to the position you are aiming for.

Step 7: Decide on Additional Marketing Tools

In addition to the resumé and cover letter, there are a number of other ways you can market yourself to your target audience.

Networking, an important marketing tool, will be discussed in the next chapter. The following are some additional tools you can use to complement your resumé and cover letter. But if you're struggling in your search, or want to go the extra mile for a position that is your idea of perfection, it might be time to get creative.

Portfolio

Usually it is only the creative types that actually have a portfolio of their work. After all, if you're a designer or artist, you can't get hired without showing off your wares. But what if you're in finance or consulting? Why not have your own portfolio of projects?

As you look back over your base resumé, there are possibly a dozen ways you can physically demonstrate your strengths to your target market. It may be a research report you created for your boss. Or a project plan you mapped out for your team. Think about how powerful it

> **Good to Know:**
> As you start to think about your marketing tools, don't forget one of the most important marketing tools: your references. We'll talk about how to find and manage them in Chapter 11, but for now, you may want to think about getting your reference page together and ensuring it matches your resumé and cover letter as opposed to waiting until the last minute and hurriedly dumping them in an e-mail to the recruiter.

would be in an interview to say "I have a copy of a report on that project, if you're interested in seeing it." Here are a few things to consider when putting together a portfolio:

- Buy a professional binder (leather if you can afford it) and the clear sleeves (document holders) that hold documents.
- At the front of the portfolio, put a copy of your resumé and reference sheet (we'll talk about how to compile references in Chapter 11).
- Choose work samples from each of the jobs listed on your resumé. Go for the visual—a project plan or a model you created are ideal. A hard copy of slides from a presentation you created and/or delivered is also an option, as are reports, memos, or research you compiled.
- Whatever you choose, go for brevity. Presentations should be no more than a few slides; research or memos should be no more than a few pages. Think highlights, not a thesis.
- Make sure you align your portfolio contents with your resumé. If you're including a project plan, select one that is from a project mentioned in your resumé.
- Don't reveal company secrets. Don't include documents from top-secret projects, and on documents you do include, remove any proprietary information and/or provide pseudonyms for names.
- Have several copies of each so you can give one to a particularly interested interviewer if the situation allows.
- Carry your portfolio with you, but don't force it on anyone. Mention that you have examples of your work to see, if there is interest.

Personal Business Cards

If you're currently employed you don't want to give out your business cards because you don't want a prospective employer calling you at work. If you are not currently employed, you don't have cards to give. So why not create some of your own? Most printing and graphic design stores can create small batches of 100 to 200 cards that can be used in interviews, inserted in thank-you letters, or given to networking connections.

If you choose to make cards, make sure they look professional. They should be on heavy card stock (the same used for company business cards) and they should not look homemade. They should also be simple, with your name and contact information easily visible (and spelled correctly!) on the front. For an added touch, put your marketing message or profile on the back as a reminder. Here's what the front and back of Bill's cards look like:

Front:

> **BILL MCCARRICK**
>
> **Business Development and Marketing Manager**
>
> 37 Marston Circle • Atlanta, GA 12345
>
> (440) 555-7789 (cell)
>
> billmccarrick@emailaddress.com

Back:

> Marketing and business development professional with over nine years of success finding and growing business opportunities, and strong presentation and financial forecasting abilities. Aggressive in lead pursuit while maintaining patience and professionalism during negotiation.
>
> *Open to full-time mid-level business development positions in the Atlanta, GA, area*

Proactive Work Samples

Another way to market yourself is to create a proactive work sample for your target market or for a particular company or position. It's called proactive because you are demonstrating to the company what your work would be like if you were hired for the position. Such a sample could be a project plan, memo, design, or work product that might address one of the tasks included in the job description, or it might tackle a problem the company or department is facing.

For example, if you are interviewing for a sales position, you might create a sales plan for the market the position would cover and share that plan with an interviewer or recruiter. If you're in finance, you might examine the company's public financial statements, and write a memo on your insights or suggestions based on your review. If you're in marketing, take a stab at researching a new audience for the company with suggestions on how they might reach that audience.

Proactive work samples are probably some of the most risky marketing tools, but they can also pay off in huge dividends. To determine whether you should take the chance, evaluate the job description and research the company carefully. If the position is very specific, and if there is enough data on the company to allow you to offer solutions that are constructive (and well thought out), it might be worth it.

Be careful, however, not to overstep your bounds. As with your portfolio, you want to share the proactive work sample carefully, offering it up at an appropriate point in the conversation. You also want to be sure the sample is good. No, really. This isn't a feat for amateurs. If you're not completely sure that your insights and work are original and well thought out, don't take this risk.

Professional Blog

Technology savvy professionals would like to think the whole world knows what "blogs" are, but in reality, a Weblog is still a pretty new concept to some people. Weblogs, called "blogs" for short, are a way that professionals share their daily musings, insights, and revelations about their experiences and day-to-day work. There are blogs out there on almost every topic imaginable, including recruiting and job searching. (Note: Appendix B contains a selection of some of the most popular recruiting and job-searching blogs.) Good blogs are updated regularly (often daily or more than once a day) and allow readers to comment online to each posting. This creates an online audience or network of the blog's readers.

For a job-seeker, blogs are a great source of research. Companies such as Microsoft, Honeywell, and Google all have blogs run by recruiters and current employees that help provide insight into the hiring process and life at the company. Blogs can also be a great marketing tool, and, according to some experts, may replace resumés in the future. Since recruiters spend so much time sourcing, or searching for candidates, they often pull up professional blogs in their Web searches when looking to hire professionals in specific fields. So if you're comfortable with technology and have an expertise to share in your field, you might consider starting a blog as part of your job search. It's not only a great way to get noticed by recruiters searching for talent, it's also a great networking tool.

9

Making Connections

After you find the perfect job opening, you still have to convince actual people why you should work there. Of course the strength of your marketing message matters, as do your marketing tools. But there's still someone on the other end—a human being—who has to assess you: "Do I really want to buy this product?" A crucial step in getting in the door is to make as many personal connections as you can.

Think about it like this: Let's say a company is considering buying a new photocopying machine. The more people who can explain to the CEO why the new machine is needed and how it will help the company perform better, the more likely the CEO will be to approve the purchase. Your getting hired is no different. The more people who can support your candidacy and speak on your behalf, the easier the decision will be. This is not the only reason that networking connections matter. They can:

- Alert you to job opportunities you might not have heard of otherwise, whether you're actively job searching or not
- Give you insight into a company's culture or insight into field or industry norms and trends (remember your Level 2 research?)

> **Good to Know:**
>
> Don't think networking contacts are only professionals in your field or industry. Essentially, *anyone who can connect you to someone else who can help your job search is a networking contact.* Don't limit yourself to your inner circle. The best connections are the ones you don't know about that come from the people you don't think to ask: friends in other professions, or family members or people who know you well, such as teachers, clergy, or even your hairdresser. After all, you're not her only client. She might be cutting the hair of your future boss.

- Speak or e-mail on your behalf to a hiring manager or recruiter
- Serve as an official reference during the job-search process
- Introduce you to other professionals in your field or industry

Connections are also an important part of your career development when you are not in the job-search process. If you are in sales or marketing, you already know how important connections are to finding new business or making new deals. If you have even a few years of work experience, you probably already have a circle of contacts you turn to for advice and insight.

While statistics vary, it is generally believed that more than 50 percent of jobs are found through networking contacts. Ideally, this means that you should be spending 50 percent of your job-search time networking. But that doesn't mean you're at a cocktail party nibbling on mini hotdogs three to four nights a week. It just means you are actively making connections for the purpose of seeking out potential job opportunities in your target field or industry.

If you're just starting your search, your networking strategy should have three parts:

1. Making sure everyone you know is aware that you are job searching and what your interests are.
2. Learning who the key contacts are in your target field/industry in the geographical locations you are interested in.
3. Finding and making at least one contact at each company you are interested in.

It's easier than you think.

Letting people know about your job search is an often overlooked but important way to make connections. Think back to the last time you were in a job search. How many people in your contact list or address book actually knew about your search? How many were surprised to get your "I'm changing jobs" e-mail? Probably more than should have been.

Executing Your Networking Strategy

Unless your job search is top secret (and really, how can it be?), it is important to let as many people as possible know about your search. If you are currently employed, you might not want to let your boss or colleagues know, but you should reach out to as many people as you can.

The reason this is important gets back to networking basics—the more people who know you are searching and what you are searching for, the more people can help you. Also, letting people know about your search will help with the second and third parts of your networking strategy, finding contacts in your target field, industry, and/or company(ies). Surely you've heard of the idea of "six degrees of separation" and people who don't know each other can be connected to each other through six degrees: "I know John who knows Carlos who knows Rochelle who knows Aliyah who knows you, Bob."

The best method of communication to start with is a simple e-mail. It's a quick way to reach as many people as possible and it allows for an easy response:

1. Make a list of everyone who ought to know about your job search without endangering your current job situation. By this, I mean everyone from your annoying brother-in-law to your ex-girlfriend (as long as you are still on speaking terms). Here's the test: If you saw someone walking down the street and know them well enough to stop, say hello, and chat for a few minutes, that someone belongs on your list.

2. Create a short, three-paragraph e-mail:

   Paragraph 1: Say hello and let your contacts know that you are in the midst of a job search and writing to ask for their quick help.

   Paragraph 2: Use a brief version of your marketing message. Tell them first what you are looking for and then remind them of your background and strengths.

   Paragraph 3: Close by making your request—you're looking for contacts in a specific field, industry, or company. Be sure to let them know that if they have contacts to share, you'll follow up to find out the most appropriate way to reach out to those contacts. Offer thanks in advance.

3. Send the e-mail to your entire list, making sure to BCC (blind copy) all of your contacts. There is always some joker who thinks it is fun to "reply all" and you want to avoid clogging everyone's inbox after you've just asked for a favor.

Here's what Bill's networking e-mail looks like:

Dear Friends,

Many of you may know I have been thinking about the next step in my career for some time now. Well, I have decided to start a job search after spending time on determining what would be the best career move for me and my family. As part of this, I am writing to ask for your help.

Since Alison and I have made the decision to remain in the greater Atlanta area, my search is centered around business development manager roles, specifically in the consulting industry. I would be particularly interested in helping a national or international firm start or grow their business in this area. While this is a change from what I have been doing in healthcare, it is a natural progression from my over nine years of marketing and sales experience. Since I tend to be both aggressive at finding new business and patient in the negotiation process, and have strong presentation and financial forecasting abilities, I am excited to see where the search leads.

The reason I am writing to you is to ask if you'll stop and thumb through your own list of contacts for a moment. I am in search of contacts in the consulting industry and in connecting with business development professionals in and out of the industry, whether or not they have any openings. I am also looking for contacts at the following companies: AER Consulting, Xynex, Bosch and Simon LLP, BroadLine Consulting, and Washington Ellis. If you are willing to share any of your contacts, just let me know and I will be in touch with you to learn the most appropriate way to make the connection. I will certainly be respectful of their time and position.

Thank you in advance for any help you can provide.

Best regards,
Bill

Once you send out the e-mail, you'll be surprised how many people respond with contacts—more results than you could ever achieve while balancing a plate of mini quiche in one hand and glass of wine in another. Wine and quiche shouldn't be ignored, however (at least not when served in the presence of some very interesting people), and because you will need a number of contacts to get your search going, you should explore both traditional and technological ways to make contacts.

Attending a networking event is one of the most common ways to make contacts. Whether it's a fancy, happy-hour cocktail party or a room filled with folding chairs and "HELLO MY NAME IS" tags, you never know when you might meet the person who can connect you to your next job. If you're attending these events only when you're job searching, you're missing the main reason these events work—they're more relationship builders than request builders.

Bill's networking e-mail was a request builder—asking for contacts and following up with those who offer them up. Networking parties and events are designed more for meeting people in a social situation and then building a relationship with them. You might get a job contact, but it won't (and shouldn't!) be your primary reason for going. Some people get frustrated with this mass form of networking because there's usually no immediate payoff. Think about these events as long-term networking investments that you should be making throughout your career and not just when you're looking for a job. A networking event might help you now, but more likely it will be more beneficial in the long run.

If you haven't already joined the local chapter of your field or industry association, consider that as an option. You can also join local business professionals groups as another way to make some quick contacts now and build longer-term networking relationships for the future.

Hors d'oeuvres aside, if your job search is in the need of contacts, you should consider the power of technology. Blogs are a way to learn about companies, network with others, or can even be used as your own marketing tool. In addition, online networking sites are another way to pinpoint the contacts you're looking for. These sites take the "six degrees of separation" concept to a new level by connecting you with other people visiting the site and then giving you access to their network, and their contacts' networks, and so on.

Online Networking Sites

First, you create a profile for yourself on the site. Using your marketing tools, you upload your resumé as well as a brief description of who you are (time for the marketing message, anyone?). Then you select what types of connections you're open to from a list that includes partnerships, job opportunities, and requests for expertise.

Once you've set up your own profile, you can search the system for companies where you've worked or colleges you have attended to connect with people you know who are already in the system. You can also invite friends and colleagues who aren't in the system to join your network and create networks of their own. The idea is that these contacts create huge, spider web–like networks and you can search contacts who are one, two, three, and more degrees away from you. When you want to make a connection, you can get introduced through the chain of contacts.

It may sound complicated, but really it isn't. And Web sites such as www.linkedin.com and www.ryze.com make it easy to search your extended network for contacts at a specific company or in a specific field. Recruiters often search these sites to find contacts who might be interested in a potential job opportunity they have open.

The huge alumni databases that colleges and universities maintain are another good online source. The schools use them to raise money, but alumni can

use them to find potential networking contacts. If you're not sure if your school·
has one, visit the school's Web site and click on "alumni." You'll probably find
loads of contacts in your field or industry you weren't even aware of. What better way to introduce yourself then to compare notes on a college football ri-
valry? Keep in mind that the point of this resource is the common bond you
have with the connection, having attended the same university, so most likely
you won't be able to get a list of alumni contacts unless you attended the school.

You should also think about any other group or association you have been a
part of over the years. Fraternities, sororities, religious, social, and volunteer groups
all have local networking events and also may have contact databases. And if you
have a common bond with a potential contact, it'll be that much easier to make a
connection. This is all part of your marketing strategy. You have to determine the
contacts you need, consider all of these options, the best place to find them.

Once You Have Your Contacts

Once you have contacts you have to strategize what your desired outcome is in
talking to each of them. Be well prepared. While some of the same rules apply
to research contacts (Chapter 6) as to networking contacts, in some cases they
are a bit different. So here are some specifics for making the most of a networking contact:

1. **Determine the goal of your conversation**

   Beyond learning about the field, industry, or company, what do you hope
   to get out of the conversation? Because this isn't just a research call, you
   want to make sure you're clear about what you need.

2. **Do background research**

   If someone referred you to a contact, ask him what he knows about the
   contact's work habits, the best way to reach the contact, and any other
   important background information. Web-search your contact's name
   and determine whether it's a busy time for their field or industry (you
   don't want to call an accountant at the end of March or beginning of
   April.) Most important, research their company's Web site and take note
   of any and all job openings that may be of interest.

3. **Don't expect immediate replies**

   Your contacts are busy. They will probably want to help you but can't always respond immediately. Give them some time. If you make a call or

send an e-mail, give it at least ten days until you try again. When you do, be sensitive to the fact that you already contacted them once.

4. Cater to your contacts

As with your research contacts, and perhaps even more important here, make your schedule amenable to theirs. Cater to their availability. Ask what days or times work best for a conversation and plan around their schedule. After all, they are doing you a favor. Don't schedule hour-long calls. Instead, aim for fifteen- or twenty-minute conversations. You should be able to get all the information you need in that time.

5. Prepare, prepare, prepare

In order to make the best use of the fifteen-to-twenty-minute conversation, you have to be well prepared.

6. Own the conversation

Remember, you are the one who scheduled the conversation and you are responsible for initiating the call, starting up the conversation, knowing when it's time to move on to the next question, and to end the call. You may have more in-person meetings at this stage (again, you're the one reaching for the check) so if you're budget conscious be judicious about who you choose to meet with. But saving $40 on lunch isn't worth losing the perfect career opportunity.

7. It's now the 75/25 rule

While you primarily sought to learn from your research contacts, now it is a combination of research and selling. You want to make sure you make a good impression on the contact by making clear how you could benefit the organization and what your strengths are. However, this isn't a time to be overly boastful or monopolize the conversation. You should devote about 75 percent of the conversation to getting tips and insights from your contact about the field, industry, or job and 25 percent to selling yourself to the contact. He or she could be an ally in getting you in the door and into an interview.

8. Mind the time

Time is always important. Especially to contacts who are going out of their way to help you. If you scheduled fifteen minutes, take only fifteen minutes. And as time winds down, say something like "I want to be respectful of your time; are you able to answer one more question?"

9. Be grateful and show it

Favors are just that, they're favors. Be sure to thank the contact at the beginning and end of the conversation. Then, follow up with an e-mail or a personal, handwritten note to thank them again. A little gratitude goes a long way—don't ever forget that. If the connection leads to an interview or even a job? Take it a step further and thank the contact with a gift—flowers, wine, a gift certificate—because it was their kindness that led to your success.

Making the Most of Your Connection

Getting an interview or a job as a result of a connection may seem like an ideal solution, but just as with any other source at your job-seeking disposal, you've got to do some work to make the most of the opportunity. You can do the minimum (some background research and a quick Web search) to get by. If you want to maximize a great networking connection, you've got to prepare. To do this effectively, you've got to research your contact, plan for the conversation, and be as well prepared as possible. One way to make it simple is to set up a worksheet like the one on page 149 to use with all of your networking calls.

The worksheet is designed to track the "who, what, where, when, and why" of the call and make it easy for you to get the most out of the contact's time. The better the impression you make, the more likely it is the contact will go out of his way for you.

Get organized ahead of time to make the best impression possible. Have your marketing message ready and your goals for the connection established before you speak or meet with the contact.

Post-Connection Strategies

Making and connecting with contacts may seem like the most important part of the process, but what do you do afterward? What are other strategies for using your connections strategically?

Networking Connection Preparation Worksheet

Who	
Name and title of contact	
How was contact made?	
What are the personality traits of the contact?	
Preferred method of initial contact	
What	
What organization does s/he represent?	
What is the status and title of contact?	
What is the status of contact's organization?	
What is the latest news that affects the contact?	
Where	
Where does the contact work?	
What should connection environment be like?	
When	
When should you connect with the contact?	
How should you connect with the contact?	
How long should the connection last?	
Why	
Why are you connecting with this contact?	
What can this contact do for you?	
What are your top three goals for the connection?	1) 2) 3)
Connection 1 (method, date):	
Preparation	
Connection Results	
Next Steps	
Connection 2 (method, date):	
Preparation	
Connection Results	
Next Steps	

- **Gratitude**

  By now, you should be well versed in the importance of thanking your contacts. It's so important, I'll remind you once more: Thank your contacts. For contacts that go out of their way or are especially helpful, thank them with a gift. Gratitude is one of your best allies in the job-search process.

- **More contacts**

  Ask your contacts if they have contacts. "James, you've been so helpful, I was wondering if you could suggest anyone else I might speak with at XYZ company or in ABC industry who might also help my search?" If a contact has extensive experience or expertise in a field, she likely has her own list of contacts that helped her get there. So why not ask for access to those as well?

- **Referrals**

  Are you interested in the company where the contact works? If so, tell him. Even if there isn't a position open, the contact can keep you in mind when one does become available. If there is a position open, formally ask for a referral: "Heather, I really appreciate your time. Your insights have made me even more interested in XYZ company. Would you be willing to refer me for the open financial analyst position?" Because so many companies have referral programs, it's likely your contact could be monetarily rewarded if you are selected for an interview or you're hired.

- **Follow-up meeting**

  If you are pursuing a position at the company where your contact works, ask if you can check back in as you go through the process. Your contact may have additional insights about first and subsequent interviews, and be willing to coach you through them.

- **Down-the-road check-ins**

  It is easy to say, "Oh well, thanks anyway" when a contact tells you there are no open positions at her organization, but don't write off that contact just yet. Stay positive and reiterate your interest in the company. Track the connection in your electronic workbook and reconnect with her later in your search to see whether any new positions have opened up. Remember, the burden is on you. Even if the contact promises to let you know about new openings, chances are she'll forget. Stay on top of the contact and on top of your search.

Showing What You've Got

Once you've got your foot in the door, you don't want to stumble. Interviews are challenging, chiding, and changing whether they are case (a business problem you're asked to solve in front of an interviewer), behavioral (a series of questions asking how you behave in certain situations), or panel (two or more people formally asking you prepared questions). Here you'll learn how to prepare and avoid falling over your own two feet.

Organizations still make hiring decisions based on the interview. As I have said previously, the resumé gets you in the door and the interview gets you the job. Interviewing takes the selling process to the next level.

STOP Many people think they don't need help with interviewing. If you can talk, you can interview, right? Not a chance. Interviews are actually the part of the job-search process where people usually need the most help and don't know it. Interviews are make or break—the only chance you get to sell yourself for a certain position. Your entire job search may depend on how well you interview.

You've already mastered your marketing message and created your marketing tools. Now you're about to deliver your message in person. Think QVC or Home Shopping Network. You're about to demo your product live for a captive audience and you hope the audience sees that they must have your product.

Before you can waltz in and start selling, you have to know what to expect. Depending on the position, the organization, or the people you will be working for, the process is going to vary. Ideally, the organization already has a good idea of what you say you can do. Now they want to see how you would perform in their organization. You already have the baseline skills and knowledge (otherwise you wouldn't have gotten the interview). The interview assesses your behavior and performance. How would you use those skills in their organization? How would you perform?

For example, you might have extensive experience in customer service and can boast about your expertise in managing and retaining unhappy customers. The hiring organization is intrigued—this is exactly what they are looking for. They bring you in for an interview. But they also bring in five other people, each of whom have similar experience in customer service. How does the organization decide who to hire? All five candidates may have similar skills and experiences but, faced with an irate customer, may behave differently. The company uses the interview to understand how each person would perform with both customers and colleagues. If you fit the job description perfectly but aren't a fit with the team, your boss, or an existing client account, that's reason enough for the company to pass on your candidacy.

You have already created your Career Kaleidoscope, so you know where your performance strengths lie. You just need to be able to talk about them, but here is where most people trip up. You can't simply walk in, answer a few questions, and expect to be hired. Interviewing is a skill. There's a talent to interviewing and you have to prepare and practice. Most people wait until they get the interview request to begin preparation. But you're going to beat out your competition by preparing first and customizing second. Just as you did with your resumé and other marketing tools, you want to have a base to work from.

With your resumé, you created a library of content. With interviewing, you're going to create a library of stories. While interviewers ask specific questions, in essence, they are asking you to tell them a story. Whether they ask you to tell them about a time you disagreed with your boss, or why you would be a good asset to the company, you don't want to give a mere answer, you want to tell the story behind it.

Let's say that three information technology professionals are interviewing for an IT managerial position and the interviewer asks each one: What would make you a good manager?

Candidate one gives a weak answer that basically repeating what is on her resumé:

> "I would be a good manager because I have served as IT manager at Century Systems, working to manage all IT systems and IT staff. I have also managed numerous projects and have just finished a course in IT project management. My experience and my history of being a good project manager would make me successful at your company."

Candidate two gives an average answer, at least making an effort to reference his marketing message but not providing any specifics to make his answer come alive:

"My detail-oriented, strong leadership abilities and project-management skills make me a good project manager. As you can see from my background, I have the experience as an IT project manager and have worked with systems and staff. In addition, my team has always cited me as a good manager. I like managing people but I also do a good job of making sure I meet my budgets, too."

Candidate three (that's you), gives *The Right Job, Right Now* answer, combining elements of the resumé and marketing message, along with self-confidence and a well-structured story as an example:

"I have a unique combination of managing processes to make sure that a project is done correctly and an excellent ability to visualize the end result. Specifically at Polytech, when I managed the software implementation launch in 2004, I was able to ensure on-time and under-budget delivery while simultaneously making project adjustments to meet the CIO's changing needs. A good project manager is adaptable to change while bringing stability to his team, and that's what I would do for your firm."

To give the best interview possible, you shouldn't simply answer the question about what you would do or why you would be good in a certain position or at a specific company. You want to make it real with an example of how you've already done it for someone else, and what you can do for them.

A library of stories is essentially a collection of on-the-job performance examples. While your resumé may showcase a specific skill and result, in the interview you're going to bring it to life. This is where the behaviors from your Career Kaleidoscope will give you the edge. While your competitors are simply detailing their skills, you're telling a prospective employer *why* you're good at that skill and making it much easier for them to see how you'll contribute to the organization.

There are more specific reasons the story library works:

- **Edging out your competitors**

  If a company brings in five candidates to interview for a position, they might all be able to do the job and do it well. But just as a company's success is only as good as the ability of its sales force to market and sell the product, sometimes your chance of getting the job is only as good as your ability to sell your fit for it.

- **Better familiarity with your stories**

  Creating a story library forces you to reexamine all of your successes inside and out. You must reexamine your work experience and become much more comfortable with discussing it. That way, you will appear much more confident in an interview. It's not impressive when a candidate is asked about an experience or success at a previous job and has to struggle to re-member the details of what she did and why.

- **Better customization and preparation**

  Once you have story library, you can pick and choose the stories that are of most interest to a potential employer and tailor your answers to their needs. If an interviewer asks about a time you held a leadership role, you might choose a different story based on the hiring organization's industry or needs. Having stories in mind also helps with preparation. Surely you've been in an interview and been asked a question you weren't prepared to answer. A story library will help you eliminate any chance of giving your interviewer a blank stare.

- **Better structure**

  Ever find yourself answering an interview question only to forget the point you were trying to make? Or spending so much time setting up the story that you rush the ending or the result? Creating a story library helps you structure your stories. However, you can't just memorize what stories to tell, you actually have to know how to tell them. Next up in this chapter, you'll learn how to do this.

- **Saving time**

  The average candidate sits down the night before an interview and thinks of a few examples to use in his interview. All you will have to do is pull up your story library and choose the examples you want to use in your interview. Then, you can spend your night-before time on other interview-preparation strategies, such as getting enough sleep and good directions to the interview location.

Creating a library of stories is as easier than you think. First, you need to compile a list of topics you may be asked about. Then, come up with a story for each one and structure each story so you can set up the situation, describe the details, and emphasize the result. Finally, determine what the "takeaway" is for each story. You should start out by creating a new sheet in your electronic workbook and creating your interview story grid.

Interview Preparation

Topic	Story	Structure	Takeaway

As we go through the creation of your library, you'll learn how to complete each section of the grid.

> **ACTION:** Set up a grid in your electronic workbook.

Interview Topics

The content of the interview may depend on the organization, field, or industry. On page 162 I'll cover the different types of interviews you may encounter. Regardless of interview type, you'll still need your library of stories. The best way to start is with a list of topics. Remember, rather than trying to anticipate what questions you will be asked (you can never guess them all), it's easier to have an inventory of stories to pull from. This way, you are well prepared, but can be flexible depending on the interview situation.

Topics for stories can be behaviors or skills—the idea is that they are something an interviewer would potentially want you to elaborate on or would provide a good example to back up the answer to a straightforward question (like the example with our IT manager above). For example:

- Leadership: "Give me an example of a leadership role you took on in a previous position."
- Data Analysis: "This job requires an extensive amount of data analysis. Can you talk about a time when you had to take a large amount of data and distill the best insights?"
- Persuasion: "How would you go about selling our product?"

The topics you choose for your interview story library should be a combination of concerns common to many jobs, which highlight elements of your Career Sweet Spot and are common to your field and/or industry.

> **ACTION:** Create your list of interview topics.

For each topic you list, you should be able to address it with a story that includes examples of skills and behaviors. The list below gives you an idea of common topics or examples you might include in your list.

- Leadership role
- Problem client or customer
- Lack of resources
- Disagreement with boss
- Workplace crisis
- Challenging situation
- Commitment to teamwork
- Innovative solution
- Stretch role or additional work
- Specific reasons you like field/industry
- Recent trends in field/industry
- Future of field/industry
- Instance of failure
- Instance of success

We will get to commonly asked questions but no matter what the question, the topics and library of stories are your tools. The idea is if you combine these tools with your marketing message, you c an address any question or interview that comes your way.

Bill's grid looks like this so far:

Interview Preparation

Topic	Story	Structure	Takeaway
What is the topic you might be asked about?			
Challenging Situation			
Problem Customer			
Innovation			
Disagreed with Manager			
Exceeded Sales Goals			
Led a Team			
Business Development Philosophy			
Career and Goals			
Time of Crisis			
Future of Business Development			

Interview Stories

Now that you have a list of topics, you want to think of your story ideas. For each topic, what is the story you're going to use as an example? You are not writing the story out yet—you're just thinking of stories to use, in which the role you played strongly demonstrated your skills and behaviors. For example: "Allied Health $3-million equipment deal, 2003" or "Jansen Inc. Internet product launch, 2001." You will want to have your Career Kaleidoscope and resumés in front of you so you can refresh your memory about your experiences and begin to select the stories that fit best. You will also want to refer to your cover letters to ensure you include those stories and that they complement and expand on your cover letter examples.

> **ACTION: Create your list of stories.**

Bill is beginning to fill out the story portion of his grid, and he often has more than one story for each topic. This is extra work, but as you did with your resumé, it will allow you to customize your answers to interview questions.

Interview Preparation

Topic	Story	Structure	Takeaway
What is the topic you might be asked about?	What is the story you're going to use as an example?		
Challenging Situation	Allied Health (2005): West Coast healthcare forum		
Problem Customer	Allied Health (2004): Capital Investments security breach		
Problem Customer	Canton Pharmaceuticals (2002): Washington Medical Group patient heart study		
Problem Customer	Canton Pharmaceuticals (2000): Atlanta Doctors' Alliance		
Innovation	Allied Health (2005): unique large investor marketing strategy		
Innovation	Canton Pharmaceuticals (1998): new packaging material for drug		

What Bill has now done is create a list of stories he can choose from when the interviewer asks him a question. He won't have to pause or stutter. Instead, he'll mentally thumb through his list of stories and choose the example that best answers the question or highlights the skills and behaviors the question is targeting.

Interview Structure

Your stories have been chosen and now it's time to bring them to life. Many interviewees lose their chance at the job because they ramble on, can't get their point across, or don't have a point to their answer. But not you. Your stories are easy to tell, easy to understand, and easy to impress.

There are many different ways to structure interview stories. The idea behind them is the same: Set the story up, describe what you did, and close with the result. There are two structures that I think work the best: "SOAR" and "PCAR." Both SOAR and PCAR are acronyms to help guide you while composing and answering questions.

SOAR stands for:

- **S**ituation
- **O**pportunity
- **A**ction
- **R**esult

(Some experts change SOAR to STAR with the "T" standing for "Task" as in the task you completed.)

PCAR stands for:

- **P**roblem
- **C**onstraint
- **A**ction
- **R**esult

Your best bet is to choose the structure that will best describe the situation. Was it a problem you fixed? Was there a situation you led or an opportunity you took advantage of? For each story, spell out the elements by letter. For example:

- **S**ituation: "When I arrived at XYZ company they were just beginning to launch a new product."

- **O**pportunity: "I took the opportunity to recommend an online complement to the launch."
- **A**ction: "I created a prototype Web advertisement along with associated market data to demonstrate the need for the online complement."
- **R**esult: "The director of marketing approved the concept, my team executed the advertisement, and sales in week one were 30 percent greater than forecasted without the complement."

Here's how Bill is mapping out his stories on his grid:

Topic	Story	Structure	Takeaway
What is the topic you might be asked about?	What is the story you're going to use as an example?	Map out your structure for each story. SOAR (situation, opportunity, action, result) or PCAR (problem, constraint, action, result)	
Challenging Situation	Allied Health (2005): West Coast healthcare forum	P: The firm was hosting its first West Coast forum as a way of increasing business on the West Coast and the scientist who was doing the research presentation was stuck in an airport because of inclement weather.	
		C: There were no other scientists present at the time at the forum and the presenter did not have access to videoconference equipment.	
		A: I rearranged the schedule so the presentation would be the following morning and worked with the presenter by phone that night to fully learn the presentation's content while also weaving in my own sales techniques.	
		R: I delivered the presentation the following day, collecting questions during the speech with a follow-up answer session scheduled for after the break (so I could connect with the scientist.) Post-forum ratings averaged 4.7/5, slightly above the previous year!	

Another example:

- **P**roblem: "The company's stock fell further than expected, and the CFO ordered immediate cost-cutting and budget revisions for all departments."
- **C**onstraint: "We had less than seventy-two hours to review the new budget submissions for errors and compile a new master budget."
- **A**ction: "I called an emergency team action meeting and assigned analysts to partner together to work on assigned departments, rather than the usual method of working alone while I abandoned my strategic projects to work alongside teams that needed assistance."
- **R**esult: "While the review was occurring at record speed, the analysts partnering together ensured that our error rate remained below 1 percent despite the speed of review, and we completed the review exactly on time."

Your interview answers won't be so short or general, and you won't be memorizing and reciting them word for word. By using the SOAR or PCAR structures, you can work on getting your stories organized and making them powerful, while not losing the attention of the interviewer.

To complete your story grid effectively, you might find it helpful to tell your story to another person (see what questions they ask!) or write your stories out first. You can then choose the most important elements for your grid.

Story Takeaways

Studies say most people only retain 10 percent of what they hear. That's why the last column of your interview grid is so important. What's the one thing that you want the listener to remember? For each story you write, determine the one element that is the most important to sell. After all, the interview is just another step in selling you as a potential employee.

When writing your takeaways, make sure you have your Career Kaleidoscope and your marketing message in front of you. The takeaway from each story should connect back to what you are trying to sell in the first place. You're the total package—make sure the interviewer knows it.

> ACTION: Determine the takeaway for each story in your grid.

As you work on your library of stories, remember that all this work isn't only for one job search. You can add stories as your career progresses and continue to use the library as ammunition for promotion and future job searches. It's a great place to add successes as they happen.

Topic	Story	Structure	Takeaway
What is the topic you might be asked ? about	What is the story you're going to use as an example?	Map out your structure for each story. SOAR (situation, opportunity, action, result) or PCAR (problem, constraint, action, result)	What's the one thing you want to make sure the listener hears about your story?
Challenging Situation	Allied Health (2005): West Coast healthcare forum	P: The firm was hosting its first West Coast forum as a way of increasing business on the West Coast and the scientist who was doing the research presentation was stuck in an airport because of inclement weather.	I was able to react with a quiet confidence, quickly assess and take control of the situation, and ensure the company is always presented in its best light.
		C: There were no other scientists present at the time at the forum and the presenter did not have access to videoconference equipment.	
		A: I rearranged the schedule so the presentation would be the following morning and worked with the presenter by phone that night to fully learn the presentation's content while also weaving in my own sales techniques.	
		R: I delivered the presentation the following day, collecting questions during the speech with a follow-up answer session scheduled for after the break (so I could connect with the scientist.) Post-forum ratings averaged 4.7/5, slightly above the previous year!	

Now that your library of stories is complete (for now), you've done your basic preparation. Now, it's time to customize again. In order to customize, you have to have an idea of what to expect.

When you get the good news that a company has been impressed by your marketing tools and wants to interview you, you have to ask some basic questions and gather some basic information. Your library of stories will be even more impressive if you know how to use it.

First and foremost, you want know how you will be interviewed. Companies

Good to Know:

If you have had a hard time remembering your successes or trying to come up with stories that demonstrate how great you really are, it's time to do a better job of tracking your accomplishments. As soon as you start your next job, create a document on your computer labeled "achievements." When you close a big sale at work or get an e-mail thanking you for your hard work, note your success immediately in the document. Then, when it's time to apply for a promotion, or conduct a job search again, you're better prepared.

structure their interviews in many different ways. The table below outlines the most common types of interviews.

A company is not likely to give its interviewing secrets away, but you can ask something like, "Can you tell me how the interview will be structured?" and the recruiter or company point of contact should give you some idea of what to expect. When you do get called for an interview, there is some specific information you need in order to interview like a champ. Some of it may seem obvious. But when you're basking in the excitement of getting that call, you'd be surprised how quickly you might forget to cover the basics. The recruiter may share this information with you, but if not, there are additional questions you should ask.

Common Types of Interviews

Type	Description
One-on-one	A one-on-one interview, the most common interview type, is where you are meeting with one interviewer. The questions will likely be straightforward and can be focused on the job that's open or on your experience as a professional.
Behavioral	A behavioral interview is one where the interviewer has been trained to assess how you would behave in certain situations. The questions are focused for you to provide specific examples of times you faced different situations (being a leader, facing a crisis, a time you failed) in the workplace. This type of interview is becoming more and more common in the workplace.
Panel	A panel interview allows multiple people to interview you at once. They're often used when a quick decision has to be made or a consensus needs to be reached.
Group	A group interview brings several candidates together to see how they share the spotlight. You may be asked questions as a group or given an issue to solve or a problem to address as a team.
Case	A case interview requires responding to a case study question, which may or may not be related to the position. The question will test your ability to analyze and respond to an issue and usually includes a workplace or business problem to solve.

- **When will the interview be held?**

  Be sure you get the month, day, and time so there is absolutely no confusion whatsoever. If it is a phone interview, confirm the time zone (and then reconfirm it). Anyone can make an error; you just don't want that error to be yours. If the recruiter offers up a day or time that won't work, be honest. You don't want to do a phone interview with screaming kids in the background nor do you want to rush an interview so you can get back to work for an important meeting. Suggest several alternative times, and be as accommodating as you can. We're all professionals here but you don't want to come across as needy or picky.

- **Where will the interview be held? For a phone interview: Will you initiate the call or should I?**

  The recruiter may assume you know where the company is located. Even if you do, be sure to ask what floor or suite to go to. You don't want to be searching at the last minute for where you should be. If traveling from some distance, the recruiter will likely offer to make travel arrangements, but if she doesn't you can ask whether you should make your own. If you are coming from a distance, most companies will offer to pay for or reimburse your travel expenses, so save those receipts. For phone interviews don't forget to verify time zone changes!

- **Do you have good directions to your location and can you recommend a good place to park?**

  If you will be driving be sure to ask for directions. While online mapping systems are a cool invention, they aren't always correct and this is not the time to be frazzled or lost. Knowing where to park is also important, especially if the interview location is in an urban location. Ask if there is a local parking garage and fork out the money to park there if you can swing it. You don't want to be fishing around for quarters to feed the meter minutes before interview time.

- **Who should I ask for?**

  Some recruiters may be interviewing you, or may want to meet you first. In other instances you may have to ask directly for the person you'll be interviewing with. Don't get flustered at the front desk—know who you're supposed to meet . . . and the correct pronunciation of his or her name.

- **How long do you expect the interview to last?**

  If you're currently employed, you might be interviewing on your lunch hour. But what if the interview lasts longer than that? What if you can't spare more time than that? Be sure to ask how long the interview (or interviews) is scheduled to last. Then add at least thirty minutes. Inevitably you will have to wait for someone to end a phone call or for a recruiter to find the person you'll be interviewing with. Nothing ever goes quite as smoothly as planned and no one knows that better than a recruiter.

- **May I ask who I will be interviewing with?**

  This is a biggie—and most people forget to ask. If you do ask, and the recruiter tells you, suddenly you are armed with information. A quick Web search on your interviewer(s) may yield amazing results: a work history, a speech or presentation he gave, a press release with his name, or even the results for the last marathon he ran. Imagine the impression you will make armed with this background information. Plus, you can make better small talk, too.

- **Can you tell me the steps in the interview process?**

  Knowing where you are in the interview process is key to navigating each step. Many candidates go in for an interview expecting it to be a first round when it is really the only round, or worse, just a courtesy or informational interview. It's also a good idea to verify the position you'll be interviewing for. You might arrive only to find they think you are a better candidate for a position you don't want.

- **I assume attire is business professional, is that correct?**

  You should always, let me repeat, always, plan on wearing a suit to an interview in the business world unless told otherwise. For example, a creative or informal organization may allow its employees to dress down and they won't want you to stand out. Ask to be sure.

- **Are there any sources of information you'd recommend that would be helpful in preparation?**

  Not everyone is comfortable asking (or recommending that you ask) this question. But it can give you some great information. You may not know of an industry or field resource that the company relies on heavily. Or the recruiter may offer up additional company materials that may be helpful. Either way, the worst thing the recruiter can say is "no."

Now that you've got the information you need, you're ready to prepare. Make sure you are using your electronic workbook to track your resumés and interviews. Once you start getting calls, you don't want to be caught off guard or be ill prepared because you weren't tracking your leads.

If you've never been in sales you may not immediately grasp the importance of leads. But every good salesperson knows how important it is to track, research, and follow up on leads. It's the best way to get a sale. Since you're in the business of selling yourself, you have to make sure you are tracking and following up on every lead you had. It would be impossible to remember all the things you need to do for your search. Imagine if a salesperson tried to remember all of his leads in his head. He'd easily get confused, forget to follow up on certain calls, and miss out on great opportunities. The same goes for you. Don't take that chance. You've done too much work to risk it all now.

Next, you should revisit your Career Kaleidoscope and examine the fit between the position and your Sweet Spot. You may see a really good fit in some places, but not in others. Using the Career Kaleidoscope, you can compare it to the job description and what you know about the open position, and determine how it fits with what you have to offer and what you want in return. The comparison will help you figure out where the gaps are, what research you need to do, and what questions you need to ask during the interview process regarding both what you have to offer and what you want in return.

For example, the environmental and cultural factors in Bill's Career Sweet Spot are challenge, travel, and structure. From one job description he has read, Bill knows how much travel he can expect, but he needs to clearly understand the structure of the firm and learn more about who his boss would be before knowing whether the position is a good fit.

Because it's hard to know right away if a position is a good fit for your Sweet Spot, that's why you look for a close match with the job description before you even consider applying. Then, once you are in the interview process, you can ask good questions and do your research to determine if the fit is really there.

Preparing for the Interview

There are two types of preparation: basic and type-oriented. Basic preparation is what you do for every interview. Type-oriented is the research that is specific to the type of interview you'll be participating in. Many people make the mistake of doing research slowly as they go through the interview process. It's more effective to do as much research as you can up front. The more information you have, the more power you have to decide what to use.

Basic Research

You've probably already done some research on the company or you wouldn't have applied there in the first place. Now you've got to take your research to

> **Good to Know:**
>
> As you conduct your research, enlist the help of a librarian. Librarians are trained to help you locate the most helpful sources for the information you need. Librarians also know which resources will work most quickly in your case and help you save much-needed time.

the next level if you want to compete. Most candidates will do a Web search on a company and learn the basics, but how many know the history of how the company's stock has performed? You might not need to know or use all the information you gather but the more you have, the more opportunities you have to stand out from your competitors. At the end of the process the company can only choose one candidate and you want to make sure you do everything in your power to put yourself in front of the competition. The information you need to gather during the basic research process is outlined on page 167.

As you do your research, you may find that some Web sites (like Hoovers.com or Vault.com) may charge a fee or require a subscription to access parts of its site. It most cases, the basic information you can access for free will do the trick. If it doesn't, before you fork out the extra cash, check with your local library or your college or university. Many college and universities offer library resources online that alumni can access for free. Additionally, some college and university career services offices offer access to career research resources such as Career Search, an online tool available only by subscription that allows you to compile lists of target companies and specific details on competitors, employees, and company news.

To find company news articles, you may also want to check in with your local library or undergraduate or graduate institution. While Web searches are great, they will likely only feature popular news about notable events, including financial issues and company mergers and acquisitions. The news articles most relevant to the position for which you are interviewing are only going to be found by searching research databases like Dow Jones or Factiva.

Finally, as you do your research, you are also going to come across a number of opinions. Many online research sites have message boards where users trade experiences about working at a certain company, or answer questions about the company culture, workload, or salary. These sites can be helpful, but take them with a grain of salt. They are often a place disgruntled employees go to vent, or are monitored by recruiters or human resources staff. It's better to use the strategies you learned in Chapter 9 to find contacts at companies you are interested in and get the skinny from them directly.

Interview: Basic Research

Information	Detail	Where to Find it
Company Basics	The company business model, their division or lines of business, and their mission and vision.	Company Web site and/or company literature.
Company Locations	Where the company is located both nationally and internationally. Know which location is the headquarters, and where the job you are interviewing for is located.	Company Web site and/or company literature.
Company History	How the company started, who the founders were/are, and how the company evolved to where it is today.	Company Web site and/or company literature.
Financial Performance*	If the company is public (traded on a stock exchange), which exchange they are on, what the ticker symbol is, what the stock has been trading at and how it has performed in the past several quarters. If the company is private, financial information may be harder to obtain, but you should at least know how much the company is worth, how it is currently doing, and how well it has done.	The company Web site, annual report and proxy, financial Web sites such as Yahoo! Finance, finance and industry blogs, industry and/or association Web sites.
Competitors	Who is competing against the company for business in the marketplace, where they stack up against their competitors, and what their plans are to continue to compete.	Company research Web sites such as Hoovers, current and former employees.
Company Culture	What the culture is like at the company. What they look for in employees and what the environment is like that employees work in.	Company research Web sites such as Vault, news articles, current and former employees, company blogs.
Company News	What has happened to the company most recently. What press releases they have issued, any legal issues they have faced, or any studies or articles they have been featured in. News on employees or executives is also important.	Press release or investor relations section of a company Web site, Google searches, database and library searches.
Company Positioning	How the company positions itself in the marketplace, who its customers are, and what its customers are like.	Company research Web sites, current and former employees.
Company Outlook	Where the company is headed. What its growth plans are and its vision for the future.	Current and former employees, company Web site.
Executive Team and Company Governance	Who is running the company and the directors' backgrounds and experience. If the company has a board of directors, who is on the board and what are the companies that board members are affiliated with.	Company Web site, company research Web sites, annual report and/or proxy statement.

*If you are interviewing for a job in finance you will want to do much more in-depth research on the financial performance, stock history, and financial trends of the company.

Research for Each Interview Type

In addition to basic research, you also want to do some research based on the type of interview:

Type	Research Needed	How to Succeed
One-on-one	Make sure you do a Web search on your interviewer(s) to get as much individual background information on them as you can.	Prepare answers to common questions in advance and be sure they are succinct (see table on page 169). Practice answers in front of a mirror or on a tape recorder to make sure you're not rambling. Maintain good eye contact with the interviewer, good posture, and be sure to answer the question that is asked.
Behavioral	Talk to current and former employees to learn how people are successful at the company. This will be a sign of what behaviors the interviewer might be assessing when interviewing you.	Make sure you know your library of stories very, very well. Remember, there is no right answer to any question and the interviewer will want you to be yourself. Use your story structures: Don't spend too much time giving the history of the situation. Instead, focus on the action you took and the result of your actions.
Panel	Do Web searches on all of the panelists or interviewers if you can. This way, you can learn what they might be interested in and customize your answers based on who asks the question.	Be prepared that with multiple interviewers, a panel interview might run longer than a typical interview situation. Be sure to make eye contact with all of the panelists and not just the one asking the question.
Group	Ask the recruiter or point of contact who else will be in the group. Research the history of the group process by talking to current employees and asking why it is used and what the interviewers are most interested in seeing.	Make sure you get enough attention but also make sure you don't hog the interview time. Know that they may be assessing your teamwork skills in addition to how you answer questions. Listen to what others answer and be sure to chime in when you have new information to add, rather than reiterate what another candidate has said.
Case	Know the company's business well and the type of work they do. Be sure you have read current newspapers or	This interview type is rare but also one of the hardest. It is often used in large companies, particularly in banking, finance, strategy, and consulting. Your research should reveal whether you can expect this interview type. Many university career

Type	Research Needed	How to Succeed
	business publications so you know the latest trends and can use them in your case analysis.	services offices have case interview guides, as do bookstores and online career development Web sites, such as Vault.com.

Types of Questions

Depending on the type of interview you have, you can also try to plan ahead for the sorts of questions you might be asked. You can never anticipate every question, but you can use the list of common questions below to draft answers and choose which stories might work best for which interviews. It is also very common to have interviews that combine some of these methods, so make sure you review and prepare for multiple types.

One-on-one

Common Question	How to Answer
Walk me through your resumé.	A good opening question, don't repeat verbatim or recite your resumé word for word. Use your marketing message to describe who you are now and then walk through how your career progressed through each position, why you left that position, and conclude with why you are now interested in the position you are interviewing for.
Why do you want this position?	Share elements of both what you have to offer and what you want in return. Focus first on what you can do for the position and the company, and then briefly mention how important the role is in your career progression and why.
Why do you want to work for our company?	Your research should have uncovered details about the firm and its culture. Here's where you can demonstrate your fit. Be sure to focus on how you can help the company meet its goals and strategy.
Where do you see yourself in five years?	Use the vision you created, but focus more on the general direction of your career rather than the exact position. You want the interviewer to see a long-term fit for you at the company and not think you are going to leave after just a year or two.
What are your strengths and weaknesses?	This is a tough (and common one) so we've got a special section on page 171 on this question.

Bottom line: Be confident and back up your answers with stories from your library. Be prepared for creative questions and to think on your feet if you get caught off guard.

Behavioral

Common Question	How to Answer
Tell me about a time you were in a leadership role.	This is a chance to demonstrate your leadership style. Choose a story that shows you led a group of people to a satisfactory result.
Walk me through a disagreement you had with a manager.	Be sure you demonstrate that you understood your manager's point of view, but had a different point of view for a different reason. Don't put down or talk negatively about your manager. Focus on why you made the recommendation you did.
How would you handle an irate or dissatisfied customer or client?	If patience or listening skills are among your strengths, this is a good chance to demonstrate that. Choose a story that shows a turnaround—how you were able to turn an unhappy customer into a happy one. Be sure to focus on the importance of the customer and customer retention.
Talk about a time when you faced a problem at work.	Choose a situation where a project or event didn't go as planned and talk about how you recognized the problem, what you did, and the end result. Use the PCAR structure and focus more on the solution than the problem.
Walk me through a difficult team situation you were a part of.	Select a team situation where you were one of many members so you can demonstrate how you work in diverse situations. Again, don't talk negatively about any of the team members. Simply walk through the problem the team faced and describe the solution. Make sure you focus on what *you* did. Don't use "we" throughout the entire example.

Bottom line: This is where your library of stories will really come in handy. Take a deep breath and feel free to pause before launching into your example so you can follow your structure and clearly demonstrate your behaviors in the situation.

Case

Common Question	How to Answer
Estimate the size of a certain product market in the United States.	For all case questions, the most important thing is to have a process. The interviewers aren't necessarily looking for the right answer. They are more concerned with the process you go through to get to that answer. Try outlining the steps you would take first, then go back and determine the information you would need for each step.
A client wants us to implement a new software package. Plan for the implementation.	
Evaluate the worth of this company using the data provided.	

Bottom line: Make sure you know that you are going to be "case interviewed" and practice, practice, practice. And don't forget your calculator. You might need it if you are asked a numbers-heavy question.

The Famous "Strengths and Weaknesses"

For some reason, the strength-and-weakness question continues to be a perennial favorite no matter how useful (or pointless) it might be. If you have done your Career Kaleidoscope (or know yourself at all) you should be familiar with your strengths. It's not hard to know what we do well. But how should you answer the question about your strengths? You should know before going into the interview what matters most to your audience. What strengths are they looking for? If you have them, great. If you don't, reconsider why you are applying for the position. Don't say something is a strength if it isn't. You may think you can compensate when you get into the position, but you can't instantly make something a strength if it isn't, and your future boss will pick up on this pretty quickly.

What about your weaknesses? Everyone has them. No one can be good at everything. Think long and hard about where you typically struggle in the workplace. If you're having trouble coming up with examples, pull out old performance evaluations or connect with your old managers or bosses to get their input. Once you do, think in the opposite way as you did for your strengths. If your weakness matches something that is important to do the job well, reconsider why you are applying for the position. As with strengths you may not have, you may think you can compensate for a weakness when you get into the position, but if the company views this ability as very important to the job, they'll see through you pretty quickly.

Do you just answer the question by saying such-and-such are my strengths and such-and-such are my weaknesses? No, that's what the other candidates are going to do. You're going to use a little technique called the "positive sandwich." Here's how it works:

1. Share your strengths and demonstrate to the listener how they will benefit the position and the company.
2. Share your weakness and indicate what you are doing (and have done) to work on improving on that weakness.
3. Reiterate your strengths and reinforce to the listener that your strengths are what the position demands.

Strengths, then weakness, then strengths again. That's the sandwich. This technique works because it allows you to show that you are aware of your weakness but at the same time are working on improving yourself in that area. It also ensures you end your answer on a positive, rather than a negative, note: "While I am working on my quantitative skills and trying to become more comfortable with financial data, in this role, I can really leverage my communication skills and my ability to learn quickly to best meet the needs of the firm."

How Much Do You Want to Make?

Whether you're working for the money or for the love of your field, you still want a paycheck in return. Companies know this, but they also know their own financial limitations. It used to be that money wasn't even a subject of the interview process until an offer was made. But companies want to make the best use of their time and yours. If you are looking for a salary that's more than they can pay you, it's not a good use of their time to drag you through the interview process.

As a result, many companies are asking for salary information in the preliminary or first-round interviews to avoid the expense of interviewing candidates they can't afford. This is a controversial topic. Some experts will tell you to avoid the salary question like the plague. Others will tell you to highball the recruiter just to test him. At the end of the day, it is your choice, but you have to answer the question. You can try to hedge the recruiter if you want, but it's usually not a good idea. If they ask, it's in your best interests to give them an idea, even if it's with in a broad range (i.e., 10k–15k).

If the recruiter is asking, it's likely that there is a budget for the position. It doesn't mean you can't negotiate, it just means you aren't wasting your time or theirs.

You determined three salaries in the rewards section of your Career Kaleidoscope—this is your range. You can either disclose to the recruiter a minimum or a portion of the range, or you can turn the question back to them. Here are a few scenarios.

Scenario 1

Recruiter: *"Chris, before we get started, I'd like to get a sense of what your salary expectations are."*

Chris: *"Actually, I was hoping to learn more from you about the position first."*

Recruiter: *"Sure, well, let's chat about the role and the firm and perhaps that will be enough to help you answer?"*

Chris: *"That would be great."*

Scenario 2

Recruiter: *"Chris, before we close the interview today, I wanted to learn your salary expectations."*

Chris: *"I think I would look to you to give me guidance on the range budgeted for the position."*

Recruiter: *"Sure. We have a wide range for this position, from $80,000 to $100,000, depending on the candidate's experience and expertise."*

Chris: *"Thanks. My range is in line with that."*

Scenario 3

Recruiter: *"Chris, before we close the interview today, I wanted to learn your salary expectations."*

Chris: *"Well, actually, I would look to you to give me guidance on the range for the position."*

Recruiter: *"We don't have a set range that I can share with you at this time, but I do need to know the range you are working within, in order to continue the process."*

Chris: *"Okay. In that case, I would say my expectations are in the $80,000 to $85,000 range. Of course this depends on the opportunity and the fit as well."*

Recruiter: *"Thanks, I wanted to make sure we were at least on the same general page before proceeding further in the process."*

These options should be enough to answer the initial salary question. If you need more guidance, or are asked for more detailed salary information from the recruiter, Chapter 12 discusses job offers and negotiation.

Testing

Another component of the interview process may include testing. Some companies (such as Capital One) are well known for the batteries of tests job candidates have to take in order to get through the process. There are laws governing what companies can and can't test and it's likely that if a company is asking you to take a test, they have already verified its legality. If you're skeptical, though, consult with an attorney or ask the recruiter.

Personality tests are the most common, especially at middle and senior levels in a company. It is a good way for a company to assess that you will fit in with the team or company culture. There are a variety of common tests and testing services employed by some companies, while others may create tests of their own to best meet their needs.

Aptitude tests are also common. A company may want to test your writing skills or knowledge of a certain subject, such as finance. Law firms require new associates to have passed the state's Bar exam because it proves that the associate has a baseline of knowledge of the law (and of course, allows a person to legally practice law in a given state). Companies may also give you problems to solve, research to analyze, or may ask you to build or create something on the spot. One major manufacturing firm in the Midwest was famous for giving job candidates Legos and asking them to build a creation as part of the interview process.

Fields like law or teaching may require certain tests or certifications to practice the profession. Be sure to research your field or industry carefully to make sure you're aware of any baseline requirements. In Chapter 15 we'll talk more about certifications and tests you can take to boost your credentials and advance your career (but are not necessarily required).

What to Expect in an Interview

As you get ready for your first interview, it's important to know what to expect. Your interview process may be only one or two rounds, or it could be four or five. You should expect to meet with multiple people in the organization, and go through several rounds. The more experienced you are, the more complicated or lengthy the interview process will likely be.

Organizations with strong recruiting functions may move more quickly, scheduling interview rounds as close together as possible. Other organizations may spread the process over a month or more if they are not as organized, or if they aren't in a hurry to hire for the role. It all depends on the organization and the industry.

You also should come prepared to fill out an application. Even if you're applying for a senior-level position, many companies (for legal reasons) require you fill out an application. Make sure you have information on references, work history, and the names and phone numbers of all of your past managers. This information is likely just for record-keeping purposes, but it still makes an impression, so make sure you have what they are asking for.

Keep in mind too that these applications are general—likely used for every employee at every level. So don't balk if it asks for the name of your high school or how many words you type per minute. It may ask for salary information, so even if you're not asked in the interview process you may have to share it on the application. You can leave it blank but if the recruiter goes looking and sees a blank space under salary desired, she will probably just pick up the phone and ask you directly.

Make sure you shake hands with everyone you meet, and request their business cards. You want to make sure you can follow up with everyone, if only by e-mail, to thank them for their time and to ask additional questions. If you have a business card of your own, be sure to offer one as well to each person you meet.

What to Wear

It's just as easy to dress correctly as it is to lose a job opportunity because of what you're wearing.

1. **Find out what you're supposed to wear**

   Corporate dress code is one of the things you should ask about when you set up the interview. You don't want to be over- or underdressed for the company, field, or industry. If you aren't given any direction, you must wear a suit (whether you like it or not). When in doubt, ask your contacts. Some fields, like banking, are very conservative and require a white dress shirt and simple tie. It's better to fit in than to stand out.

2. **Go for business hours, not after hours**

   Even if your fashion sense is the epitome of New York's hottest runway, remember that you should be dressing as a business professional. You don't want to look like you're headed to a club after the interview. Women: Skirts should be knee-length or right above your knee and necklines should be very conservative. Men: Pants should at least graze the tops of your shoes but not touch the floor. Hair and jewelry should be conservative and understated. If you sport an accessory like a nose ring, consider carefully whether you should keep it in or not. Some workplaces are more conservative than others. That said, don't lose your personality. You want to make sure you don't compromise who you are.

3. Make sure you match

Men: If you're wearing a black suit, wear black shoes, black socks, and a black belt. Accessories should match. Athletic socks are a no-no. In most cities hosiery is absolutely necessary. If you live in a warm climate, again, ask your contacts what's appropriate. The idea is to look like you fit in, not stand out.

4. Go for perfection

Nothing says "I don't pay attention to detail" like a wrinkled shirt or suit with threads hanging from it. If you don't iron, make sure your suit is fresh from the dry cleaner. Have a friend or spouse give you the once-over to make sure you don't have any excess threads, wrinkles, or stains. Please, don't eat lunch right before the interview. You know what will happen.

5. Keep up with the times

You may think your interview suit from 1990 is still in good condition, but it's probably out of style. Even if you're not the most stylish person, make an exception here. You don't want to look like you don't fit in, or worse, like you're too old! Ageism is illegal, but that doesn't mean age doesn't affect opinions. Companies are more likely to hire people who they think have many years of work left in them. If you've got old-fashioned glasses or a head of gray hair it might be time for a change.

6. Test out your outfit

New shoes? Great. Slipping in the hallway of the office building? Not so great. Be sure you scuff the bottoms of your shoes, and try on your entire interview outfit before the morning of the big day. Make sure that when you cross your legs your pants or skirt are not too short. Have backup hosiery in case you find a last minute run or hole.

7. Don't wear the same suit throughout the interview process at one company

If it's been a while since you've had to wear a suit, you might be tempted to wear the same one and just change the shirt or tie. No way. You can't show up in the same suit three times for three different interviews, even if cheapskate is your middle name. You must, and I repeat must, invest in three suits for any good job search. Save up, find a bargain, do whatever you have to do. You don't want to look like you can't pay the bills.

8. There's no better time for new purchases

Last but not least, if you're thinking about springing for a new suit, new glasses, or a new purse or bag, now is the time. When you look good, you feel confident, and that comes across to the interviewer.

Questions to Ask

I'm sure you haven't forgotten the "what I want in return" part of your Career Kaleidoscope. While selling yourself during the interview should be your focus, you can't forget that you are also responsible for assessing how the opportunity fits with your needs and Career Sweet Spot. Almost every interview closes with the interviewer asking "Do you have any questions for me?"

For every interview, you should have three or four questions pre-prepared. The questions should get more detailed with each interview and should not be repeated. Interviewers talk to each other and share details. You don't want to be labeled as unoriginal. Early questions should focus on the company's performance, expectations for the role, and why the position is vacant. Bring a portfolio with a pad of paper inside that has your questions already written out. Then, as the interviewer is answering them (and be sure to note which interviewer answered which questions!), take notes. Good ones. You'll need all the information you can get to follow up with your interviewers and potentially make a decision on whether to accept a job offer.

As you get further through the process, you can ask more detailed questions about the structure, the function, the current projects, and the weaknesses of the firm. Only in the final round and after you receive an offer should you ask pointed questions about salary and benefits. They are certainly key to your decision-making process, but you can always get this information before you make a decision and it makes a better impression if you focus on the content of the job first. Don't forget to ask about the interviewer, too. Interviewers love to share their own success stories.

Don't waste the interviewer's time. Don't ask questions that you can easily find the answer to yourself, such as "What are your lines of business?" or "Who is your CEO?" There is a reason you did all of that research in the first place. It's not only so you can answer questions better than the other candidates. It's so you can ask better questions, too.

Good questions depend on the opportunity, and, more important, on your Career Sweet Spot. What's essential to know in order to determine if the role is a good fit? Here are some questions to get you started. Choose the ones that best fit the job you are interviewing for and your personality. Be sure to come up with some on your own, customized to the job itself. Regardless of the questions you choose, remember that questions regarding benefits and salary are best held off until the end and should most likely be addressed to the recruiter or hiring manager.

Question	When to Ask
I understand you've been at XYZ firm since its inception. Can you give me more details on your background and the secret of your success here?	Any round
What are some of the current projects your department/function is working on?	Any round
I understand the culture of the firm is very [entrepreneurial, structured, etc.]. Would you agree with that? What other words would you use to describe the culture here?	Any round
What type of person is most successful at XYZ company?	Any round
What are some of the greatest challenges you see the firm facing in the coming year?	Any round
Is this a newly created position or has someone vacated the position?	First round
Can you walk me through the structure of the department/function?	First-second rounds
What are the most important qualities of the person you're looking for to fill this position?	First-second rounds
How does XYZ company contribute to the community?	First-second rounds
What do you like most about working at XYZ? What do you like least?	First-second rounds
I read this week that your major competitor is considering [product launch, acquisition, etc.]. How will your company respond?	Second-third rounds
I understand the job requires about 20 to 30 percent travel. Can you describe the nature and length of some of those trips?	Second-third rounds
One of the things that is most important to me in my next role will be the level of challenge it provides. How will the person in this role be challenged?	Second-third rounds
What distinguishes your benefits package?	Final round
Are there other benefits that the firm is considering offering?	Final round
What is the salary range for this role?	Final round

Last But Not Least

Before you walk out the door on the day of the interview, go through this handy checklist:

☐ **Have you reconfirmed the interview with the organization?**

Last-minute changes happen. Always call or e-mail the recruiter or contact person the day before to reconfirm the place and time.

☐ **Is your interview outfit ready to go?**

Be sure you know what you'll be wearing and make sure it's appropriate for the interview. If you have not been given guidance on what to wear, go with a conservative suit and tie (for men) and a skirt (knee-length or lower) or a pantsuit (for women).

☐ **Do you know where you're going and how long it will take to get there?**

Be sure you have directions to the interview location and allow thirty extra minutes to get there. You can always wait in a nearby coffee shop or in the downstairs lobby.

☐ **Do you have your materials?**

Be sure to print out a few resumés on professional paper in case they are needed during the interview. While the interviewer was probably routed a version of your resumé from the recruiter, it may be buried in a file folder, stuck in their inbox, or in an electronic file (sent directly from the Recruiting Management System) they can't access. Be sure to carry your resumés inside a nice portfolio in an equally attractive purse or bag.

☐ **Do you have information for the application?**

Don't forget that you need reference, salary, manager, and work-history information to complete the application, if asked.

☐ **Do you know your resumé and your stories inside and out?**

Make sure you know your resumé extremely well. You don't want to look surprised or be caught off guard if the interviewer mentions a long-ago job, or a small piece of information at the end of your resumé. You never know what will catch someone's eye.

☐ **Are you well prepared?**

Bring notes on important research points about the company and examples from your work experience that you can share. If you arrive early for the interview you will have something to study.

☐ **Have you reviewed your field or industry lingo?**

Whether you're new to the field or a seasoned veteran, pull out a textbook or go online to one of the many field or industry associations featured in Appendix A. If you can't talk the talk, you won't be convincing that you can do the job.

☐ **Have you read the newspaper today?**

It's never a good idea to walk into an interview unaware of major news in the business world or in your firm or industry. At the very least, at the last minute, skim the headlines of a major business newspaper or two as well as publications in your field or industry to make sure you haven't missed any recent or breaking news.

Interview Time

You're ready to walk out the door and make the best impression you can. You know your library of stories and you've done your research. What now?

Don't forget your marketing message. On your way to the interview, think about your marketing message and what impression you want to make. After all, you've got a product to sell—you! You also want to make sure you are confident. Most people hate to talk about themselves, but this isn't a time to be modest. Unless you're normally very aggressive, it's not the time to be shy. You're in sales mode and need to be focused on why the consumer should buy the product, that is, why the interviewer should hire you.

It's important to be patient. If you're a good fit and make a convincing initial sales pitch, you'll be invited back for subsequent rounds of interviews. Don't try to sell everything on the first round or get all your stories out. Choose your words and the elements of your sales pitch carefully. You don't want to overwhelm the interviewers to the point that you aren't invited back for subsequent rounds.

Think ahead. How are you going to sit? Where are you going to put your bag, purse, or coat? You don't want to look frazzled or disheveled, so imagine how the situation will play out. Listen to yourself and watch the number of "ums" and "uhs" you say. If you've practiced, your answers should come out sounding concise and confident.

Pay attention to body language. Sit up straight and fold your hands in your lap just like Mom taught you. It's less likely that you'll fiddle if you do. Maintain eye contact. It's surprising how often job candidates look around the room and up at the ceiling when they interview. It's not only distracting, it's rude! Your eyes should be in only one of two places—the interviewer or your notes (the latter, infrequently). Think of the interview as a formal business meeting and you'll be just fine.

There are a few common mistakes that even the savviest of interviewers make. Don't fall into the trap of:

- **Not answering the question that is asked**

  This may seem ridiculous, but I can't tell you how often people skirt the question or miss the point altogether. There is a reason the structure in your story library is important; it helps you structure your answers. If it helps, try repeating the question or parts of the question to make sure you frame your answer: "A good example of when I was in a difficult situation was when . . ." Don't end every answer with "Did I answer your question?" That's annoying. Make sure you do so you don't have to even ask.

- **Interrupting**

  You may have the greatest point in the world to make but if an interviewer is talking, let him or her finish. Even if you feel like you're not getting to talk enough or aren't selling yourself effectively, interrupting your interviewer will only make you look unprofessional.

- **Talking about the fun you had**

  One of the most common (and ill-advised) responses when asked about an experience is to say "it was fun" or "it was a really good time." The interviewer doesn't care if you had fun, he cares what you learned from the experience that you can bring to his firm. Fun is for describing carnivals, not jobs. (Unless you're interviewing for the circus).

- **Getting personal**

  You may be desperate for this job because you've just gone through a divorce. Or you may be having financial issues. No matter what your personal problems are, leave them at home. An interview is not a time to talk about personal issues or the interviewer will think that you'll bring those issues into the workplace.

- **Time mismanagement**

  You have only a brief time to make your impression. Use it well. Try to keep an eye on the clock (if it is visible) or your watch (if you can see it without pulling back your cuff). You don't want to look like you have somewhere else to be, but you also don't want your answers to be so long-winded that the interviewer has time to ask you only two more questions.

- **Taking control**

  The interviewer is in charge here. While you have taken control of your job search, networking connections, and sales pitch so far, in the interview you have to let the interviewer take the lead. Don't try to ask questions in the middle of the interview or take control of the questions asked.

- **Thinking you're too good to practice**

  Even if you're the greatest business executive the world has ever seen, you still need practice for your interviews. Use a tape or voice recorder and try practicing answers out loud. Ask friends, colleagues, mentors, or networking connections if they have time to listen and critique your answers. Check with your undergraduate or graduate career services offices; some offer free mock interviews for alumni. If you think you're too good to practice, or you don't practice at all, you'll be surprised how disappointed you feel when you walk out of your first interview.

- **Going overboard**

  Showing your enthusiasm is one thing, but going over the top, or just coming off as plain weird is another. The interview is a formal business process, so don't do anything you wouldn't normally do in the workplace. Mentioning your interest in cooking to the recruiter is one thing but bringing her freshly baked bread is odd. If you're trying anything risky or creative, test it first. Ask networking connections in your field and industry how they would perceive it. Then decide. If you're in a creative industry you'll likely have a little bit more leeway.

Ending on a High Note

You've gotten through the interview and asked all of your brilliant questions. What now? Ask the recruiter or hiring manager if there is any additional information you can provide or any areas you haven't yet covered for them. You don't want to leave the interview without reiterating your interest for the job:

> "Before we close today, I just want to let you know how impressed I was with everyone I met today. I am extremely interested in the position and in the firm."

Some experts also recommend asking about the next step. While it's risky, and you may not feel comfortable doing it, it can work:

> "After meeting everyone today, I am even more committed to this opportunity. I'd like to continue in the process and have a chance to share more about how I can contribute to your company."

After closing with confidence, make sure you make a smooth exit, and ask for business cards from everyone you have met. Otherwise you can't follow up, which is not only a way to say thank you but one more way to make your sales pitch.

Etiquette may seem old-fashioned, but everyone likes to be thanked for their effort. Thanking your interviewers is a no-brainer. You may choose e-mail or snail mail (hard copy), but whatever you do, do it fast. Interviewers may be convening to make a decision that afternoon or in the next few days and this is your last chance to make an impression. A thank-you letter should be short, but it should also be detailed. Simply thanking the interviewer for her time isn't enough. Try this simple structure:

1. **Thank you**

   Thank the interviewer for his or her time, lunch, or dinner if it was provided, and, simply, the effort they put into the day.

2. **Refer to something specific the interviewer said**

   Go back to your notes and mention something the interviewer said about the firm or gave as an answer to one of your questions that was particularly interesting to you.

3. **Reiterate interest**

   Reiterate why you want the position and why you are a good fit for the firm.

Choosing e-mail or snail mail is a harder decision, but because time is of the essence, most people choose e-mail. But how many e-mails do you get a day? If you really want to stand out, bring formal stationary or note cards with you and write your notes immediately after the interview is done. Your interviews will still be fresh in your mind and you can better tailor the notes to the recipients.

You can then hand them to the receptionist or front-desk attendant and ask that they be delivered. Now *there's* a way to make an impression.

Were you referred by a current employee? They get a thank-you note, too (and a complete update on the process). The more they know, and the more you thank them for their efforts, the more likely they will help you again in the future.

Why Interview?

Think about interviewing like going on a date. You already know you have some things in common and there is a basic interest, and now both parties are seeing if there is an even greater interest. With each date (interview) you learn more about each other, while at the same time you highlight your best qualities. And finally, after several dates (interviews), you decide whether it makes sense to make a go of it, or politely part ways.

As you go through your job search, you should find yourself going on many, many dates. It doesn't make you a Casanova, it makes you thorough. Like dating, you don't have to take every interview that comes your way. Just the ones that have real potential. Few people marry the first person they date. This isn't to say it doesn't ever happen, but it's rare. It's the same with interviewing. You can strike gold on the first try, but more often than not, it is going to take some time. So be patient. But now that you have created your Career Kaleidoscope and isolated your Career Sweet Spot, you'll be able to spot the real thing much more easily. That's the whole point. Don't just take a job to take a job. You've done the work to find the perfect match, and you'll find it sooner than you think.

Closing the Deal

While other candidates are waiting by the phone, you're planning behind the scenes to make sure you're the one who gets the offer.

When you walk out the door, it may seem as if your fate is in someone else's hands. And you'd like to believe that, too. After all, you have already done so much work you'd almost rather sit back at this point and wait to see what happens. But just because the interview process is over doesn't mean you can relax. If you really want the job, there are a number of things you can do to check in, remind the recruiter and hiring manager how qualified and interested you are, and help them decide that you're the one they want.

The Decision-making Process

To understand how you can affect the decision-making process, you have to understand what happens after the interview is over. Whether you're interviewing for the first or fifth round, most recruiters will have evaluation sheets for your interviewers to fill out.

Depending on the sophistication of the firm, and how advanced and technology-focused its recruiting function is, the evaluation process and the decision timing will vary greatly. Some firms have electronic feedback forms, allowing for completion and routing of interview feedback forms via e-mail. Others manage the feedback process through a database, with interview feedback compiled and routed to the recruiter in real time. Still others do it the old-fashioned way, with paper interview forms routed by interoffice mail.

The sophistication of the forms also varies. Some (see page 186) are very general and streamlined for the entire organization; others are tailored to a specific business unit on department, or to the position itself. It is so important to have networking contacts at every organization where you interview because you can ask your contacts for insight on how the evaluation process works at that organization.

Sample Interview Evaluation Form

XYZ Company   **Candidate Feedback Form**
(Please return form to Recruiting Department, Suite 750, within 24 hours of interview completion.)
Candidate Name: _____
Position: _____
Date Interviewed: _____
Interviewer(s): _____
Round: ❏ First   ❏ Second   ❏ Third   ❏ Final

Experience   ❏ 5   ❏ 4   ❏ 3   ❏ 2   ❏ 1
(Please rank this candidate's experience as it relates to the position: 5=Superior, 3=Average, 1=Poor)
Comments: _____
_____
_____

Leadership   ❏ 5   ❏ 4   ❏ 3   ❏ 2   ❏ 1
(Please rank this candidate's leadership potential: 5=Superior, 3=Average, 1=Poor)
Comments: _____
_____
_____

Teamwork   ❏ 5   ❏ 4   ❏ 3   ❏ 2   ❏ 1
(Please rank this candidate's ability to be a team player: 5=Superior, 3=Average, 1=Poor)
Comments: _____
_____
_____

Firm Potential   ❏ 5   ❏ 4   ❏ 3   ❏ 2   ❏ 1
(Please rank this candidate's fit and long-term potential at the firm: 5=Superior, 3=Average, 1=Poor)
Comments: _____
_____
_____

Recommendation: ❏ Hire   ❏ Hire with reservations   ❏ Need more information   ❏ Do not hire
(Please check your recommendation above and justify your decision below. Use the back of this form if more room is needed.)
_____
_____

Just as the forms vary from company to company, so does the timing of the decision and who actually has the final say. Companies that are very good at recruiting do things quickly. They know that they are more likely to have a candidate accept an offer if they move fast. If you interview and then don't hear anything for several weeks, you assume the company isn't interested. Sometimes that's the case, but at other times, the company is moving slowly.

Large companies, or those who hire often, typically have a more streamlined process. When a company is starting up, or even in high-growth mode (like a newly public company), the focus isn't on Human Resources processes but on making money. On the other hand, some small companies have excellent recruiting processes. You should go into the process knowing that the smaller the firm, the more patient you might have to be with the recruiting process.

The decision-making process varies. Customarily, the recruiter manages the process. Recruiters are usually assigned to certain business lines, departments, or functions and know their staff and workloads well. This helps the recruiter work more effectively, form a bond with the department or function, and make the decision-making process go more smoothly. This matters to you because you have to know who's talking about you and when.

Recruiters aren't necessarily to blame for a slow process. Recruiters want to fill open positions as soon as possible. They are going to do everything they can to gather feedback and prompt the department or manager to make a decision, so they can move on to filling other open positions.

Much depends on how the company actually makes the decision. In some companies interviewers score the candidate on a number of different variables and weigh each variable depending on how important it is to the job. Other companies simply collect interview feedback and route it to the hiring manager or decision maker for the final say. Still others bring all the interviewers together to make a live decision. There are also companies that use a combination of these methods. If you have networking contacts at the company where you interviewed, you can ask them for insight in the decision-making process. When in doubt, assume that everyone you have met with will have a say, including the recruiter.

Post-Interview Strategies

Time isn't always a bad thing. The more time a firm takes to make a decision, the more time you have to follow up on your interviews and make that final sales pitch. Here are a few ways to do just that:

- **Articles of Interest**

  If you had a good topical conversation with one or more of your inter-viewers about an industry trend or issue of interest, find an article or on-line source you think the interviewer might be interested in and send it along a few days after your thank-you notes. It will keep your name fresh in the interviewer's mind and reinforce your level of interest and knowl-edge in your field or industry. Don't overdo it, though. If you use this strategy, use it with the one or two most influential decision makers and not every single person who interviewed you.

- **Thanking the Recruiter**

  Have you thanked a recruiter today? Sending a follow-up note to the re-cruiter, thanking him for his help and time "regardless of the decision made," will earn you some extra brownie points. Make sure you mean it. If you don't, it will come across as insincere or hokey.

- **Re-thanking the Hiring Manager**

  You've already sent a note thanking the hiring manager after the inter-view. And the recruiter has already told you "You're a strong candidate and we are in the process of making a decision so we will be in touch soon." Why not send a follow-up note to the hiring manager to thank her again and reiterate your interest in the position. When in doubt, a lit-tle extra interest goes a long way. If you choose this strategy, be sincere and keep it short and sweet, too.

- **Using Your Internal Contacts**

  There's a reason you worked so hard to network and find people you know at the company. Now it's time to use them. This is important, es-pecially if you were referred by a current employee. Make sure you up-date your contacts on the interview process and keep them in the know about any information (or lack of information) from the recruiter. They can also put in an extra good word for you, follow up with a letter of rec-ommendation, or support your candidacy after the interview process to reaffirm their belief in how great you'd be in the position.

- **Getting Questions Answered**

  Interviewers and recruiters are serious when they say "Please don't hesitate to let us know if you have any questions." And asking insightful, well thought out questions not only demonstrates your interest but allows you to check in on the process at the same time. As with the questions you asked in the interview, make sure your questions aren't so simple you could have found the information on your own.

- **Checking In**

    Many job seekers want to check in after they've interviewed to see if a decision has been made. It is crucial to check in (every job seeker should follow up to see where he or she is in the process), but can be risky if not done in the right way. Check in too often and you'll be seen as overbearing. Not checking in at all is a sign of lack of interest. Find a happy medium and vary the ways you check in. If your phone call isn't returned, try e-mail. Don't be offended if there is no answer. Recruiters can't always follow up with every candidate.

While post-interview strategies are a great way to try to close a deal, everything's better in moderation. Choose one or two ways to follow up and then do it once or twice after the interview has come to a close. You don't want to be seen as overeager or unprofessional.

There's also a fine line between keeping in touch and nagging. Because the recruiter often does have a say in the hiring decision, you don't want to check in too much with her or with the hiring manager. As much as you would like to think the open position is their top priority, in reality it is probably one of many things on their "to do" list competing for attention. To avoid becoming a nag, when you get in touch with a recruiter, ask for a time frame: "Jennifer, I don't want to interrupt you, but I am really interested in the position and eager to hear your decision. When would it make sense to check in with you again?"

Framing your question that way makes it easy to get an answer, and may also give you insight into your status. If the recruiter seems bothered or responds with a curt "If we are interested we'll call you" you may have caught her at a bad time, or it may be time to take a

> **Good to Know:**
> Don't ever underestimate the power of the recruiter. Do what you can to make the recruiter's life easier. Respond to requests for information quickly, or offer before even asked. Don't disrespect or give the recruiter the brush-off; recruiters often have more power or say than you think. If you get the recruiter on your side, he or she might make a case for you, or help you find a more suitable position if you don't make the cut for the one you applied for. If you really believe you are a perfect match and the recruiter won't give you the time of day, ask your internal contacts to do a little detective work and find out why.

hint. But you can't always read into a recruiter's response. You can only be respectful of her time and of her request. At the end of the day, if they are interested they will let you know. If you push too hard, you may ruin any chance you had in the first place.

When in doubt, as a rule of thumb, check in with the recruiter when told to do so. If the recruiter says "We will get back to you in a week" don't call two days later, expecting an answer. If you aren't given any instruction, don't forget to check in. It can be seen as a sign of lack of interest. Instead, give it four working days, and then contact the recruiter by phone. If you don't hear back in another two days, follow up with a short e-mail indicating that you are "just following up with the message I left . . ." After that, checking in once a week is fine until you hear back or are told otherwise.

A company may make a decision in two or three days, but you may not be notified until weeks later. Many companies automate the process and send rejection letters through their Recruiting Management Systems only after they've had a candidate accept (which may take some time). Don't be offended if you feel like you met a hundred people at the company and still get a form letter. The automated systems can be set to send the same letter to all rejected candidates, changing only names and addresses.

The other misstep you want to avoid is to disrespect someone who referred you for a position. Follow their instructions and don't go over their head. Companies usually have referral policy rules, and in order for your contact to be rewarded if you are hired, you have to follow the rules. Some job seekers often ask a contact to refer them for multiple positions without considering which would be the best fit. You are a reflection on the person who referred you and you want to behave that way.

References

While more of an old standby than a creative marketing tool, references are almost always part of the job-search process. Most of the time, we wait until we are asked for them and then quickly dump them into an e-mail to the recruiter. Why not go the extra step and create a reference page ahead of time that supports your marketing message? This way you can offer it before you are even asked, or have it ready to go as soon as it is requested. Recruiters always appreciate candidates who can respond to requests for information immediately. It makes their job easier.

References *aren't* just people who know you. They are people who can speak well on your behalf. You want to choose former managers or colleagues who you know can testify to your strengths in a variety of ways. To choose references, follow these rules:

1. Select three or four people who are familiar with your work and who you have kept in touch with (even if irregularly). Make sure you aren't choosing people for their titles, but rather people who actually have direct knowledge of your work.

2. Choose people at a variety of levels, including a boss, colleague, and staff member who reported to you, and make sure the references have worked with you recently. A boss from ten years ago won't cut it. If you are in, or applying for, a client-facing role you might also want to include a client as a reference. You can also choose someone who has worked with you in a volunteer capacity if the work was significant.

3. Contact each person in advance, updating them on your search and providing details on the position and on the interview process. You don't want a reference to get a call out of the blue without even knowing you are in a job search or without having granted you permission to serve as a reference.

4. Ask whether they are willing to furnish a reference, and if so, when would be the best time to be contacted and what contact information they prefer you share. The easier you make it for the reference, the more likely the reference will say nice things about you. Be sure to ask if their company allows them to serve as a reference and what they can say. For legal reasons some companies have strict rules about what information references are allowed to share.

5. Follow up with an e-mail confirming your request and reaffirming the details about the position and the company. Provide the name and title of the person who might contact them as well as what the person might be most interested in learning about you.

6. Choose backup references (and get their permission in advance, too) in case a recruiter has trouble reaching a reference you have provided. Even the best of references might be swamped at work or might not have time to return a phone call in the time frame requested.

Once you have your references, match your reference page to your resumé and cover letter. Use the same font, style, and header so they work as a package. Put your header (name and contact information) at the top, followed by references in the order that you prefer they be called. It's also helpful to include some background information on how you know each reference, so the recruiter or hiring manager has a sense of context when they get in touch with them.

Your reference page might look something like this:

Bill McCarrick
37 Marston Circle | Atlanta, GA 12345
(440) 555-7789 | billmccarrick@emailaddress.com

REFERENCES

1. Sondra Mikowski
Vice President, Business Development and Marketing
Allied Health
401 Vantage Parkway, Suite 200
Alpharetta, GA 40004
smikowski@alliedhealth.com
(404) 555-9809 (office)

Sondra is my current manager at Allied Health. She is responsible for all business development and
marketing activities in the firm and I have been reporting to her since 2004. Sondra would prefer to be
called at her office number during the morning hours. She is aware that I am in the midst of a job
search.

2. Brian Carmichael
Marketing Analyst
Allied Health
401 Vantage Parkway, Suite 200
Alpharetta, GA 40004
bcarmichael@alliedhealth.com
(404) 555-9875 (office)

Brian is one of four to whom I directly report at Allied Health. He is responsible for tracking and
reporting data on marketing and business development activities. He is aware of my search and can
be reached at any time.

3. Allison D'Agostino
Vice President, Sales and Marketing
Canton Pharmaceuticals
2100 34th Street, 4th Floor
Atlanta, GA 40010
Allison_dagostino@cantonpharma.com
(404) 555-1154 (cell)
(404) 555-2374 (office)

Allison supervised me in multiple capacities during the majority of my tenure at Canton. She was
previously Director of Sales and now oversees all sales and marketing efforts. She is aware of
my job search and prefers to be contacted on her cell first and office second in the afternoon
hours.

If you are currently in a job search your current manager, boss, or company
doesn't (or can't!) know about, be sure to let the recruiter know this when you
send along your reference page. Otherwise they will wonder why you didn't
include references from your current firm.

Finally, make sure you follow up with your references and thank them for
their efforts. Because your references might be contacted more than once during your job search, your best strategy is to send a thank-you note after they

have been contacted, and then, after you have accepted a new job, follow up with a gift such as a bottle of wine, a gift certificate, or a book. You never know when you might need them again.

Background Checks and Testing

The reference check is usually the last step before you get an offer (or you may receive an offer contingent on a successful background check). Once reserved for military and government personnel, background checks are now a requirement at many companies. They help minimize risk and ensure that a candidate is who he says he is. With the increase of lawsuits and security breaches, companies would rather be safe than sorry.

A background check is a way to ascertain that you've told the truth and to verify the information you have provided. Most companies outsource background checks to organizations who specialize in them rather then doing them on their own. It also ensures consistency and reliability of information. Companies will ask your permission to perform a background check (and you'll have to give it if you want to be hired) by having you sign the bottom of your application. If you haven't had to sign anything by your last interview, be sure to ask the recruiter if there are any forms you need to fill out to continue in the process.

Background checks may differ depending on what kind of job you're applying for—government, education, and other industries may require extensive checks. The basic background check for a full-time position in the business world usually includes:

- Full legal name, previous legal names, and contact information
- Current residence and previous places of residence
- All educational institutions attended and their accreditation status, degrees attained (some companies may also request transcripts for details on all grades received and any academic suspensions or probations)
- All companies where you have been employed and the dates employed
- All job titles
- Any criminal record you have or may have had

Information that may or may not be included:

- Salary information
- Promotions

- Names and titles of managers
- Reasons for leaving

Companies will also likely do a credit check on you to make sure you are in good credit standing and not in legal trouble. Your permission is legally required for companies to perform a credit check, and it is usually granted when you sign the application (read the fine print carefully!).

Companies may also contact your previous employers to get information your background check left out, such as exact salary or reason for leaving. Some companies have policies about what information they can and can't release so it's important to be aware of any policies your current or former employer might have.

Finally, you may be asked to get fingerprinted or take drug or alcohol test as a condition of employment. This is usually the case if companies deal with a great deal of secure information (i.e., financial services firms) or if you will be operating a company car or traveling a great deal for a company. Like background checks, these are often administered by outside companies on an organization's behalf. In the case of fingerprinting, you may have to make the trek to your local police station to have your fingerprints made and delivered to the organization. For alcohol or drug tests, you might have to schedule an appointment at a local testing center. Either way, if you are asked to do any of these things, make sure you get detailed instructions from the recruiter, find out how long each one takes, and the date by which the recruiter needs them. You don't want your offer to be held up because you haven't made time to take the test. And by all means, don't try to "fix" the test. It won't work and it's just plain dumb.

When dealing with these checks, never, never, never lie. I can't make that clear enough. There is nothing worse than going through the application and interview process, receive an offer contingent on a successful background check, and be denied because you lied or gave misinformation. If you're concerned that a past misgiving might hurt your chances, it is better to be honest upfront than to be disappointed later.

Can I stretch the truth?

It depends. If you graduated with a 3.47 grade point average and your resume says 3.5, that's fine. But if your 3.5 is in your major and your overall grade point average is a 2.9, you better darn well make that clear.

Will I be automatically denied an offer if I lie?

Probably. No company wants to employ someone who can't tell the truth. However, there are no absolutes. If you're an amazing candidate, and the lie is insignificant, you might be able to slip through. But do you really want your future to rest on that small chance?

What about salary? I don't want to lie, but I make so much less than I am worth.

Don't lie about how much you make. The company can probably find out and you'd be denied an offer for lying. It's not worth the risk. We'll talk more about salary negotiation in Chapter 12, but even if you're making peanuts now, it won't necessarily affect what you might be offered.

I have a less than perfect credit history. Can I be denied a job because of it?

Companies aren't worried if you paid your electric bill on time. But they might have cause for concern if you've filed bankruptcy or are in a ridiculous amount of debt. Companies will also look to see whether you have any required payments (such as from back child support or losing a lawsuit). These payments are sometimes required to be taken directly from your wages (called wage garnishment) and the company would then be responsible for deducting that payment from your paycheck.

I was convicted of a crime. Can I be denied a job because of it?

You might be. It depends on the severity of the crime. A company won't care if you got caught going 80 mph in a 65 mph zone. But if you were convicted of stealing or assault, they might not want to take the chance that you'll commit the same crime in their workplace. Other offenses, such as drunk driving, will depend on the sentence, and whether it was a first-time offense. If you have ever been in legal trouble, you should be sure to contact a lawyer specializing in employment law to make sure you are aware of your rights.

I know that some negative information will come up on my background check. When should I tell a prospective employer?

This is up to you and depends on the severity of the information. But the best advice is to wait until the end of the interview process. During the final round of interviews, ask the recruiter or hiring manager if you can have ten extra minutes to talk to them and use the positive sandwich technique discussed earlier when addressing weaknesses. Reiterate how much you are interested in the job and what a good fit you are for this position. Then share the negative information, letting the recruiter know that you wanted to be as upfront and honest and possible. Include anything you are doing or have done to remedy the situation and close the conversation with a statement reaffirming your commitment to the organization and your hope that it won't affect their decision-making process.

All in all, background checks and pre-employment testing should be pretty painless. But if you have an issue that you think might affect the results, be honest with your employer and with yourself. It could hamper your job search. If the issue is a legal one, be sure to seek the advice of a lawyer. The expense will likely be worth your protection and the future of your career.

Waiting for the Offer

You've written your thank-you notes, your references have been checked, your background check is in process, and you've already covered a few post-interview strategies. Even if you're ridiculously confident an offer is imminent, don't neglect or stop your search. The offer may be delayed, the salary proposed may be much lower than expected, or you may be passed over. Continue your job search at full speed until you've accepted an offer. The worst that can happen is that you'll get multiple offers and you can use them to negotiate.

12

Taking and Making the Job

The phone rings and you've got yourself a job offer. Congratulations! Before you jump up and down like a three-year-old on his birthday, take a deep breath. First you've got to follow these six steps:

1. **Thank the recruiter and let them know you're really pleased to receive the offer.**

   It's important that you convey your enthusiasm even if the salary you are quoted isn't what you'd hoped for. When you go back to negotiate, you can use your enthusiasm and interest as a bargaining tool.

2. **Ask when you can expect to receive the formal offer in writing.**

   You should never proceed or make a decision until you have the offer in hard copy. Offers aren't ever 100 percent legally binding, but you're much better off having it in writing before trying to negotiate or accepting the offer. Most companies will provide you a job offer in writing, but if you don't get one, ask.

3. **Ask how long after you receive the formal, written offer that they would like a decision.**

   It's important to know the amount of time you have to make your decision, and to be able to ask for more time if you need it. You'll want to closely evaluate all aspects of the offer (including salary and benefits) as well as involve any relevant family members in the decision-making process.

4. **Ask who the best person to talk to is if you have any questions.**

   You're likely going to have questions about the offer and want to negotiate. Make sure you know who your main contact is for this process because it may not be the recruiter.

5. Ask what the desired start date would be if you accept the offer.

If they give you a date that's impossible, you can ask whether there is room for negotiation, but it's better to wait and negotiate a start date when you negotiate other items, such as salary and benefits.

6. Hang up the phone

Now you can freely dance around the room and celebrate. You've worked hard and should be proud of yourself for making it this far. Sit back and wait for the written offer, but until you formally accept it, don't drop the ball on the rest of your job search. Your search for *this* job may be over, but you may yet be searching for others.

The written offer may come by mail, e-mail, or overnight delivery, and should include all information associated with the offer: salary and other compensation, signing bonus details and delivery, benefits information, and any agreements you have to sign to make the offer binding. If you haven't yet given permission to do a background and/or credit check, forms for that might be included as well.

Ensuring the Right Fit

Now you're going to use your Career Kaleidoscope to validate the offer. You've spent a considerable amount of time in the interview process with the company as they tried to learn as much as they could about you. But have you learned all you need to know about the company? If you have unanswered questions or the smallest of doubts, just because you're offered a job doesn't mean you should take it.

Remember how we compared interviewing to dating? Well, now you're about to get married. Think of taking a new job like walking down the aisle. You're about to make a big commitment. Sure, you can get out of a job after you've taken it, if it doesn't work out. But isn't that the point of doing all of this work to avoid making a bad choice?

The work you have been doing now leads up to this point. If the position matches your Sweet Spot and the other top elements of your Career Kaleidoscope, it should be easy as pie to determine that accepting the offer is the right thing to do. Before you say yes, compare the position one last time to your Sweet Spot and identify any questions that may linger.

STOP If you find yourself on the fence, or making excuses why you should or should not take the job, then there's something wrong. Either you weren't honest with yourself when creating your Career Kaleidoscope, or you know the job isn't a fit but you feel like you have to take it. If you aren't struggling financially and don't have to take a job for the income, don't cave into the pressure. Taking a job that isn't a fit with your Sweet Spot just means you'll be unhappy, and forced to leave and start this process all over again. Stay true to why you opened *The Right Job, Right Now* in the first place.

You should not have many questions because you will have asked most of them during the interview process. Any questions now should be more focused on the finer nuances of who you will be reporting to, your benefits and rewards, start date, and/or offer contingencies (which will be discussed shortly).

Group any final questions you have into categories (i.e., salary, reporting structure, start date) so that you can address them with the recruiter in one very organized conversation. One of your questions about salary might be "can you give me more?" Before you pick up the phone to initiate your final round of inquiries, you have to be prepared.

Negotiation

The last remaining issue you may have about your offer may be ascertaining that the rewards and benefits portion of the offer fits your Sweet Spot. Maybe you're psyched about the job, but already agreed with your family that you need to make at least $5,000 more than in your old job to make the transition work. Or maybe the position is contingent upon a move to another city that you hadn't bargained for. Whatever the hesitation is, you can try to negotiate the point. Does negotiation always work? No. But it's worth a shot and if done well won't lose you the offer or alienate your recruiter or whomever you are negotiating with.

Needing to Negotiate

Nothing is ever written in stone, including your Career Kaleidoscope. If money is the only thing between you and the perfect job, now isn't the time to give up. Only you can decide if the money is right. Where does money fall in your Career Kaleidoscope? How important is it to you? To your family?

Many job seekers make the mistake of negotiating when they don't need to. Don't negotiate just because you can, negotiate because you need to. Without getting into the psychology of it all, know that if you don't have a clear reason why you deserve more or why you need to make more, it's going to show through and the negotiation won't work. Make sure that the need is actually there.

What's Negotiable

If you decide to negotiate, and many people do, think about salary negotiation like buying a car. Most people only try to negotiate the sticker price of the car. But that's just one portion of the price. Everything's negotiable, from free oil changes to licensing fees to the sticker price. A job offer works the same way.

Monetary Compensation

Of course the money is negotiable, but compensation includes more than just your salary. It may include a signing bonus (money you get for accepting the job), performance bonus (money you get for reaching or exceeding predetermined goals), or stock options (the ability to purchase shares of company stock at a set low price).

> **Good to Know:**
> Companies don't concoct salaries out of the blue—there's a methodology, *and* a number of human resource professionals and executives behind compensation structures. Many companies have a compensation strategy that outlines their policies and philosophy and guides how employees are rewarded. The more you can learn about the company's structure and their philosophy, the better you can negotiate. Unless you're interviewing for Chief Something, they likely won't go outside their bounds just for you.

When you get your offer, be sure to factor in all of these types of compensation to determine the total value of the monetary portion of the offer. Be forewarned, though—if you are given an offer that is more than 50 percent bonus or performance money, it may affect your financial situation. Many loan and mortgage companies won't consider performance income as real income unless you have a letter from your company guaranteeing that you will earn it. If they can't give you the salary you want at this time try negotiating for an interim performance review, through which if you meet certain goals by, say, month six, you'll get an automatic increase.

Benefits

Many job seekers think benefits aren't negotiable, and to some extent they aren't. For example, healthcare plans are usually set in stone, but you may be able to wangle extra days of vacation. Also, depending on your job level and the type of benefits offered by the company, you may be able to trade off one benefit for another. Some companies actually have this built in already—called a cafeteria plan—where you get a set amount of "dollars" to spend on benefits and you can choose the ones that make most sense for you. For example, if you are single and childless, you can choose to spend your benefit dollars on a fitness benefit rather than childcare. Make sure you fully understand the benefits before you try to negotiate them. You don't want to waste your breath fighting for something you already get.

Promotion/Title

If the company can't afford a higher salary, many savvy job seekers try to negotiate a title or promotion, asking for a senior manager title instead of manager or the promise of a promotion within a certain amount of time. This creative negotiation requires proactivity on your part—a company isn't likely to offer it. So be sure you have good reason to back up your request.

Start Date/Moving Options

You can also negotiate your start date in order to enjoy some more time off before starting your new job, or to tie up loose ends at your old company. This option is a good one if you know the company has flexibility, and/or if your vacation time is limited at your new job. You can also negotiate moving benefits if you'll have to move in order to take your new job. Everything from a moving van to transportation expenses to temporary living arrangements is negotiable.

Regardless of what you try to negotiate, the most important thing to be realistic about is your job level. Most often, the more senior the position, the more ability you will have to negotiate. For example, entry-level candidates often have little negotiation power and unionized positions or employers may not have any negotiation ability at all.

Power Trip

Generalizing the negotiation process is impossible. Every situation is different and carries a certain level of risk. It's up to you to determine how risky it would be to negotiate and how to proceed. The first thing to do is to get a sense of who has the power. How badly did the company fight for you? Are you a perfect fit for the role, or are they taking a chance on you? Do you have competing offers and does the company know about them?

Usually one party (the company or the candidate) has more power than the other depending on the situation (and how you answered the questions above). As the candidate, you can shift the power base somewhat in your favor by being in the know. Basically, the more you know, the more power you can control. You might know what others make in the company, in your field, or in your industry. Or you might know that the company needs to fill the position as quickly as possible because of an important client or project.

You also may have negotiation power when the economy is strong, when demand in your field or industry is high, when an employer is busy and profitable and hiring like crazy, or when you are uniquely qualified and have a great deal of experience.

On the flip side, the company may also have second- and third-choice candidates waiting in the wings. They may be hiring many people for the same job (i.e., sales representative), or they may have a budget that simply can't be adjusted. The more you do your homework, the more informed you will be and the better you can make a decision about what to negotiate, if anything. At the end of the day, as with any negotiation, the goal is to make both parties happy and ensure a fair deal on both sides.

How to Prepare

The more information you have, the better able to negotiate you will be.

Use Your Contacts

Yet another reason why having inside contacts matters, networking contacts inside the company may be able to divulge insider knowledge about salaries and negotiation strategies. Contacts in similar fields, industries, or positions may be willing to share information on what they are making or what the going rates are.

Review Your Interview Notes

Throughout the process interviewers, hiring managers, or recruiters may give subtle hints leading to negotiation opportunities. Look back through your notes to see whether they mentioned anything about how crucial it is to fill the job, the importance of a specific start date, or a budget for the position.

Get Educated

Whether you believe it or not, there are a ton of online resources to benchmark or compare salaries in specific fields, industries, or geographies. Web sites such as Salary.com feature interactive salary searches for different fields, industries, and geographies. Others such as Vault.com feature message boards where you can anonymously ask about salaries. Keep in mind that Salary.com charges a fee for anything beyond a basic report, and the strength of Vault.com's message boards depends on the people who are on them at any given time. (Appendix A has more salary resources.)

To prepare for your negotiation:

1. *Do your planning.* Use your three predetermined salary figures: bottom line, acceptable, and ideal. Make sure you have involved your spouse, partner, or relevant family members to determine these figures.
2. *Do your research.* Use contacts and online resources to determine the norm for your field and industry, based on your experience and expertise.
3. *Know the company.* Get a sense of what you can and should negotiate, based on the strengths and weaknesses of the organization.
4. *Understand the offer.* Before you attempt to negotiate make sure you understand every piece of compensation and every type of benefits. If you don't, ask. Benefits like stock options and incentive compensation can be confusing.
5. *Look at the total offer.* Consider all aspects of the offer (not just salary) when thinking about what to negotiate. The salary might be a little bit less than you expected, but if you don't have to pay for parking, or you get a benefit (like dental or medical) you didn't have before, you may actually be making more than you think.

The Negotiation Process

When it comes time to make the phone call, have all the information you need at hand. In addition to knowing what you want to negotiate and how far you're willing to go, here are some other hints for success:

- Never negotiate immediately. Start out the call by thanking the recruiter, reiterating your excitement about the offer, and asking any questions remaining from the interview process. Then begin the negotiation.
- You shouldn't negotiate without a written offer in front of you or you run a greater risk of losing the offer altogether.
- Know how low you are willing to go. If you don't get the figure you've deemed acceptable, are you willing to accept your bottom line? Do you know what your must-have benefits are and what you are willing to trade off?
- Be realistic and don't overvalue yourself. Your offer may be revoked if you come back with a figure that's completely unrealistic.
- Be patient. You might be negotiating with a recruiter who has to go back and get permission to offer you more money or more vacation. If she does have to get back to you, ask politely how long it will take and when would be a good time to check in.
- Be the one who wants to be fair. Offer creative compromises when you can, such as a salary review in six months or more vacation instead of more money.
- Listen for verbal cues. Know when pushing any further could be a mistake. If you push too hard or drag the process out too long, the employer may give you an ultimatum. After all, he has a job to fill. If the employer makes a good-faith effort to work with you, don't go beyond two counteroffers unless you are at the executive level.
- Don't take it personally. If a company can't give you what you want, it may not be because they don't want to. Oftentimes they're restricted by budgets, internal politics or policies, or poor company performance.
- Get the final offer in writing. Once you've reached the negotiation compromise, let the recruiter know you'll be accepting as soon as you receive the final written offer. Make sure she knows your intent, but that you need to see any changes to the original offer, no matter how small, in writing.

Checking for Contingencies

A background or credit check and drug testing might be contingencies of your offer, meaning you have to be successful in all of those areas for the offer to stand. But there are two other common contingencies you should be aware of before formally accepting an offer.

One of these is called a non-disclosure agreement. If your offer is contingent on you signing a non-disclosure agreement, it means you have to agree to keep certain company information confidential. These agreements vary from company to company, but usually consist of the following parts:

- **Definition**

  This is where the company defines what information is confidential. It may apply to all information shared by the company to the employee or only certain types of classes of information, such as client or financial data.

- **Confidentiality Rules**

  This section details the rules of confidentiality. It will normally cover the ways in which information is received as well as who owns the information, how it can or can't be used (i.e., the employee can't use the information to sell or make his own products), and when or if confidential information has to be destroyed.

- **Miscellaneous Rules and Policies**

  This is mostly the legal mumbo jumbo—the city or state under which the agreement is binding, the term of the agreement, how and when the agreement can be modified, and who is responsible for legal fees if such action were to occur.

The other agreement you may have to sign is a non-compete agreement. This agreement covers issues relating to company competitors and may include the following sections:

- **Employer Definition**

  This spells out the type of business the company is in, so there is no confusion about what would constitute a competitor.

- **Covenant Not to Compete**

  The main section of the agreement, it prohibits you from leaving to work for a competitor within a certain period of time after you leave or within a certain geographical area. It also forbids sharing information with competitors, or using information to start a company of your own that would compete with the company within the specified time period and geography.

- **Solicitation of Employees**

   This section, also based on a certain period of time, forbids you from hiring company employees after you leave, or encouraging company employees to leave the organization.

- **Miscellaneous Rules and Policies**

   As with the non-disclosure agreement, this section covers the legalese— the city or state under which the agreement is binding, the term of the agreement, how and when the agreement can be modified, and who foots the legal bills in the event of a lawsuit.

Both the non-disclosure and non-compete agreements are legally binding documents that can be upheld in a court of law, so you'd be smart to have them reviewed by a lawyer before signing them, just to be safe. If you don't want that expense, at least make sure you ask the recruiter or hiring manager for complete clarification on any clauses that you find confusing or that you don't understand. You don't want to sign away your rights without fully understanding any document you are required to sign. Don't say I didn't warn you.

Accepting or Turning Down the Offer

At the end of the negotiation, you can accept the offer, decline the offer, or ask for more time. If you ask for more time, make sure it is for a good reason. The recruiter might worry that you are wavering and might ask why you need more time. The longer you delay, the longer the position remains open, and the more time they lose in finding the right candidate if you say no. Asking for more time is a risky move. Some companies may also time your signing bonus or other compensation— the longer you take the less you make. Make sure that you ask

> **Good to Know:**
>
> If you feel like the job is a really good fit, but have doubts about one specific element of the position, be honest with the recruiter. He may be able to set up a call with you and your potential boss or the hiring manager to talk specifically about the concern, so that you can make your decision. Don't try to talk to everyone in the interview process again—business has to go on at the company whether you accept or decline the job.

for more time only if you truly need it, and don't ask more than once. It's not fair to the company.

If you decline the offer, be sure you do so politely and respectfully. Recruiters and hiring managers know that it's a business decision and they won't be offended, but they will be disappointed. If you can, deliver your decision personally rather than by e-mail or a voicemail message. This way, you can thank the recruiter for his or her time and reiterate that the decision was tough and you're sorry you'll be unable to accept the offer. If you can't get in touch with the recruiter directly after a number of tries, then you can follow up with an e-mail. But be sure to be just as polite and respectful in the e-mail as you would be on the phone. You never know when your paths might cross again.

If you decide to accept the offer, congratulations are in order. Make sure you have reviewed all of the documents associated with the offer and that you don't have any remaining questions. Only then should you contact the recruiter with your acceptance. You may also have to sign a letter of acceptance and any associated contingency agreements. To make the best impression, sign all of the documents before making the call so you can send them in immediately.

When you do make the call, verify the start date and any remaining details associated with the offer. As mentioned earlier, make sure you've already received all of your promises in writing. Otherwise, they're less likely to happen. Make sure you ask when you can expect your first paycheck. With a new job, it takes a few weeks for the paperwork to be processed and the first paycheck to be delivered, and you'll need to plan ahead.

If you are currently employed, you also need to let your current employer know of your decision to leave. Standard notice is two weeks, but this and other resignation protocol are discussed in Chapter 18.

Preparing to Start

With any luck, you have had some time off to refresh yourself, and you are energized and excited to start your new job. Well, at the very least, somewhat excited. It's like getting ready to walk down the aisle at your wedding. You may be nervous or second-guessing your decision. But, in the end, if you have done all of the work to make sure it's the right fit, and you've matched your Sweet Spot and your vision, you should be confident in your job change.

Your first day on the new job may depend on a number of factors. If the organization is in high-growth or start-up mode, or your position is key to a major project that's under way, you might be thrown into work immediately. Or, as is common at many large or well-established companies, you might have a formal orientation program along with other employees who are also starting work that day. You and your "start group" will learn all about company history, structure, strategy, and policies. Companies that have formal orientations often include everyone from the new receptionist to the new CFO.

Whether it's a formal or informal process, day one also brings a pile of paperwork and a potential administrative nightmare. You don't have to complete all of the forms at once, but the more you prepare ahead of time, the more you can cross off your "to do" list and move on to more important things—like your job. Take a minute to learn (or remind yourself if you've started a new job before) what you'll be signing and reading.

Form	What It Does	What You Need
Tax forms	Ensures you pay the correct amount of taxes to both the federal and your state government. If there is a city or wage tax where you live, you will have to fill out a form for that, too.	Know your social security number, your number of dependents, and the amount of deductions you plan to take.
I-9 (U.S.)	Proves you are a citizen and/or have a legal right to work in the United States.	Bring your drivers license and social security card or a valid passport (in the U.S.).
Direct deposit	Eliminates a paper paycheck and deposits your salary electronically into an account you specify. Gives you the opportunity to split your pay between accounts and have a portion go into checking and a portion go into savings or another account.	Have the account number(s) and routing number(s) of the bank accounts where you want the money to be deposited. If the account is a checking account, you will also need a voided check.
Life insurance	If offered by the company as a benefit, gives you a minimum amount of life insurance protection at no charge and you can choose to purchase more.	Know how much (if any) life insurance you have already, and if your spouse has any through his/her job. Have the names, birthdates, and social security numbers of whom you'll name as beneficiaries.
401(k)/403(b)	Invests a portion of your pretax salary. You choose	Know your social security number and how much

Form	What It Does	What You Need
	the investments from a number of options the company has already preselected. 401(k) is the name of plans used by for-profit companies, 403(b) refers to plans for nonprofits.	(percentage) of your salary you want to go into the plan.
Stock/ESOP forms	Allows you to purchase company stock at a lower price (usually) than it is selling for on the market.	Know your social security number and the amount of company stock/options already given to you as compensation so you can decide how much more (if any) you want to buy.
Health benefits	Gives you and your family members/dependents health and/or dental and/or vision discounts or coverage.	Compare the company plan to any plan your spouse or partner's company offers (that could cover you). Know any preexisting health conditions that have to be covered and give yourself plenty of time to compare company options.
Reimbursement accounts	Allows you to save a certain amount of pretax salary to be used toward eligible medical and health expenses.	Know how much your family spends on healthcare and other eligible expenses each year; if you use this account you want to estimate as close to the right amount as you can since you usually don't get any money back if it's not used.
Transportation	Allows you to save a certain amount of pretax salary for transportation costs—often limited to public transportation costs.	Know how often you plan to take public or other eligible transportation to work and how much it costs.
Personal information	Gives the company a record of all of your contact information and emergency contacts.	Make sure you know who your emergency contacts are and you have all of your personal data at hand.
Security/ Property	Gives the company a record of property loaned to you while an employee (such as a computer) and affirms that you will secure the property and return it if you leave.	Make sure you know the type of equipment you'll need to do your job and the terms of use in any agreement you sign.

(*continued*)

(*Table Continued*)

Form	What It Does	What You Need
Other	Credit cards, travel preferences.	Have personal data to register for any credit cards, and airline, hotel, and car-rental frequent-user numbers for any travel preference sheets.

Helpful Hints

- If you can afford it, max out your 401(k) or 403(b) from the beginning—if you start out at the highest level, you'll get used to it being taken out of your paycheck instead of having to adjust to a bigger deduction later.
- If you're single or don't have a partner or children, avoid the expense of purchasing extra life insurance unless you think your parents, siblings, or whomever you designate as beneficiaries depend on your salary for financial support.
- Use the split account option for your direct deposit—it will help you automatically save money every month. Because it is being deducted electronically, you won't even miss it.

Day One

Now that you are aware of the mound of paperwork that awaits you, you're ready for the first day of your new job. On day one, make sure you know:

1. **Where you are going**

   You'd be surprised how many people aren't sure which of the company buildings or entrances to use.

2. **How to get there**

   If you came to the interview from the airport, or interviewed at a different location, make sure you have directions to where you're supposed to be on day one. You might be coming from a different place and your first day isn't the time to get lost.

3. **What to wear**

   You might have worn business attire to the interview but the corporate dress code is business casual. Maybe you've seen various types of attire worn throughout the building and don't know the rules. Ask ahead of time. First impressions are important on day one and you want to make sure you start off on the right foot.

4. Whom to ask for

Are you going through a formal orientation? Or will you go right to your office or cubicle and get started? Either way, you need to know whom to ask for when you get there.

5. Who did the job before you and who wanted your job

It's no fun to start a new job when one of your staff members is angry that you got the job instead of her. If you can, ask ahead of time who you replaced and if anyone already in the company was up for the position. Knowing the politics ahead of time can help you prepare for any animosity or tension.

6. What to expect

Will you be expected to dive into a project headfirst? Is day one jam-packed with meeting new colleagues or with filling out forms? You don't want to be caught off guard on your first day, so make sure you know what your schedule will look like, or if you'll be on your own.

Day One Advice

No first day on the job is the same for everyone, but try to fill out as much paperwork as you can, to get that out of the way. If the company hasn't scheduled time for you to meet with the people in Human Resources, be sure to keep a running list of benefits and other HR-related questions.

You may have been the head honcho at your last job, but you're in a new place now and you may have to ask for help. Whether it's asking where a certain office is, or how packages are sent, remember that every other employee was once new, too.

Another important "to do" you want to get started on is learning who is who. You don't want to be in the company kitchen with the CEO and not be aware of it. First, ask your direct manager who are the most important people for you to know. Then, if the company has a directory, use it to learn the names and titles of the senior officers. Many companies now have online directories to make this process much easier. Be sure to also ask for a directory for your department.

You also want to make sure you've found the basics. It may sound simplistic, but knowing where the bathroom, kitchen, copy room, supply room, and mail room are, can be just as important as knowing your colleagues. You can't get by without them.

Focus on listening. Soak up everything you can in your first few days. Sure, you were hired for your brilliance, but hold off on letting the world know just how smart you are (unless asked of course). You want to learn where your smarts can be used first.

At the very least, you should walk away from your first day feeling like you made a good choice. If the company tries to switch bosses, offices, or job responsibilities on you right away, it is cause for concern and an immediate talk with your boss is in order.

Day Six Advice

Your next major turning point comes on day six. As you start your second full week of work at your new job, you may feel like you know the basics, but there's still a great deal to learn.

You may be getting to know your colleagues, but if they mention an acronym or person you don't recognize, speak up. If you don't understand something, better to learn it now instead of being confused later. You don't want to miss an important point or get an assignment wrong just because you were too shy to ask.

Day six is also a good time to begin forging relationships. This doesn't mean dating your colleagues, but rather taking the time now to get to know the people who can help you later. How can you do this? People love free food. Set up lunches with the people in the company you think are key, and are close to your level. Setting up lunch with the CEO is only a good idea if you're high enough to make it worth his or her time.

It's also time to start saying "thank you." You probably already have, and will continue to, ask for help from peers and managers. Don't forget to thank anyone—from executive to administrative—who helps you, even if only for a moment. It's crucial to making a good impression and gets you started off on the right foot. If you haven't already, now is also a good time to make sure you get a copy of the company performance evaluation for your position. You should know how you will be evaluated and what the measure of your performance will be. You should also plan to sit down with your manager, regardless of your level, and set goals for the coming months and years. You don't want to make the mistake of assuming you know what you're supposed to accomplish only to find out after the fact that you were supposed to be doing something else.

Week Three Advice

By week three of your new job, you've gotten your feet wet, know your way around the office, and may even be doing some work. But before you get in too deep you want to make sure you've covered the basics.

Have performance goals been set? It's dangerous to go more than a few weeks without knowing where you are headed. Managers and bosses get busy and may forget you require some direction. It's okay to remind them—gently but firmly—that you need to know what's expected. If you can, ask for it in writing. This way there's no argument later about what you should have done or what you should be doing.

Create and review your own plan of attack. What resources do you need to get started? How long will certain goals or projects take? How do you prioritize your work, and what can wait until later? Once you have direction in the form of goals, you have a direction to move forward with your first projects.

While it's good to get comfortable with your colleagues, don't forget you're still the new kid on the block. Surely they will welcome fresh ideas, but they'll also get sick of you saying "At my old job we did it this way . . ." Offer up suggestions carefully and constructively. You don't want to hear a new colleague whisper "If they did everything so well at his old job, why didn't he just stay there?"

Month Three Advice

After you've been at your new job more than three months, you'll be settled in, plugging along, and crossing things off your "to do" list. Before you get too comfortable, there are a few final new job checks.

Are you on track to meet your performance goals? Most companies will do six-month reviews, twelve-month reviews, or both, so be prepared. Performance goals are only as good as the effort you make to reach them; leaving them buried in your desk drawer sure won't help your career. Try posting your goals in a place where you can see them every day. Constantly reminding yourself of what you have to accomplish will make it that much easier to do so.

What have you done for your boss lately? Surely you aren't one of those brown-nosers we have all come to hate, but there's a fine line between doing the right thing and sucking up. You don't want to offer to pick up your boss's dry-cleaning or clean his office, but you can offer to buy him lunch once in a while. Month three is a great time to treat your boss to lunch, catch up on how you are doing, and ask for any advice going forward. By month three you've learned the ropes, but may be making some missteps you hadn't realized. Lunch with the boss is a great time to figure that out before you get too comfortable.

It's important to not ignore what got you to this point in the first place. It's important to revisit your Career Kaleidoscope and your vision on a regular basis. Why not post your Kaleidoscope next to your performance goals? This way you aren't just reminding yourself where you are headed, but what is of importance along the way. If your performance goals aren't in line with your vision, how will you ever achieve what you've set out to do with your career? Your Career Kaleidoscope will help you make sure you aren't venturing too far off course—easy to do in a new job when you are in boss-pleasing mode.

PART THREE

Managing Your Career: Staying Challenged, Sane, and Motivated

Once you find and get that perfect job, you aren't allowed to be complacent. You should keep your Career Kaleidoscope, and especially your vision, close at hand so you don't strike the wrong key.

Many professionals make the mistake of thinking that career management ends when the new job begins. After all, you've just made a good career move and plan to stay there for a few years, right? Well, whether you're in your new position for a few months or a few years, from salary to performance, you need to keep tabs on how you're doing, what you're making, and how you'll get ahead.

13

You DO Work Hard for the Money

Money isn't everything, but it *is* something. In fact, it's often the primary reason we get a job. Would you continue working if you didn't get a paycheck? But do you really know what goes into your paycheck? And how you get it? Getting complacent about money is easy. Until you realize that you should be earning more. Or, you're not sure how the company decided what exactly you should earn. It's time to stop being clueless and get in the know. You can't ask for more unless you know how it all works.

> **STOP** In this chapter, we're focusing just on the money. Although the cash may matter most to you, it's hardly the only aspect of your compensation. If you're dealing with or trying to negotiate or understand certain benefits, jump ahead to Chapter 15.

Before you can understand how your company decided on your lofty salary, you must understand what makes up your paycheck. You may be paid biweekly or once a month. You may receive a yearly bonus based on performance or a commission every time you sell a certain amount of products or bring in a new client. It doesn't matter when you get it, it's all cash.

Regular Salary

There's nothing more reassuring than knowing that money is coming in on a regular basis. Whether it's the reassurance that you can pay bills or pay for a night on the town, it's that very reassurance many professionals come to grow and love. The regular paycheck is the most common element of compensation, but as no paycheck is the same it's important to make sure you know the details:

- **How often do you get it?**

  It may seem like a dumb question, but just because you were paid every two weeks at your last job, doesn't mean you'll be paid that often at a new job. Ask upfront so there are no surprises later.

- **How do you get it?**

  Some companies may offer paper paychecks while others offer a direct-deposit or an electronic option. Again, no company is the same, so you have to ask to be sure.

- **Exempt or non-exempt?**

  Companies often use weird terminology and "exempt" and "non-exempt" are no exception. Used to classify employees, these terms refer to whether an employee is eligible for overtime pay or not. If you are non-exempt, it means your cash compensation is low enough (typically below $500/week) that the company is required by law to pay you overtime for any extra hours worked. If you are exempt, you are exempt from overtime, meaning your cash compensation is high enough that the company is not required to pay you overtime. The rules about which category you fall into, and the compensation amounts that define those categories, change from year to year, so if you're confused about your status ask the HR staff at your company to explain how the law applies to you.

- **Are there exceptions?**

  Some companies pay employees for holidays, others don't. Some may allow you to take unpaid vacation, others don't. Knowing the rules ahead of time avoids any confusion later.

- **When does a pay period start and when does it end?**

  Depending on the company, you may get a paycheck right away, or it may take some time. Even if the company pays every two weeks, don't assume that your first paycheck will automatically arrive two weeks into the job. And since you can't postpone rent or mortgage, this is one oversight you don't want to make if you're counting on the cash.

- **Why is my net pay lower (or higher) than I expected?**

  Taxes are always more than you expect. Often your first paycheck at a new job may be lower than you expect. Much depends on the amount of deductions you took when you filled out your federal and state tax returns. If you think the taxes are too high, consult with your company's HR professionals to see if you are taking too many deductions. You may also find that due to varied start or end dates, you may see a higher or lower paycheck. It may take time for your paperwork to be processed and you may receive your first biweekly paycheck three weeks into the job. You might also find that company reimbursements or bonuses are included in your paycheck amount. Don't ignore your checks, especially if you do direct deposit and/or receive an electronic confirmation of your deposit. Review the amounts closely and make sure you understand any variation from the norm. Mistakes can happen.

Above and Beyond

The regular paycheck is nice but for many professionals, it's only one type of cash they receive for their hard work.

- **Merit Increase**

  If you remain in the same job and it never changes, it might be that your salary won't change, either. Most professionals receive an increase in salary as your performance and your job responsibilities increase. Often this is dependent on how strong the economy is and how well the company has performed. Standard merit increases can range anywhere from 3 to 20 percent. Don't get greedy, be grateful for any increase you receive, but if you feel slighted, ask how the increases were calculated and why the amount was set at the percentage it was.

- **Commission**

  Common for professionals in sales, or those responsible for finding new customers, clients, or business, a commission means you receive a certain cash amount based on your sales. Commissions are often tied to the cost of the product or service sold (you receive X percent of the sale made) or to your performance goals (you get X percent when you bring in one amount and Y percent when you bring in another). If commission isn't common in your field don't expect it. If it is, make sure you understand every single detail of how the pay structure works and whether you receive a commission on top of a base salary or if you are working strictly on commission (a risky, but often lucrative proposition). Companies often promote the average commission a salesperson makes as the salary you can expect, but those commissions usually aren't guaranteed.

- **Performance Bonus**

  A common form of additional compensation is the performance bonus. If you reach a certain goal, or your performance evaluation is above a certain level, you receive a certain bonus. Some bonuses are paid out yearly, others may be paid out multiple times a year, and some are for individual achievement while others are team based. Most bonuses are described ahead of time so you know what you have to do to make a certain amount of money. But the rules may vary, so make sure you know the specifics.

- **Gainsharing**

  Like a bonus, gainsharing is a cash reward that's based on performance. However, instead of individual or team performance, gainsharing is based on how well the company does. The idea is that what you do in your job contributes to the company as a whole. If the company does well, then you are rewarded. Gainsharing is usually revealed ahead of time so you know how well the company has to do and what you get in return (typically a percentage of your salary). This compensation is also often tiered. The more senior you are, the higher the percentage.

- **Spot Award**

  Sometimes cash appears when you least expect it. This is an unlikely scenario unless your company gives spot awards or spot bonuses. These one-time, cash awards are usually given by surprise to an employee who has done exceptionally well or gone out of his or her way to achieve a goal, handle a customer, or bring in a new client. Some companies may also give spot or one-time awards at specific times during the year, such as the holidays or the company's anniversary.

- **Stock Ownership**

  If your company is public, that is, traded on a stock exchange, a

> **Good to Know:**
> Unlike your paycheck, the rewards from stock ownership and stock options are never guaranteed. A company could have a bad month or a bad year and the value of the stock could drop dramatically. When evaluating how much this form of compensation is worth, look at the company's performance to date, the value of the company and its prospects for success. If you don't know a heck of a lot about stocks, don't be embarrassed. Instead, ask one of your contacts who's in the know, to help walk you through what the stock price means.

major component of your cash compensation may come in the form of stock ownership. This means you are given actual shares of stock in the company, in the hope that you'll work hard, the company will perform well, the stock will go up, and you'll accordingly reap the monetary rewards. Stock ownership is often a form of compensation used with mid-to-senior-level employees, so don't expect it right out of the gate unless you're working for a start-up company that plans on going public.

- **Stock Options**

  Getting stock options as a form of compensation is another way you can be paid. Although some people see options as a benefit, either way you stand to gain cash from options if the company does well. Getting a stock option basically means you are given the option to buy a certain number of shares of the company stock at a price usually quite lower that the price it's trading at (which is how you stand to make the extra dough). Options are also reserved typically for mid-to-senior-level employees.

Standards of Living

You shouldn't only be concerned with how much you're earning, but also with where you are working. Let's say you're making $100,000 in Omaha. You're living very well. Then your company transfers you to New York City. Still living the good life? Not so much. Not that Omaha is better than New York City or vice versa, but the simple fact is that things cost more in New York City. Your $100,000 will get you much further in Nebraska. Fair? Maybe, maybe not.

Instead of making judgments about cities, most companies just adjust salaries for the cost of living in those cities. Cost of living adjustments (COLAs) are common for companies with offices or locations in many places. If you are transferred from Omaha to New York City, you should expect a company to adjust your salary accordingly. If you are being transferred, or if you're negotiating a salary for a city in which you have never lived, make sure you take the cost of living into account as part of the salary discussions.

Know that most companies use standardized government and salary data to determine employee COLAs when needed. They aren't pulled out of a hat. So if you're comparing your salary in Charlotte to that of a peer in San Francisco, don't be disappointed if you make a little bit less. It may just be the cost of living.

Deciding Who Gets What

Companies aren't only scientific about how they decide cost of living adjustments. There's significant data, planning, and structure behind your salary, though you may not know it. Like almost every other job-related practice, there's no one right way to pay employees. Companies may base their decisions on the industry they are in, how well they are doing, or what a competitor does.

The most important thing is to make sure you understand how *your* company does it.

1. Objectives and philosophies

A company has to decide how much it wants to pay its employees and what it hopes to gain from paying them. Do they want to compete by paying the most money they can? Or do they want to save money on compensation so they can use the money elsewhere? Some companies want to match what their competitors are paying while other companies can afford to pay less because of their name or their business. Other companies want to be known as paying the most so they can get the best talent. It all depends.

2. Lining up employees

Once a company decides what its compensation strategy is, it has to figure out some sort of structure. After all, what company pays every employee the same amount? Depending on the company, its business, and its industry, employees might be organized very hierarchically, like in steps on a ladder, or they might be grouped together in bands. If they're organized in steps, this is usually based on job responsibilities and seniority: The higher the step, the more the employee can make. There may be set salaries for each step, or, more likely, a small range for each step. If employees are grouped in large bands, there is likely a very large range for the band and employees of many levels may fall within the range. This is the most complicated part of the process, so if you don't understand how your company does it, don't be afraid to ask. The flatter your company's structure, the more likely there are broad salary bands.

3. Looking to the outside

After a company organizes its employees, it has to see what its competitors are doing. Companies often pay for elaborate salary surveys and data that allow them to compare their numbers to what others pay. If a company didn't do its research (just like you're encouraged to do if you want to stay on top of your earnings) it wouldn't be able to effectively compete for talent.

4. Defining a structure

With their employees organized and an understanding of outside data, a company can now plan its own compensation structure. This includes the aspects of cash compensation discussed above, as well as benefits (to be covered in Chapter 14). It's the combination of cash and benefits that companies have to design. They may look at what their competitors are doing but also at what matters most to their employees or how they can encourage the best performance.

5. Planning for the future

Finally, a company will project where it is headed. The strategy a company uses to reward its employees has to match the strategy for the company's success. Companies also want to look ahead to keeping their employees happy. Ignoring changes in the market, the economy, or in a certain function may result in employees leaving for better paying opportunities. Companies especially want high-performers to stay a long time.

How can you use these steps?

Knowing how your company determines the numbers on your paycheck will make it easier for you to understand why you are paid a certain amount and whether you can and should ask for more. In this case, knowledge certainly is power (and money!). Don't assume—ask if you don't know.

Long-term Relationship

Taking a new job is exciting, especially if you are getting a bump up in salary. In fact, getting a salary increase is one of the most common reasons professionals take a new job. But saying good-bye to your old job and hello to more money doesn't mean you'll always be in salary heaven. Even if you were underpaid, chances are your new company won't be able to give you a hefty raise if they hire you at a high salary.

Do your research. If cash is the only reason you are leaving a job, think twice. If you stay, you can use other offers, market data, and industry knowledge to make the case to get a raise. Sometimes a long-term relationship with one job can be more profitable that hopping around to several. After all, background checks will show how many jobs you have had and even how much you may have earned. On the flip side, know that not all companies are competitive on salary, so leaving for money reasons may be the right decision. If you've made your case to your employer to no avail, go back to your Career Kaleidoscope to make sure you are making the best decision for you.

Asking for More

If you do decide to ask for more before walking out the door, don't just walk into your boss' office and blurt it out. Like every other aspect of your career, you've got to do your homework and have a strategy.

1. **Ask yourself why you deserve more**

   If you can't tell yourself why you deserve more money, how can you tell your boss? Companies don't just give out cash at random (though it would be nice). You have to know that you are underpaid compared to the industry or field, or that you are doing more than your current set of responsibilities.

2. **Do your research**

   Once you have a legitimate reason for being paid more money, you need to find the data to back it up. Use the salary resources in Appendix A to find comparable salaries in your field or industry. If you're angling for more money because you're doing more, compare your current set of responsibilities to what you're actually doing, or to what the next-level position does. It's also important to make sure you've researched how the company calculated your salary, and what their compensation structures and philosophy are. It sounds like a lot of work, but the more you know, the better you can plan.

3. **Plan your attack**

   Even with the best data, you can't expect a handout. You've got to time your attack. Don't corner your boss at happy hour or in the hallway. Set time aside to talk to her when her mind isn't on other things or she's not rushing to another meeting. It also gives you time to make your case, understand the response you receive, and ask questions. Be wary of where the company is in the performance review cycle, too. Many salary increases are often given only in conjunction with reviews, so you may want to time your request accordingly.

4. Ask away

Start out the conversation by being positive—about the company, the job, and your team. Then make your case for more money. Whatever you do, don't make idle threats. Telling your boss you'll leave if she won't give you more may make her less likely to compromise.

5. Be patient and willing to compromise

Your boss may not be able to answer you right away and may have to check with her boss or with Human Resources. If you don't get an immediate yes or no, don't fret. You also should be willing to compromise. If you can't get the money you want, you ask for more vacation or another benefit. If you can't get the whole increase you want, will you be happy with half?

7. Know what you'll do if you don't get it

Even the best plans don't always pan out. You might have the best argument this side of the Supreme Court, but there simply may not be money in the budget. Or your boss might just say no. Plan ahead for what you'll do if you don't get an increase. Will you wait? Will you trust a promise that an increase will be considered in several months or a year? It's up to you, but you certainly don't want to be caught off guard.

Planning Ahead

Last but not least, most compensation is cash you can count on, so it's important to think ahead and plan for where you want your salary to go. Years of experience doesn't always equate an increase in salary, especially if you are moving to a new state, changing careers, or taking a position with less responsibility. This is why it's so important to know your salary thresholds and the amount of cash you need to live on. There are some chances you don't want to take.

You also don't want to think only in terms of dollar signs. Cash is a good thing, but it's not the only thing. And while you might make more cash in one job, the benefits and perks from another may actually make it more highly compensated.

Money Isn't Everything

Cash may be king, but it isn't the only way you're compensated. If you're evaluating an offer for a new job or trying to decide that your current one is worth it, you want to take into account both cash and benefits. After all, a certain benefit may save you cash that you would otherwise have had to spend. You may think you know what benefits are, but do you, really? Take the time to fully understand not only what's a part of your current job, but also what's out there, so you know what your options are.

Saving and Protecting Your Money

A penny saved is a penny earned. If you can't save your money, you might have to work forever. A scary proposition, eh? That's why any benefits a company offers that will help you save and protect your income are key.

- **Health benefits**

  Health benefits may be the most important and the most common benefit. If you don't stay in good health, or you can't afford to get medical care when you need it, you might not be able to work. And then you're without a job and without an income. Medical, dental, and vision care can cost a pretty penny but benefits can be convoluted and confusing. Pay attention to what is covered, how much you have to pay out of pocket (a deductible), and how much you have to pay (co-pays) for simple things like doctor's visit. Even if "healthy" is your middle name, make sure you understand every detail of your healthcare benefits. You never know when you might need them. Planning to have children? Have a medical condition that you need coverage for? Look closely at benefits that already apply to you now or that will someday soon. If you can be covered by your spouse's or partner's plan, be sure to compare and make the best choice for your family.

- **Retirement**

  If you have visions of a chair in the Florida sun and an umbrella-laden drink, you better start paying attention to your retirement savings now. Even if you plan to work well into your golden years, knowing that you will have income to count on is more important than you think. Look closely at the retirement options provided by your company. The most popular, a 401(k)—or 403(b) for nonprofits—allows you to save pretax money toward retirement. Some companies will also match your contributions up to a certain amount—so contribute as much as you can. This way it gets matched and you get used to having it deducted from your paycheck. Other companies may allow you to roll previous 401(k) savings into your new plan. Just ask.

  If you ever leave the company, savings can be transferred to other financial savings plans, such as an IRA (Individual Retirement Account). It's also important to be aware that in many cases, if you leave a company before your 401(k) is vested, or deemed by the company to be of full value, you walk away with only the contributions you have made and not the company's match. Check with your organization to be exactly sure what its rules are. All in all, take advantage of as many of these benefits as you can, even if retirement seems light-years away. Trust me—you'll thank me later.

- **Life insurance**

  Another common benefit is life insurance. It may sound grim, but basically, if your company offers coverage, it means your survivors and/or estate will receive a cash payment upon your demise. Typically, if this benefit is offered, it is a basic level (i.e., $10,000) with an option to purchase more. Consider this purchase option carefully. If you're single and have no dependents it's probably not necessary. If you're married or have dependents, you may want to consider the extra coverage unless you already have a personal policy.

- **Savings plans**

  The other option companies may provide is a chance to save money from your paycheck. A company may provide a savings option for you, or it may simply provide an opportunity to split your paycheck between your own personal checking and savings account. Either way, although these sound like simple benefits, their worth can be tremendous. Having money go directly into a savings account before it even gets to your hot little hands helps you save instead of spend.

Work/Life Balance

Money and savings aren't everything; you have yourself and your family to think about, too. Increasingly, companies are offering benefits that help you and your family live a better life. Work/life balance benefits aren't offered only because they're trendy, they're offered because they make your own life a little better and, with any luck, that satisfaction carries over to your work life. So take advantage of (or even suggest!) as many of them as you can.

- **Health and wellness**

  Gym memberships, company-sponsored athletics, and fund-raising or volunteer events can do wonders for your body and your mind. Working to lose weight? Some companies have group sessions at lunch. Not only will you reach a personal goal, but it helps the company save money on health costs. Want to give back to the community? Join or start a firm-wide volunteer event. Not only will you feel better but you'll make some good internal networking contacts, too.

- **Family**

  From childcare to family events, companies are trying more and more to cater to working men and women who are raising children. Some companies may offer time for you to coach a child's sports team or attend a school-related event. These benefits aren't common, so if your company doesn't have them, ask. You may be the one to get them established.

- **Self**

  It's easy to forget to put yourself first when you get caught up in work and family responsibilities. Some personal benefits, including on-site massages, free or discounted dry-cleaning, or even transportation benefits, may seem insignificant but in reality, they may be the one small thing that makes a difference. After all, how many times have you missed picking up your dry-cleaning?

- **Scheduling**

  One of the most common work/life benefits (and perhaps the most important) is flexible scheduling. It may be working part-time (less than forty hours), working a compressed workweek (forty hours in less than five days, i.e., four ten-hour days), or sharing your job with another co-worker. If you're interested in this type of benefit, and if your company offers it, you might make it work, though it may require altering your schedule or lessening your compensation. If your company has such a program, read the rules carefully before you apply for it. They may require a certain amount of tenure under your belt or a high performance rating. If your company doesn't already have a formal program, it doesn't mean it will never happen. Sketch out a proposal that demonstrates not only what you're asking for, but how the arrangement will work and how it will benefit the company. Be sure to check with HR to see if anyone else has made a similar request and what worked for them.

Extras

When the economy is good, companies often have lots of money to throw around and can get creative with benefits. Even if the tables turn, sometimes the creative benefits remain.

- **Allowances**

  From a laptop to a company car to a ski condo, many companies make lending arrangements with their employees or provide them allowances for certain perks. These are not as common as they used to be, as employees would often rather see the perk in cash. They shouldn't be ignored. Use of a company car is one less thing you have to pay for out of your own pocket.

- **Gifts/awards**

  In lieu of cash, your company may thank you for your service in the form of a trip, a clock, or a fancy plaque. Sure, some gifts and awards are better than others and may rank more highly on your worth scale. But don't forget the value in recognition. Even if you didn't need another paperweight, it's still nice to be noticed.

- **Fun, fun, fun**

  All work and no play makes Jack a . . . well, you know the rest. And companies know it, too. So don't think they're just being nice when they send you and your team to an amusement park for the day, or sponsor a company-wide happy hour. "Work hard, play hard" is a motto that some companies live by and work hard to support.

Final Thoughts

You may have heard the term "total compensation." Total is the key word. You've got to look at all of your compensation and benefit options to really get a sense of how you are rewarded. Then you can go back to your Career Kaleidoscope to see if there is a fit with what you want in return. You already know that you are going to have to make tradeoffs, but you can't make tradeoffs unless you know everything you have to work with. You know that you've got to take the total cash and benefits package into consideration when making decisions about taking or keeping a job. But you also shouldn't ignore each cash and benefit option on its own. These reward options can be complicated, and may have facets to them you hadn't even realized, or that you don't know how to use. Even if you don't think you'll ever use or need a benefit, or if you don't have any money to invest right now, learn about *all* of your options. Read the literature that the company provides and ask questions about how a reward works. You don't want to miss a single thing.

15

You've Only Just Begun

If you want to move up instead of out, you need to stay on top of your industry, your field, and your skills. From M.B.A. and Ph.D. to C.P.A. and P.M.P., advanced degrees, training, and certification options can seem like a confusing alphabet soup of accreditations. You'll need to learn about learning and development options and determine how and when to use them.

What You Have to Work With

You were hired for your job not only for the skills and behavioral attributes you have, but also for the education that supports them. Whether you've got your G.E.D. or your M.B.A., the options to supplement your hard work vary, from degrees to certifications. To determine what you need to move forward, you need to know where you're headed, and take stock of what you have.

Your Career Kaleidoscope can keep you on track. For some professionals, the status quo is all they strive for. They may prefer a steady job that may be interesting and challenging rather than a career path that leads up the corporate ladder. Other professionals strive for the exact opposite—a series of career advances that build on each other and ultimately culminate in a leadership position. Still others want to advance their careers but, rather than move up into management, they want to specialize and be subject-matter experts in their fields.

One choice is not better than another. The question is: What is best for you? There's no career judge or jury here. The reason your career goals matter is that you want to align your education and training with where you want your career to go. Let me give you an example. Nadine and Stephen are both financial professionals. They both have undergraduate degrees from a college in the

United States, and both have three years of work experience in finance in U.S. companies. Both are interested in advancing their careers and want further education to help them do that. There is a wide range of options: getting an M.B.A., getting certified in one of the many specific areas of finance, or enrolling in ongoing training from one of the national finance associations.

Nadine and Stephen know what they have to offer and have taken stock of their skills and expertise. In order to decide how to further their careers, both of them have to have some idea of where they want their careers to go. Career direction was the vision part of your Career Kaleidoscope. Where do you see yourself in the next five or ten years? Remember, you don't have to know the exact position, company, or industry, but you do have to have an idea of the type of career you want.

For example, Stephen has always been a keen student of finance. In college, he loved learning the theories behind financial decisions and was good at looking at a problem and determining possible finance solutions. On the other hand, Nadine was also a finance-problem solver, but she liked to use her answers to fix broader problems. She was interested in why finance matters to a company and the role the finance function plays. Although both Nadine and Stephen have been in financial analyst roles, working out complicated financial equations and analyzing their impact for their company, Nadine prefers the impact part while Stephen prefers the equation part.

Nadine and Stephen want to advance their careers, but should they take the same steps? No—they don't want the same things. Stephen wants to be more of a subject-matter expert, someone who is called upon to solve a complicated financial problem with sophisticated data analysis. Nadine would rather climb the finance ladder and someday be a controller or CFO. She likes the idea of being in charge of making strategic financial decisions.

In her case, it might make more sense for Nadine to pursue a broad graduate degree, like an M.B.A., to help her understand the broader applications of finance to business and other functions. Stephen, on the other hand, might be better served by getting a degree that will advance his subject matter expertise, like a Master of Science in Finance (M.S.F.) degree. These two finance professionals with similar experience and backgrounds have completely different educational goals.

Formal Education

The most common type of career-related education involves earning high school, college, and graduate degrees. A formal education requires a lengthy time commitment (and often a monetary commitment) and is rewarded with a degree that demonstrates you have learned and mastered knowledge and application. A formal education is usually the baseline for many jobs—job postings may require a certain degree or level of completion.

If you're a professional, most likely you need at least an undergraduate degree. A very high percentage of professional positions will require this degree. You can get away without having one—there are dozens of examples of professionals, especially entrepreneurs, who have ascended to professional success without having gone to college (or even high school, in some cases). Steven Spielberg, Peter Jennings, Bill Gates, and National Public Radio's legal correspondent Nina Totenberg didn't go to college. Jennings, in fact, never finished high school.

It's your choice. But if you can make it work (there are a bazillion student loans and grants, by the way), having a degree at least gives you a baseline of credibility and assures that you won't get overlooked for a job that requires one. The question may be which degree to get or whether to get more than one. If you're trying to decide whether to spend the dough, consider the following:

- **Do you need the degree?**

  You've heard the term "career student." Some people go to school simply to avoid working! For the most part, making the choice to go to school is specific to a career goal or need. But make sure you're not going to school only because you don't know what else to do, or because you've given up on your current position or everyone else is doing it. If you can defend your choice to a unbiased party, you're probably making a good one. And if your choice aligns with your Career Sweet Spot and vision then you're definitely making the right one.

- **Do you have a specific interest?**

  Degrees come in all shapes and sizes, so make sure you aren't choosing your focus area arbitrarily. If you really aren't sure what you want to do but want a general education, go for a degree that can be applied widely. If you want to do something in the business world but don't know what, choose a general business discipline rather than majoring in interpretive dance. If you go the graduate degree route, you should be thinking as a specialist, not a generalist. Either way, you shouldn't go into the process without some vision. You'll likely have to explain in an essay or an interview why you want that degree and what you're going to do with it.

- **Do you want to be a subject-matter expert or a manager?**

  Like Nadine and Stephen, having an idea of whether you want to manage and make strategic decisions or be relied on for some specific area of expertise, can help you choose which degree to pursue. Explore the types of careers in your area of interest to see which degrees are required to pursue the path you want.

- **Do you have the credentials required to be considered for admission?**

  Many degree programs require that you have some sort of education or work experience. A number of the top-ranked M.B.A. programs, for example, often require two or more years of work experience for consideration. Of course there are exceptions to every rule, but make sure you investigate before you move ahead.

- **What are your time constraints?**

  You may want to make the commitment to a formal degree, but do you have the time? Do you want to go part-time? Full-time? Online? The number of degree choices is as big as the number of ways to actually get the degree. Talk over your interest with family members and mentors. Visit schools, talk to admission officers, and ask about the time commitment and requirements. While going to school full-time allows you to completely commit to your education, going part-time means you can still be earning money and applying what you learn on the job. But it might be more stressful. Weigh your options carefully.

- **Do you know anyone who has already gotten the degree you seek?**

  Connect with your network to see who has done the full-time gig and who made the part-time choice. This will help you determine the best fit for you. You can also ask prospective schools if they can connect you with current students to provide an insider prospective. Be sure you visit the schools, as well. Ask to sit in on a class and talk to current teachers and professors.

- **What kinds of advances do people with a degree make in their careers?**

  Outcomes are always important. Accordingly, you want evidence of what others have done who have made the educational leap you are considering. Do your research, and ask your contacts for results. Admissions offices are also a good place to check for data: Will the degree really help?

- **Can you afford it?**

  Formal education can be expensive—there's no doubt about it. But financial help is available, too. Start with your own budget—what can you afford? Be sure to include forfeited wages, that is, the money you'd lose by going to school instead of working. Compare that with the difference in salary you would have after you actually earn the degree. You also want to make sure you can cover your costs of living if you choose to go to school full-time. Check with the financial aid offices of the schools you are interested in to find out about loans, grants, or scholarships to help you. Most graduate programs can be entirely loan financed regardless of how much money you currently make.

- **How long will it take?**

  Make sure you are clear about how long the degree program will take, either done part-time or full-time. You may start as a full-time student and change to part-time, or vice versa (if the school allows). You don't want to commit to a program you're not sure you can complete. Wasted time doesn't do anyone any good.

- **What are the noneducational benefits?**

  Getting a formal degree isn't only about the knowledge. It's a gold mine for making those important networking connections. There's no better place to make them than in a classroom of your peers, all of whom are interested in working in similar fields.

- **Where can I learn more?**

  The resources for making educational choices are so many and varied you may not know where to start. Much will depend on your goals, finances, and timing. If you care about reputation or ranking, *U.S. News and World Report*, *Princeton Review*, and *Business Week* are among the many publications that rank and evaluate schools. Many associations also have rankings or guidelines on finding a degree or school in a specific subject area, and there are also a variety of educational consultants for hire.

Like any career decision, you have to make sure you have all the information you need before you can proceed. In terms of education and training, the decision to get a degree may be one of the biggest (and most costly) career choices you ever make. So take your time, talk to others who have been through the process, and make this an informed decision.

Extra Letters: Getting Certified

Another option beyond a formal degree is to get certified in your profession or industry. Certification means that you have studied and learned a certain body of knowledge and demonstrated that you know it. Unlike a formal degree that comes from a university, takes several years to earn, and may cover multiple disciplines, certifications often don't take as long, will focus on one particular area, and often show that you can handle the practical part of the job. That is, you don't just *know* the stuff but you can actually *do* it. For example, accountants take the C.P.A. (Certified Public Accountancy) exam to show proficiency in understanding the field of accounting but also, in most cases, to be allowed to practice in their chosen field.

Other professions have certifications that just give you an extra leg up—they aren't required. In the field of human resources there are the PHR and SPHR certifications that when earned automatically give you the credential of Professional in Human Resources (if you have less than five years of work experience) or Senior Professional in Human Resources (if you have more).

If you've gone to college and already have the job, why do these certifications matter? For one, it demonstrates a baseline. Employers know that you've recently studied and understand the profession, its changes, and its laws. Since universities tend to focus more on the theory of a given topic or profession, certifications are meant as a way to show you have practical understanding.

Additionally, a certification is a way for an employer to compare candidates. A company may require a certification as a means to ensure that the candidates it interviews possess the baseline knowledge and understanding of the profession, and instead can focus on how candidates would use that knowledge on the job.

You should know for sure what certifications are popular and/or expected in your field. Otherwise you're going to come across as unprepared or unknowledgeable. Do you have to have a

Good to Know:

If you get certified pay attention to the rules. You may have to recertify several years later. Most recertifications are achieved through continuous education—seminars or work experience in your field—in order to demonstrate your continuous development. To make the process easier, track all professional development activities in a document or spreadsheet. It will make the recertification process easier, and help you see where you have made great strides and where you could still use some extra education.

certification? Not necessarily. In some fields, like teaching, accounting, and fi-nance, specific certifications may be required to hold a specific job. In other fields a certification may just be a professional advantage.

Certifications often can take months or years to earn, and may cost a pretty penny (though your company may reimburse you for this cost). Appendix A includes many associations in specific fields where you can research your pro-fession and learn about what's available. Use your networking connections as well to get the skinny on whether you need the extra letters after your name, and if you don't have to have them, what you can gain from making the effort.

Membership Has Its Privileges

Associations don't exist merely to test your brain. Associations, often nonprofit entities, are organizations that seek to educate, govern, or connect professionals in a specific field or industry. And there are thousands of them. Many professionals simply join associations in their fields or industries of interest to have access to the latest research, laws, and updates in their field, and to show they are staying connected. After all, you don't want to be so focused on your own company and job that you miss what's going on in the professional world around you.

Joining an association may give you access to the association's resources and may look great on your resumé. Associations also:

- **Provide training and development courses and events**

  How else can you learn about the latest tools and techniques if you don't de-velop yourself professionally? Associations are often one of the best sources to help you develop areas where you are weak, learn a new skill or tech-nique, or research ways other companies have successfully met challenges your company might be facing.

- **Lobby and research on your behalf**

  Associations are often the voice of your profession. They may speak to and lobby members of congress regarding laws that affect your field, or fight for better changes in the profession. They also serve to better the profession by promoting ongoing education and training.

- **Reach out to new professionals in the field**

  If you are a student, or are new to a field, many associations cater directly to you through student or new professional opportunities. Some association

Web sites have entire sections devoted to understanding and learning about a profession as well as providing membership discounts for students.

- **Provide networking opportunities**

    You may have gone out of your way to make networking connections when you were job searching, but what about when you finally got the job? It's crucial to find colleagues in the field who are outside of your company and can help you. Whether you need job advice or are facing a problem at work and want their take on how they would handle it, associations are a great way to make new networking connections. Many associations have local chapters to help you connect with professionals in the area, or may provide online or worldwide networking opportunities.

As with certification options, you want to use your connections and resources to research the most popular associations in your field. You don't want to have a blank stare on your face when an interviewer asks what the most important recent trends are in your field. If you don't know the associations in your field, or don't stay on top of the industry through news and resources, you'll have a hard time competing against candidates who do.

Keep in mind too that most associations charge a yearly fee to be a member. This will usually give you unlimited access to their resources and discounts or admission to training opportunities and networking events. However, if you can show that membership is valuable to your job, your company might be willing to cover the cost of membership or even some associated training courses.

On-the-Job Training

Training and development isn't limited to classes or testing. Much of your professional development will come on the job. This includes performance evaluations (to be discussed in the next chapter), learning from your colleagues, and taking on extra responsibilities. No one ever got ahead by sitting back and doing only what was asked of them. It may seem informal, but learning on the job is one of the best ways to grow your career and move up in the company. Here's how:

- **Ask for more work**

    It may seem ridiculous—you already have enough to do. Or do you? As you master the components of your own job, ask for more work. Just be sure you ask for specific tasks. If you want to move into a certain area, ask if you can help on a project in that area. If you've got your sights on climbing the ladder, ask the person above you if he has tasks you can help with. Make sure you're clear about why you want the extra work—you want to learn.

- **Find a mentor**

  There's no better way to learn on the job than to find someone who is in a position you eventually want to be in. Whether we admit or not, we love to help others. Find someone in your firm or in your field whom you admire and can learn from. Ask her if she would be willing to be your mentor and help you learn from her experience or mistakes. Set aside time to talk about what you hope to get out of the relationship and what you can promise in return.

- **Look for cross-functional assignments**

  It's easy to sit in your cubicle all day, do your work, and forget that there's a company around you. Ask for tasks or assignments that force you to work with other company functions or departments. Not only will you make great contacts across the company, but you get invaluable experience as well.

- **Try a rotational program**

  If you've done all the research but still have your eye on working in several functional areas (and it's early in your career), look for companies that offer rotational programs. This is where a company hires you as an associate and you spend a certain period of time working, say, in finance before moving on to marketing and then HR. Or a different combination completely. It not only gives you exposure and understanding of the broader business world, but it also gets you in the door of a company while still having a chance to try on different jobs for size.

- **Ask for a shadow day**

  Sometimes a company or a position doesn't lend itself to working across many functions or partnering with colleagues across the firm. In this case, you may want to take a day off and ask someone in a profession or position you're coveting to "shadow" them. Spending an entire day with a professional gives you a chance to see the good, the bad, and the ugly, and to imagine—what would your life be like if you moved into that kind of role?

Making the Grade

Companies and organizations have their own version of parent-teacher conferences and GPAs—it's called performance management. Staying on top of your own performance, development, and feedback is crucial to managing your career.

Why It Matters

Imagine that a company has hired you and then walked away and just let you do your job. Sounds great, but if you're a manager or CEO, you would never ignore the performance of your employees. Keeping employees who don't perform well hurts the organization. Ignoring superstars encourages them to leave for an organization that will notice and reward their work. Organizations have to keep tabs on their employees.

They aren't being selfish, though. Performance evaluations are also key to your career development. They help alert you to areas in which you need to improve, and point out your strengths and areas of expertise. Evaluations also serve as a "state of the union address," giving you a sense of where you are, where you're headed, and how long it will take to get there. Without them, it would be hard for you to progress as a professional.

Maybe your company doesn't care about evaluations. And, yes, an evaluation is only as good as the process in the company. Not all companies take these evaluations seriously, or enforce their completion. Some companies have more complicated performance evaluations than others. But if you take the process seriously, you can get the career development benefits even if the company seems to care less.

For some people, performance evaluations are a crucial component of the job—and an element of their Career Sweet Spot. They can't take a job unless there is a clear indication that the company cares about performance and is committed to the review process. For others, in-the-moment feedback is enough. As long as their manager tells them when they are screwing up, that's all that matters. In smaller organizations or start-ups, the performance management process may be informal or nonexistent. In large companies, the process may involve multiple steps or take several weeks.

If how well the company evaluates performance is very important to you, then you should ask about it upfront. Find out how the process works and ask current employees what their experience with the process has been like. If it is not on your list of what matters (or your Career Sweet Spot), that's fine. But don't you dare ignore the process; you must have feedback on how you're doing, even if it's informal.

Professional Report Cards

In grade school and beyond, most schools used the basic A through F system, modified by some plusses and minuses for good measure. You might think companies would be much more sophisticated than that, but in reality most aren't. You are evaluated in certain "subject" areas and often given a letter or number grade from an overall scale.

Gathering input and determining your "grade" in a company is more complex than in school. There's no teacher averaging all of your test grades for a final score. Instead, there may be more than one manager, boss, peer, or customer sharing thoughts on how you perform. The types of feedback include:

- **Downward feedback**

  The most common type of feedback, this comes from a manager or boss who has responsibility for supervising you. He or she evaluates your performance over a certain period of time.

- **Upward feedback**

  Becoming more and more popular, upward feedback is a way for employees to

> **Good to Know:**
> You may know what all of these feedback types are, but does your company use them? If not, set aside time to talk with your manager or with Human Resources staff to see if you can help launch a trial version in your department or function.

provide performance feedback on their managers. It may or may not be confidential, and gives companies insight into how well their managers are actually managing.

- **Peer feedback**

  Less common than both downward and upward feedback, peer feedback allows colleagues to share insights on the work of colleagues at the same level.

- **Customer or client feedback**

  Also somewhat uncommon, some firms solicit performance feedback on employees from clients or customers. It provides a unique perspective on how employees work with clients, especially in industries where much of the work is client based.

- **360-degree feedback**

  The combination of all or most of the above feedback types is called 360-degree feedback. The idea is that you are receiving feedback from all levels, essentially creating a circle. This is the ultimate form of feedback. It is usually used in organizations that believe strongly in feedback or have progressive performance management processes.

How to Prepare

The single biggest mistake professionals make with performance reviews is to not prepare effectively. If you do it right, a performance review should never be a surprise. You should know what your goals are ahead of time and what you have to do to achieve them, and what you will get and where you will be if you do. It takes some time and some effort to sort all of this out. You've got to plan ahead and be committed. There are a few ways to do just that.

1. **Know your company's evaluation philosophy and process**

   You'd be surprised how many people respond with a blank stare when asked about the performance review philosophy and process at their company. Everyone gets reviewed or evaluated in some way, but often that's all we know. That's the problem. If you don't know how, when, or why you're evaluated, you can't effectively prepare or argue for that well-deserved salary increase. If you don't know what the policies are in your company and why they were created, find out now. Like compensation, there is a methodology to how reviews are created and executed. The more you know about the why, the better your review will be.

2. Establish performance goals

It's easy to get distracted by the rigor and busyness of your job. You want to look good and do what you're supposed to do. You may know what you're supposed to do at the moment, but what about in three months from now? Six months? A year? Without goals, it's hard to know what all your hard work is supposed to lead to. Even if it is not a formal aspect of your company's performance review process, go the extra mile and ask your boss if you can set some goals with him. The goals should be set months ahead of the review so, come review time, you can be evaluated based on whether you met the goals you and your boss set. After all, if you don't know where you're headed, how can you be evaluated on whether you actually got there?

3. Determine actions for each goal

Once you have goals you need to figure out how you will reach them. Goals aren't worth much unless you know how they can be achieved and what you need to do. Once you set your goals with your boss or manager, go back to your office or cubicle and make your plan. You know what resources are at your disposal and what projects you need to accomplish. Start setting some timelines and some action plans to get you there.

3. Put your goals in a visible place

If you go to all the trouble to set goals and create an action plan and it finds its way in your desk drawer, it may not resurface until evaluation time. Move the cartoons and photographs on your bulletin board to the side and make room for your goals. If you're not looking at your goals every day it will be easy to lose sight of them.

4. Check in midway

Every company has a different timeline for evaluation. Some are done once a year, some are done twice a year—there's no magic number. It depends on the company. One of the best moves you can make is to schedule a mid-review check-in with your boss. It doesn't have to be anything formal; it simply serves as a chance for you to review your goals with your boss and ask for an assessment of how you're doing. It's the only way to understand where your problem areas are and still have time to make corrections in mid-course. Remember, your review should never come as a surprise.

5. Plan for your evaluation

Every time the performance review cycle rolls around, dutiful HR professionals write detailed instructions to legions of employees about the process, timeline, and responsibilities. And then that memo finds its way to trash cans around the working world, because people don't often read instructions or pay attention to the details. Here's one occasion when you should read the memo, follow the instructions, and plan carefully for your review. You may have to do your own self-assessment, or initiate the process with your boss.

8. Know what you want to get out of your evaluation

Evaluations aren't just a "sit and listen" conversation. This isn't the old days—you actually have input into your career development now. Go into your review knowing what you want to get out of it. A promotion? A raise? Approval to get certified in a certain expertise? Remember those pesky goals? If you don't know what you want to get out of the meeting you won't get it. A review is a two-way process. You get feedback and then ask how you can act on it. Are you performing at the highest levels? If so, ask to be promoted to the next level or request a raise. Having difficulties in certain areas? Ask for advice on how you can improve or for the opportunity to take a training class or work with someone who's an expert in that area.

Getting Your Review

Performance reviews can be nerve-wracking, there's no doubt about it. If you're a praise-hound, it's never easy to sit back and listen to someone criticize you or your work. But the latter is the best part of the review—at least you should try to think of it that way. After all, you probably know what you do well and there's no reason you won't continue doing it. But understanding what you don't do well from someone else's perspective is the only way you'll advance your career and improve.

> **Good to Know:**
> If your performance review does come as a complete surprise then something is wrong. Either you weren't paying attention to your manager's feedback throughout the year, or your manager didn't give you any feedback, or, worse yet, gave you positive feedback when in fact you weren't doing a good job. Make sure you let your manager know if the review results are a surprise and talk about why, so it doesn't happen again.

You should go into your review knowing the basic areas in

which you excel and those in which you need improvement. The purpose of the review is to learn ways you can improve and to talk about the career path you're on. Even if you're the employee of the year, you should still be prepared for some constructive criticism. No one's perfect.

The other important thing to remember is that you're not on trial here. A performance review should be a conversation and not an argument. If you go in defensive, it'll show. Listen. Let me say that again. Listen. Your reviewer has probably spent time thoughtfully preparing your review and put energy into determining where you excel and where you can improve. Respect and pay attention to his comments.

Sometimes your reviewer doesn't put in any time on your review. If this happens to you, ask questions about how you can improve, or request additional projects you can undertake or training the reviewer can recommend for you. The more interest you show in developing yourself and your commitment to the company, the more the reviewer will sit up and take notice of you and maybe spend more time on you at the next go-round.

It's easy to look at the review process as boring or a waste of time, especially if your company doesn't take it seriously, or does it as a matter of routine. If this is the case, look at the process in terms of what you can get out of it. When you're in the midst of a job search you are devoting time to your career and your next best step. When you're in the throes of a job, you're so focused on work it's easy to miss out on your own career needs. Even if no one else seems to care, make sure you do.

What It Means

The ratings process can vary among companies—A, B, and C ratings, numbers, or simple categories: poor, average, above average, and exceptional. You must understand clearly what each rating means before you go into the review. Many reviews are confusing, so if you don't understand the process or anything that's being said about your performance, don't make assumptions. Ask for exact definitions of each rating level.

It's also helpful to think about your review in terms of how new you are to the position. For example, if you're brand-new to a position, or have just been promoted, you shouldn't expect to receive the highest rating—even if you've done a really great job during the review period. In many companies, getting the highest rating on a review means you have mastered everything in your current job and are ready for the next level or promotion. If you still have some work to do or growth steps to take, you shouldn't be rated at the highest level.

If the Review Is Bad

- **What's expected**

  If you get a review that's less than stellar, it's understandable that you might be frustrated or upset. Your boss or manager will expect that. In fact, if you're flippant about it or appear not to give a damn, your boss is going to wonder about you. You don't want to be unprofessional and have an emotional fit, but you should express your concern about what you can do to improve.

- **Company trial periods**

  In some companies, below average performance means you will have to be put on a trial period. This usually means the company is giving you a specific period of time (and some guidance) to get your act in order. If you don't improve you'll likely be let go (that is, asked to resign and given time to do so) or fired (you're asked to leave immediately). A trial period is a warning. In some companies this is more common than you think. The goal isn't to scare you into submission, but rather to make sure that you understand very clearly the goals you have to achieve and take the process seriously.

- **The end of the rope**

  Sometimes a review that's below average can signal the end of the line. How you proceed may or may not be up to you. Most professionals are what's called "at-will" employees, meaning that a company can fire them for bad performance at any time. Even if you do have a choice, you might not want to fight to stay. After all, bad performance may not mean you were lazy or that you're a failure. It may mean that the job or company just isn't a good fit for you. You need to go back to square one (and page one of this book) to find a better fit.

> **STOP** If you feel like you have been wronged and your performance does not warrant being let go or fired, consult with an attorney to determine your options, and don't forget to write everything down. You'll need very explicit details on past performance at the company to proceed with legal action.

Looking Ahead

Whether you have gone through one review or one hundred, the best thing you can do when you've completed a review is to look ahead. If you dwell on poor performance or a disagreement over one or more elements of your review, it won't do anyone any good. Instead, focus on what you can do during the next performance period to avoid repeating the same mistakes.

Playing the Political Game

Democrats and Republicans aside, you may try to stay away from office politics, but it's impossible to avoid them altogether. It is possible to navigate your way from the water cooler to the boardroom without making too many enemies along the way.

Office politics are the battles we fight and strategies we create to win a certain argument, make a point known, or get a decision made. The work of finding your way through the interpersonal maze of the workplace isn't easy. Every job has some sort of social dynamic, from team meetings or disagreements with the boss to falling in love with a co-worker.

Politics can involve using your influence to obtain something you might not normally get. This is the bad side of office politics. They can also help you convince your audience to do something important, or work on behalf of others to get something accomplished. If you plan on having a successful career, you'll find yourself campaigning for things more often than you planned.

Even the savviest of professionals can't avoid office politics. They are everywhere. Even if you're working online, a chain of e-mails can be just as political as a meeting about an unhappy client. Instead of trying to avoid office politics, the best thing you can do is to navigate them. Even if political savvy isn't your strong suit, there are a few things you can do to tough it out.

Establishing Yourself

You've heard the old adage about making a first impression. It's true—it really matters. The workplace is no different. When you start a new job, a new position, or even a new project, it's important to set the stage for the kind of player you will be.

Some professionals like to be vocal and make their presence known. If this is you, you may be more likely to get in political hot water than your colleagues. The more you say, the more likely it is you can be debated or contradicted. Does that mean you should be seen and not heard? Not at all. It just means you have to know yourself so you can be prepared to combat more politics if your working style invites them. If you're the vocal one, the important thing to remember is to think through a statement (as much as you possibly can) before you actually say it.

On the flip side, if you're the quiet type you can't simply sit back and not play. Some professionals don't like to contribute to a discussion unless they feel like they have something valuable to add. There's nothing wrong with that, but there are politics inherent in that attitude, too. You don't want co-workers to make assumptions about you being uninterested or uninvolved. Make sure you pay attention. If you don't want to contribute in a large group, make it obvious that you're alert and interested. Share your ideas post-meeting with your manager or colleagues to make sure they know you're making an effort.

Of course the ideal way to establish yourself is to find a happy medium. If you demonstrate that you are someone who can contribute but doesn't overwhelm, you'll find it easier to navigate the political waters. Other tips for establishing yourself to handle the politics include:

- **Be polite**

  People can be fickle—even at work. If you're rude or you demean a colleague or co-worker, chances are they won't forget it and you'll suffer later.

- **Stay positive**

  If you constantly rail and complain, it's hard to earn your colleagues' confidence and trust.

- **Don't judge**

  The fastest way to make enemies or to lose a battle is to judge your colleagues or judge a situation before you know the truth. If you've heard that someone is hard to work with, wait until you work with him before you decide.

- **Don't gossip**

  No one ever trusts a big mouth. If a colleague asks you not to share a piece of information, then don't. If you hear negative information about your boss or another colleague, keep it to yourself. Part of managing office politics well is the ability to maintain a certain level of maturity.

- **Make it a win-win situation**

  Good politicians know that the best ideas are ones in which everyone sees the value. Position yourself and your ideas as beneficial to everyone, not to just one person, group, or department.

Recognizing Politics

Because workplace politics can involve pretty much anything that has to do with the social and interpersonal nature of work, it's important to recognize when you're in a political situation so you can consider the best way to handle it.

Some issues of office politics are obvious, such as who gets promoted to a new position in your department. Others, such as a disagreement with a colleague, aren't so obvious. Imagine that you're arguing with a colleague who just took credit for a new client you brought in. You want to read her the riot act—after all, you worked hard to earn that new business. However, what if you regularly rely on the colleague for other aspects of your job? Then you have to be political. You don't want her to get away with taking the credit, but you also don't want to anger her so that she refuses to help you. It's a slippery slope and you have to pay careful attention to where you're walking. See the following table for some common political issues in the workplace.

The Issue	Why It's Political	Common Problems	What To Do
The problem colleague	Arbitration has to come first. If you and a colleague don't agree, you can't just go running to the boss, you have to try to work it out yourselves without coming to blows.	• How to proceed on a task when you disagree • Taking credit that isn't yours • Division of responsibilities • Fighting for a promotion only one of you can have	Set aside a time to talk to the colleague one-on-one. Choose a neutral place and come prepared with suggestions for compromise. Listen to each other and make an effort to give a little. You'll both be better served if you can solve it on your own without involving your boss.
Something no one believes in	If you have an idea that no one thinks is good, or you don't have the power to try it yourself, you have to find and convince potential allies.	• Needing more money • Wanting to try an idea that is considered too risky • A failing project	Make sure the idea or concept is good enough to risk your reputation on. If it is, determine who it will affect and the how it will help each party. Find allies in each party, department, or

The Issue	Why It's Political	Common Problems	What To Do
			function to help support your cause.
Teamwork	Teams are diverse and everyone has a different view of what's appropriate and what's not. Norms of behavior aren't always set and differences of opinion can easily cause tension.	• How to proceed on a task when you disagree • A team member(s) not pulling his or her weight • Concerns about meeting goals, deadlines, and/or budgets • Division of responsibilities	Set team rules and norms before starting a project—use a team contract to formalize behavior. Set a way for team members to share disagreements and how they will be solved. Take disagreements offline if they involve only one or two members or bring in a neutral third party to help arbitrate.
Dealing with the boss	The boss has the power to hire, fire, or transfer you in the organization. You want to be honest but you don't want to risk your job.	• Not getting something done on time • Disagreeing on a solution to a problem • A bad performance review • Lack of attention from the boss	Don't ever confront your boss angry. Set up a meeting to discuss the issue, and come prepared with talking points to defend your position. Be respectful and make it clear you want to solve the problem.
Workplace etiquette	Everyone has their own idea about what's appropriate and what's not. A loud talker may not think she's loud or a co-worker who yells at his assistant may think it's deserved. Opinions about what's acceptable aren't always in line.	• Loud co-workers • Seeing a co-worker violate or abuse office policies or rules • Poor treatment of co-workers or staff	Communication, communication, communication. If someone is loud or behaving badly, you have to make the effort to politely ask them to stop or offer suggestions to change. If the behavior is so overt it borders on or is illegal, then it's time to involve HR or your boss.
Office events	Everyone has an agenda at an office event. Whether it's to get face time with a certain executive or make a good impression, office events can be a good opportunity—or a bad one—to be noticed.	• Office-wide or town-hall meetings • Holiday parties • Networking events • Company outings • Volunteer activities	Know what you want out of an event before you go, and be patient. You don't want to monopolize anyone's time, or stand out like a sore thumb. If you're trying to get face time to talk about a certain project or idea, do it carefully. The goal is to be social while at

(continued)

(*Table Continued*)

The Issue	Why It's Political	Common Problems	What To Do
			the same time advancing your agenda.
Romance at work	You can't help who you fall in love with. Or at least want to have a glass of wine with. But romance at work can be very political, especially if it doesn't work out, or a boss has to make a decision based on your romance.	• Dating a co-worker • Dating a superior or subordinate • Working at the same place as a spouse or partner	First, check company policies to ensure you're allowed to take the risk, and then go forward only if you think it's worth it. If one try at romance at work doesn't pan out, don't go for a second or third. It's a good way to get a reputation. And if it does work out? Be honest with your boss and take yourself out of situations where you might work on the same project or work with each other.

Playing the Game

As you're going to encounter office politics at some point in time, it's up to you to determine how you want to play the game.

Deciding not to get involved in office politics is admirable. Perhaps envious. However, it could be risky in its own right. As much as you may feel uncomfortable, you run the risk of losing a good opportunity or getting to play in the big league. To advance your career and move up in an organization, you need a certain amount of experience managing certain situations, including politics. Maybe you:

- **Don't like feeling like a brown-noser**

  No one will admit that they like sucking up to the boss or trying to get in good with a decision maker. But you don't have to be a brown-noser to be good at managing office politics. You just have to know how praise and admiration (in small doses) will help you accomplish your goals. That's all politics really is—a means of achieving a goal.

- **Aren't good at networking**

  You don't have to be a social butterfly to be an office politician. You won't be shaking hundreds of hands or going from one event to the next. But you do have to know who you need to talk to and when to advance your agenda or idea. You don't have to win over a big room full of executives, you need to recognize who can help you and talk to them at the right time.

- **Think politics are underhanded**

  Office politics can be sneaky or deceitful. Not always. It depends on the goal. If you aim for a promotion by sleeping with your boss, that's underhanded. If you have your eye on a promotion and set aside time to talk with your boss and other colleagues about what you need to get there, that's good politics.

Cleaning Up a Mess

No good political fight hasn't left behind some ruins. Chances are, at some point you will leave some destruction in your path, even if you don't mean to. If you get a promotion, that means someone else didn't and might be disappointed. If the boss picked your idea, then someone else's idea got squashed. No matter how hard even the best of politicians try, they can't win every vote, and neither can you.

If you find yourself in a sticky situation, or are creating enemies faster than you can count them, stop and ask yourself a few questions:

1. **Are your morals and values in check?**

   You know yourself better than anyone else. Do you have even a tinge of regret about what you are doing? Keeping to your own morals and values is essential as companies become more and more ethics-minded. If you feel as if you are compromising what you think is right, even in the slightest, stop and rethink your political strategy. If you're compromising your own morals, chances are you might be compromising someone else's.

2. **Did you anticipate the problems?**

   If you didn't anticipate causing World War III in your office, then certainly no "I told you so's" are in order. But if you did, ask yourself why you didn't do anything to prevent it. Part of being a good politician means that you can plan ahead for any fallout. If you didn't plan, and now find yourself in the middle of some serious drama, step back and prioritize who is the most significant player in the situation. Who could cause the most damage? Try to defuse the situation before it blows up.

3. **Can you smooth ruffled feathers?**

   If you have caused some damage with your politicking, the first thing to realize is that it was bound to happen. You can't accomplish your goals and please everyone at the same time. You can't undo what's been done but you can go back and calm down the people who didn't get their way. If your idea was accepted over someone else's, then focus on the benefits that person will get from your idea. If you've angered a colleague or caused someone to lose out on an opportunity or credit, tell them you're sorry and explain why you did what you did. If you can't explain why, consider your own morals or values. When you do talk with your unhappy colleague, remain professional, polite, and low key. You don't want to intentionally cause malice.

4. Is it worth it?

Many of the political choices you will face in the workplace will leave you wondering whether the sacrifice is worth it. Is being transferred worth the opportunity to date a colleague? Is having a colleague mad at you—someone who used to be a good friend—worth a promotion? There's no right answer to these questions. Sometimes it's yes and sometimes it is no. It is up to you. Use your own best judgment as well as your Career Kaleidoscope to decide what is most worthwhile.

Finding the Right Fit

It's no surprise that some careers, fields, and industries are more political than others. The more relationship-building a career requires, or the more interpersonal a job is, the more likely you are to encounter office politics. A professional who is a member of multiple teams at work is more likely to have to deal with politics than a professional who programs computer code all day.

Similarly, organization size can play a role. The bigger an organization is, the more room for politics. Not that small companies aren't political, because they certainly can be, but there usually aren't as many layers of bureaucracy or as many people to report to. The key to coping with office politics is to know yourself and your behavioral strengths. If you don't like politics, find out as soon as possible whether an organization is overly political or a position will require lots of campaigning. Like most everything else with your career, you won't know unless you ask.

No matter where you work, you can't ignore office politics. Think through situations and seek out colleagues, mentors, and friends for unbiased advice. If you get stuck, think like a politician. The more votes you have the more likely you'll ascend to the top spot. You have to make sure that when you get there, you can deliver on all those campaign promises you made.

18

The Fond Farewell

You can't imagine you'll ever leave, but sometimes good-byes are in order. To avoid letting the door slam on the way out, you'll need to pay close attention to decisions, timing, and farewell politics.

Sometimes there is no better feeling than quitting a job. You can't wait to get rid of a boss, say *adios* to a colleague, or *sayonara* to the client who wasn't grateful for anything you did. If you've read this book up to this point, you should be leaving for the right reason—a position that furthers your vision. Leaving is a natural process: We can't stay in the same job forever.

We've all left jobs before—whether it was a high-paying director's position or the cashier role at the local supermarket. You simply tell your boss you're leaving and then you leave. Right? Well, you can do it that way. But if you want to exit gracefully, maintain a strong network in your field or industry, make the transition smooth, and avoid any legal issues, there's a right way to do it.

Just as in any other aspect of your career, there are guidelines to help you leave a job well. If you simply walk out, the repercussions are huge. You have to know how to make the exit smooth and be aware of what might happen next.

STOP If you have been fired or asked to leave, there are important legal and career issues to recognize. This chapter contains important information on resigning and how to handle an invitation to leave. Each section contains valuable departure information.

Should I Stay or Should I Go?

The first question you should always ask yourself is: Am I sure I want to leave? After all, you've probably invested a significant amount of time in the job, as well as in building relationships with your colleagues and clients. Before you rush to break ties, explore the following:

- **Are you angry?**

  Just as when your partner or spouse makes you mad, sometimes we overreact to a situation that probably isn't as grave as we think it is. It may be that your boss has pushed you over the edge and you need some time to cool off. Or maybe you just left a client meeting, thinking "If I have to work with him one more time I will shoot myself." Whatever the reason, a career decision shouldn't be made rashly. Sleep on it, talk to mentors, or ask for unbiased advice from outsiders. Find a devil's advocate to bounce the issue off of to make sure you aren't unreasonably mad.

- **Can the problem be fixed?**

  Perhaps the problem is worth fixing. Whatever it is that makes you want to leave, there might be a way to remedy the problem without walking out the door. If you haven't explored this option, it's a good idea to consider it.

- **Can you move within the firm?**

  If you like the business and the company culture, consider moving within the company. Transferring across departments or divisions may allow you to keep working with a business you love while losing the boss or department you can't stand.

- **Do you have a financial plan?**

  If you leave your job it's crucial to make sure you've planned to cover the income gap. Unemployment insurance is available to you only if you are fired. If you quit or resign on your own, you cannot collect unemployment.

- **Do you know why you're leaving?**

  Make sure you can articulate why you are leaving. If you can make a good, solid case to a stranger why it's time to move on, then you probably should. When in doubt, try making your case to an unbiased party and assess his response.

- **Do you know where you're headed?**

  Leaving a job without having an idea where you will go next is a very risky proposition. Not that it shouldn't ever be done—sometimes a clean break and time to clear your head is a good thing. However, know that it's a risky move and be prepared both mentally and financially.

Making the Decision

If you've already made your decision—and can't be convinced otherwise—good for you. If you remain unconvinced, it is a smart idea to make sure you have covered all of your bases. This way, if you do decide to leave, you will do so with confidence.

Try taking your concerns to your manager and explore your options with him. You don't want to overlook any remedies that you aren't aware of, such as restructuring or staff changes. It may also be that you are suffering from a career development issue. Wanting to leave your job because there are no more opportunities for growth or promotion is common. Checking with your manager to make sure there are no other options isn't. Ask if other options exist, rather than assume that there's nothing to be done.

Being open with your manager also allows him to give you a counter-offer (if he wants to) before you formally resign. Counter-offers typically match or exceed the offer you've received in an effort to get you stay at your current company. If your reasons for leaving are pay-related or you are a pivotal part of a project or team, you might be convinced to stay. Be sure you stay for the right reasons.

If you do go to your manager, be careful with ultimatums. The "If you don't do this, I will leave" threat doesn't work in your love life and it won't work here, either. Share your frustrations and potential solutions and find out whether any of your suggested options are viable. Ask your manager for advice—what would she do if she were in your position?

Finally, your manager's response may also bolster your decision. Is she supportive? Does she take your frustrations seriously? Is she the root of the problem? Gauging her response may help you make your final decision.

Making the Break

Once you've made your decision to leave, it doesn't mean you can waltz out the door. Follow the specific rules:

1. **Review any hiring contingencies**

   If you had any contingencies when starting the job (such as a non-disclosure or non-compete agreement) make sure you review them thoroughly before offering your resignation. Be confident that any job you are about to take doesn't violate the terms of these agreements and be aware of any limitations you are about to face if you're entering a job search.

2. **Put it in writing**

   If you have made the decision to leave, it's important to put it in writing. Writing a resignation letter ensures you have covered all of your legal bases and formalizes the decision. Type up the letter just as you would a formal business letter, and address it to your immediate boss. Use the "positive sandwich" technique we talked about earlier: Indicate how grateful you are to have worked at the company, formally offer your resignation, and re-iterate your gratitude for the opportunities you have been afforded. Be sure to date the letter and offer your willingness to work with the company on your transition.

3. **Know how you'll respond to a counter-offer**

   If your boss responds to your resignation with a counter-offer to stay, it's important to know what you would do. You don't want to be caught off guard, or stall the employer who has given you an offer already. Know what would make you stay, if you're willing, and make sure you're doing it for the right reasons. Your Career Kaleidoscope should also help you clarify your decision.

4. **Set departure terms**

   It is standard to give two weeks' notice, but sometimes departing employees give more or less. Some companies may require a minimum notice, while others may ask you to leave immediately. It depends on the situation, the company, and the work you are doing. Be as gracious as you can, but don't drag it out forever. You don't want to resign and then still be working two months later. Decide on a departure date to set the official wheels in motion.

5. **Create a transition plan**

   Surely you're leaving work behind and you want someone to pick up the slack. Based on your departure date, work as amicably as you can with your manager and peers to turn over your work to your successor. If someone new has been hired, you can help that person get up to speed. If you're leaving a gaping hole in the department, wrap up as many loose ends as you can and provide instructions and organized notes and files for whoever comes next.

6. Determine your departure announcement

Determine how will your resignation be announced to your peers and to the firm, and come to a consensus with your manager ahead of time as to when a formal announcement will be made. You don't want news of your departure to be the biggest item on the company rumor mill.

7. Plan your thank-yous

To whom do you owe a debt of gratitude? During your tenure at the company, there undoubtedly have been people who have gone out of their way to help you. Write handwritten thank-you notes or take significant colleagues out to lunch. You never know when you might need them again, or cross paths at another company.

8. Offer forwarding information

When an employee leaves, questions and confusion are left in his wake. Proactively offer a personal e-mail address and/or cell phone number where you can be reached in case questions arise. You don't want a project you worked hard on to fall apart after you leave.

9. Maintain commitment

During your last few days or weeks at the firm, stay committed. Don't adopt an "I'm outta here" attitude and slack off on your work. No matter how much you want to get the heck out, work hard until the end—you want to leave on a positive note. You never know when you might meet some of your colleagues again.

10. Have an exit interview

Before you leave, it is important to meet with Human Resources. Most likely they will contact you to initiate the process. Don't blow off the meeting or decide not to go because you are leaving. The exit interview gives you an opportunity not only to learn about what happens to your benefits and final compensation (salary and any remaining bonuses or incentives) but also to share constructive criticism and praise. Employers can use comments from exit interviews to make the workplace better for the colleagues you left behind.

11. **Take only what's yours**

You may be tempted to take everything from your client files to your stapler. Legally, you likely can only take what's yours (i.e., your personal documents and performance evaluations). When it comes to data and information, that's your call. Hiring contingencies may prevent you from taking anything, so be careful. Typically, what you create or design while an employee of the company is the company's to keep. You can save your work or e-mail it to a personal address but be aware that this is risky and sometimes illegal.

12. **Leave gracefully**

Finally, even if you're about to head to the best job there is, don't consistently remind your colleagues you're on your way out. It's disrespectful and rude.

Legal Mumbo Jumbo

When you leave an organization, even if by choice, you still have legal rights. For example, in the United States, there's an act called COBRA (Consolidated OmniBus Reconciliation Act) that requires a company to provide you the opportunity to purchase the health insurance plan you have been on with the company for up to eighteen months after you leave. If you earned a pension, the company may still be required to pay it to you. On the flip side, if you signed a non-compete or non-disclosure agreement, or have stock options or other ties to the company, you may have to abide by specific rules that determine where you go next, investments you can make, or jobs you can accept.

Ask questions. Go over everything detail by detail before you leave and use your exit interview or human resources staff to help ensure that you understand all of your rights and responsibilities. If the company is trying to enforce a policy or document you think should not apply to you, try to resolve it internally first. If that doesn't work, you might need legal assistance. Appendix B has a list of resources you can use. If you encounter a troubling issue in the process of leaving, make sure you write it down and make copies of everything. You can never be too careful.

Invitation to Leave

At other times, leaving is not by choice. If the decision isn't in your hands, there's little room for negotiation but you can take steps to make it somewhat less painful, and still protect yourself and your integrity.

1. **Ask for another party to be present.**

   If you sense that you are about to be fired, laid off, or asked to resign, make sure there is more than one staff person in the room. Most human resources professionals know that they should have at least two people present, but if they don't, ask for another party to be present before the discussion goes any further. It protects you and the company should there be arry later debates about what transpired.

2. **Get an explanation and take notes, or record the discussion if they will let you.**

   Maintaining records is very important, especially if you decide to take legal action later. Even if you don't, you will want to have a good understanding to use in crafting an explanation to potential future employers of why you were let go.

3. **Ask what your rights and responsibilities are as well as the terms of your departure.**

   The company should inform you of your rights once they've communicated their decision. Will they be enforcing hiring agreements? Do you have to leave immediately? Will they allow you to clean out your desk? Will you be getting severance or any benefit extensions? Do you have to sign a document promising not to sue? Depending on the situation, a company can do anything from escorting you out immediately to helping you find a new job.

4. **Start a personal file.**

   Include copies of all company policies and write down an immediate account of what happened, as well as any previous related situations. If you can, retain copies of any documentation relating to the issues. You'll probably need it later.

5. **If at all possible, try to keep your emotions in check.**

   It's probably impossible to not react emotionally to a situation like this. But try to remain as mature and professional as you can so that you can collect all the information you need.

6. **Consult legal counsel immediately if you have any question about the company's action.**

If you don't think the company is right to fire you or ask you to resign, or you have questions about documents you are being asked to sign, get legal help immediately. You may or may not use it, but it is important to consult an expert who can give you an unbiased recommendation and ensure that you don't sign your life away. The Web site Findlaw.com is a great place to start. A number of other legal resources are included in Appendix B.

7. **Look into income options.**

From unemployment insurance to part-time work, there are a number of ways you can cover the income gap when you suddenly find yourself out of a job. Begin to investigate your options so you don't find yourself in a financial bind. Calling your local unemployment office is a good place to start.

8. **Start looking forward.**

Even if you end up taking legal action against the company, you can't look backward forever. Start thinking about what changes you can make or what you can do differently to take a career step forward. Getting fired or laid off isn't a bed of roses, but it can put things into perspective and help you stay committed and on top of your next role.

Walking Away

All in all, regardless of how it happens, leaving a company is emotional. Allow yourself time to feel frustrated, disappointed, relieved, ecstatic, or regretful. You can't anticipate exactly how you'll feel when you walk out the door, but you can allow yourself time to think through what happens next.

Go back to your Career Kaleidoscope and remind yourself what you have to offer and what you want in return. Remember you're not looking for the perfect career, you're looking for the perfect career for you.

AFTERWORD

You've now gone from understanding what your Career Sweet Spot is, and how to find a job that fits with it, to how to manage the early days on the job and, finally, how to handle the tough issues of performance, compensation, and resignation. It's a full cycle. When you're ready to move on to your next position, you can use your Career Kaleidoscope to help you determine what's next, and the rest of the information in *The Right Job, Right Now* to find your next role and navigate issues along the way.

Remember, though, no matter how many times you go back to your Career Kaleidoscope, it's great to finally find that Career Sweet Spot and feel like you've arrived, but it's not the time to settle into bliss. Not *quite* yet, anyway. When you face an issue related to your career, you should be proactive when you can, and prepared when you don't know what's to come. Step back and think about your situation and your goals, and then act.

You're always going to come across frustrating concerns, such as a colleague you can't stand, or sticky situations, such as falling in love with a co-worker. Advice columns, message boards, and blogs are full of whining and complaining about what to do. In reality, the only way you'll get past any issue at work is to take charge. You don't need to overthrow the CEO but you have to take charge of yourself.

Complacency will get you nowhere in your career. No one will ever care as much about your career as you do. So own it. Take the time to figure out what you have to offer and what you want in return. If there is an issue at work, speak up. If you think you deserve a raise, ask for it. Instead of opening your mouth to complain, get up and take action.

Proactivity, however, should be tempered with a heavy dose of respect and patience. When you found your Career Sweet Spot, you had to sacrifice some things to get there. You can't have it all, but you can find what you want the most. Be patient but not too patient. Be respectful, but not simply obedient. Be vocal but not loud. Be yourself. After all, it's your career. You've found *The Right Job, Right Now.*

APPENDIX A
Resource Center: Good Help Isn't Hard to Find

You've got your plan, so don't waste time looking for help to make progress. Appendix A is the most comprehensive and organized collection of field, industry, and career resources available today. One of the biggest mistake job seekers and career professionals make is to hide behind a computer. With more than 80 percent of jobs today attained through networking, it is important to make direct personal contacts. The goal is to consider the list below as a starting point, and to create a specific career development strategy that works best for you. Use whatever resources you need to structure your search or your advancement strategy, and to focus on your career path.

JOB-SEARCH RESOURCES AND NATIONWIDE JOB-SEARCH SITES

- 6FigureJobs.com: http://6figurejobs.com
- America's Job Bank: http://www.ajb.dni.us
- Best Jobs in the USA Today: http://www.bestjobsusa.com
- Black Collegian: http://www.black-collegian.com
- Brilliant People: http://www.brilliantpeople.com
- CareerBuilder: http://www.careerbuilder.com
- Career Journal: http://www.careerjournal.com
- Career Magazine: http://www.careermag.com
- Careers.org: http://www.careers.org
- Career Site: http://www.careersite.com
- College Recruiter.com: http://www.collegerecruiter.com
- Contracted Work: http://www.contractedwork.com
- Craig's List: www.craigslist.org
- Destiny Group (ex-military): www.destinygrp.com
- Employment Guide: http://www.employmentguide.com
- Flip Dog: http://flipdog.monster.com
- Hot Jobs: http://www.hotjobs.com
- Indeed: http://www.indeed.com
- Job.com: http://www.job.com
- Job Hunt: http://www.job-hunt.org

- Job Smart Salary Index: www.jobsmart.org/tools/salary/index.htm
- Linked In: www.linkedin.com
- Monster: http://www.monster.com
- My Stock Options: http://www.mystockoptions.com
- Nation Job: http://www.nationjob.com/management
- Networking Associations: www.job-hunt.org/associations.shtml
- Quintessential Careers' Informational interviewing: http://www
  .quintcareers.com/informational_interviewing.html
- Riley Guide: http://rileyguide.com/index.html#help
- Salary.com: www.salary.com
- Salary Expert: www.salaryexpert.com
- True Careers: www.truecareers.com
- Vault: http://www.vault.com
- Wage Web: www.wageweb.com
- Weddles: www.weddles.com
- WetFeet: http://www.wetfeet.com
- Women For Hire: www.womenforhire.com
- Work Tree: www.worktree.com

SEARCH FIRMS/EXECUTIVE RECRUITERS/PLACEMENT

- Adecco: http://www.adecco.com
- Analytic Recruiting: http://www.analyticrecruiting.com
- Drake Beam Morin: www.dbm.com
- Executive Search International: http://www.esihbc.com
- Executive Recruitment Group: http://www.erg-retail.com
- Heidrick and Struggles: http://www.heidrick.com/default.aspx
- Kennedy Information (Search Firm Directory): www.kennedyinfo.com
- Kforce: http://www.kforce.com
- Korn/Ferry International: http://www.kornferry.com/Library/Process
  .asp?P=Home
- Manpower: http://www.manpower.com/mpcom/index.jsp
- Management Recruiters International: http://www.mrinet.com
- Michael Page International: http://www.michaelpage.com
- Monster Worldwide: http://www.monsterworldwide.com
- National Search Inc.: http://www.insurancerecruiters.com
- Randstad: http://www.randstad.com

- Robert Half: http://www.rhii.com
- Robert Half Legal Staffing: http://www.affiliates.com
- Russell Reynolds: http://www.russellreynolds.com
- Spencer Stuart: www.spencerstuart.com
- Vedior: http://www.vedior.com
- Westminster Group: http://wgpeople.com

ACCOUNTING/FINANCE/VENTURE CAPITAL RESOURCES

- Accounting Net: http://www.accountingnet.com
- AICPA Career Resources: http://www.aicpa.org/temp/jobres.htm
- Association for Financial Professionals: http://www.afponline.org
- Association for Investment Management and Research: http://www.aimr.org
- CFO Magazine: www.cfomagazine.com
- DC Accounting Jobs: http://www.dcaccountingjobs.com
- Greater Washington Association for Finance Professionals: http://www.gwafp.org
- Financial Jobs.com: http://www.financialjobs.com
- Financial Jobs Network: http://www.fjn.com/default.asp
- Financial Positions.com: http://www.financialpositions.com/Main/Default.asp
- Financial Management Association: http://www.fma.org
- Jobs in the Money: http://www.jobsinthemoney.com
- Managed Funds Association Career Center: http://www.mfainfo.org/careercenter.htm
- Occupational Handbook-Finance Managers: http://stats.bls.gov/oco/ocos010.htm
- Smart Pros: www.accountingnet.com
- Street Jobs: http://www.streetjobs.com
- Venture Capital Task Force: www.vctaskforce.com

CONSULTING/CONTRACT RESOURCES

- American Association of Healthcare Consultants: http://www.aahc.net
- Association of Management Consulting Firms: http://www.amcf.org
- Cambridge Consulting: www.cambridgeconsultant.com

- Consulting Base: http://www.consultingbase.com
- Contract Employment Weekly: www.ceweekly.com
- CPRi: www.cpri.com
- Elance: www.elance.com
- Free Agent: www.freeagent.com
- Guru: www.guru.com
- Institute of Management Consultants USA: http://www.imcusa.org/index.shtml
- Kennedy Information: Consulting: http://www.kennedyinfo.com/mc/mcindex.html
- M^2: www.msquared.com
- Professional and Technical Consultants Association: http://www.patca.org/main
- Project Management Institute: http://www.pmi.org/info/default.asp

COUNSELING/SOCIAL SERVICES RESOURCES

- American Counseling Association: http://www.counseling.org/site/PageServer
- American Psychological Association Jobs: http://www.apa.org/ads
- American Psychological Society: http://www.psychologicalscience.org
- American School Counseling Association: http://www.schoolcounselor.org/index.cfm
- Center for the Study of Technology in Counseling and Career Development: http://www.career.fsu.edu/techcenter
- Chronicle of Higher Education: http://chronicle.com
- Med Search: http://www.medsearch.com
- National Board for Certified Counselors and Affiliates: http://www.nbcc.org/index.htm
- National Career Development Association: http://ncda.org/cjs.htm
- Social Work and Social Services Jobs Online: http://gwbweb.wustl.edu/jobs/index.html
- Social Service.com: http://socialservice.com

EDUCATION RESOURCES

- AGORA Language Marketplace: http://agoralang.com
- Chronicle of Higher Education: http://chronicle.com

- EDUCAUSE: http://www.educause.edu/jobpost
- Council on International Education: http://www.ciee.org
- Education Jobs: http://www.educationjobs.com
- Higher Ed Jobs: www.higheredjobs.com
- Independent School Management: http://www.isminc.com/index.php3? M=mmm1
- Library Job Search: http://www.lis.uiuc.edu/gslis/resources/jobs.html
- Job Web (NACE): http://www.jobweb.com
- School Spring: http://www.schoolspring.com
- Teachers at Work: http://www.teachersatwork.com
- Teacher Jobs: http://www.teacherjobs.com
- Teachers-Teachers: http://www.teachers-teachers.com

ENGINEERING RESOURCES

- American Society for Engineer Education: http://www.asee.org/neic/ careerscope
- Engineering Jobs: http://www.engineeringjobs.com
- Graduating Engineer and Computer Careers: http://www .graduatingengineer.com
- IEEE: http://www.ieeeusa.org/careers
- National Academy of Engineering: http://www.nae.edu
- Professional Society List: http://www.nae.edu/NAE/naehome.nsf/ weblinks/KGRG-5CKQ2U?OpenDocument
- Society for Women Engineers: www.swe.org

ENTERTAINMENT/HOSPITALITY RESOURCES

- American Hotel and Lodging Association: http://www.ahma.com
- CPB Job Line: http://www.cpb.org/jobline
- Cruise Ship Jobs: http://www.cruiseshipentertainment.com
- Entertainment Careers: http://entertainmentcareers.net
- Entertainment Employment Journal: http://www.eej.com/featuredjobs/ jobinfo.html
- Entertainment Services and Technology Association: http://www.esta .org
- Gen Art: http://www.genart.org
- H Careers: http://www.hcareers.com

- Hospitality.net: http://www.hospitalitynet.org/opportunity/By_Date/page1.html
- National Restaurant Association: http://www.restaurant.org
- Renard International: http://www.renard-international.com
- ShowBiz Jobs: http://www.showbizjobs.com/dsp_jobsearch.cfm
- TV Gigs: www.tvgigsonline.com
- TV Jobs: http://www.tvjobs.com

ENTREPRENEURSHIP RESOURCES

- Forum for Women Entrepreneurs: www.fwe.org
- Inc. Magazine: www.inc.com
- Making It: www.makingittv.com
- Small Business Development Centers: www.sba.gov
- Young Entrepreneurs Association: www.yeo.org

FEDERAL/GOVERNMENT/CIVIL SERVICE RESOURCES

- Air Force Careers: http://www.airforce.com/index_fr.htm
- Applying for Federal Jobs: http://federaljobs.net/applyfor.htm
- Bureau of Labor Statistics: http://www.bls.gov
- Corporation for National and Community Service: http://www.cns.gov
- Destiny Group: www.destinygrp.com
- Federal Jobs: http://www.fedjobs.com/jobdb/search.html?id=5NjHQDFu
- Fed World: http://www.fedworld.gov/jobs/jobsearch.html
- FedQuest: http://www.fedquest.com
- Government Jobs Zone: http://www.governmentjobszone.com/index.html
- GovernmentJobs: http://www.governmentjobs.com
- Hill News Jobs: http://www.hillnews.com/classifieds/employment.shtm
- Hill Zoo: http://www.hillzoo.com/jobs.htm
- House of Representatives: http://www.house.gov/cao-hr
- Marines Jobs: http://www.marines.com
- Military Recruit: http://www.militaryrecruit.com
- Navy Jobs: http://www.navy.com
- Peace Corps: http://www.peacecorps.gov
- Opportunities in Public Affairs: http://opajobs.com

- Office of Personnel Management: http://www.opm.gov
- Partnership for Public Service: www.ourpublicservice.org
- Roll Call: http://www.rcjobs.com
- State and Local Opportunties: http://www.thejobpage.gov/statelocal.asp
- TAOnline.com: http://www.taonline.com
- Vault.com's Government Section: http://www.vault.com/hubs/512/ hubhome_512.jsp?ch_id=512
- U.S. General Accounting Office: http://jobs.quickhire.com/scripts/gao.exe
- USAJobs (official federal government job site): http://www.usajobs.opm .gov

GENERAL/MISCELLANEOUS BUSINESS CAREER RESOURCES

- Business Journals (by major city): www.bizjournals.com
- Business Week: www.businessweek.com
- CEO Express: www.ceoexpress.com
- Corporate Information: www.corporateinformation.com
- Fortune: www.fortune.com
- Hoovers Online: www.hoovers.com
- Insurance Workforce: http://www.insuranceworkforce.com
- Jungle Magazine: www.mbajungle.com
- Venture Reporter: www.venturereporter.net

HUMAN RESOURCES/ORGANIZATIONAL DEVELOPMENT RESOURCES

- 3M Meeting Network: http://www.3m.com/meetingnetwork
- Academy of Management (AOM): http://www.aomonline.org
- American Society for Training and Development (ASTD): http://www .astd.org
- Employment Management Association: http://www.shrm.org/ema
- International Foundation of Employee Benefit Plans: http://www.ifebp .org/jobs
- International Personnel Management Association: http://www.ipma-hr.org
- International Society for Performance Improvement: http://www.ispi.org
- Kennedy information (HR and Recruiting Central): http://www .kennedyinfo.com/hr/hrindex.html
- The MASIE Center: http://www.masie.com/masie/default.cfm?page= default

- National Human Resources Association: http://www.humanresources.org
- Organization Development and Change (Division of AOM): http://aom.pace.edu/odc
- Organization Development Institute: http://www.odinstitute.org
- Organization Development Network: http://www.odnetwork.org
- Organization Development Information: http://humanresources.about.com/cs/org
- Recruiting Life: http://www.napsweb.org
- Society for Human Resource Management: http://www.shrm.org
- Society for Organizational Learning: http://www.solonline.org
- TCM's HR Careers: http://hr-careers.tcm.com/jobs/list.php3
- Workforce Online: http://www.workforceonline.com

INTERNATIONAL/MINORITY COMMUNITY SITES

- Asian Avenue: www.asianavenue.com
- Asia Net: http://www.asia-net.com
- Association for International Practical Training: http://www.aipt.org
- Bilingual Jobs: http://www.bilingual-jobs.com
- Black Planet: www.blackplanet.com
- Career Strategy (focus on Japan): http://www.csinc.co.jp/english/index.html
- Career One (Australia/New Zealand): http://careerone.com.au
- CDS Global: http://www.cdsintl.org
- Chinese Information and Networking Association: www.cina.org
- Computing Technology Industry Association: http://www.comptia.org
- Council on International Exchange: http://www.ciee.org
- Dev Net Jobs: www.devnetjobs.org
- Euro Circle: www.eurocircle.com
- International Careers Consortium: http://www.intlcareers.org
- International Careers Consortium Resource Links: http://www.intlcareers.org/resources.html
- International Career Employment Center: http://www.internationaljobs.org
- Keizai Society: www.keizai.org
- LatPro: www.latpro.com
- MiGente: www.migente.com

- National Association of International Educators: http://www.nafsa.org
- One World: www.oneworld.net
- People Bank (UK): http://www.peoplebank.com
- Wall Street Journal Asia: www.careerjournalasia.com
- Wall Street Journal Europe: www.careerjournaleurope.com

LAW RESOURCES

- American Health Lawyers Association: www.healthlawywers.org
- Army Jobs: http://www.goarmy.com/index04.htm
- Emplawyer: www.emplawyernet.com
- Equal Justice Works: www.napil.org
- Find Law Career Center: www.careers.findlaw.com
- Hieros Gamos Legal Research: www.hg.org/employment
- Hispanic National Bar Association: www.hnba.com
- In House (of Counsel) Jobs: http://jobline.acca.com
- Law Bulletin Career Center: www.lawbulletin.com
- Law Jobs: www.lawjobs.com
- Law.com: www.law.com
- Legal Staff: www.legalstaff.com
- Legal Hire: www.legalhire.com
- Lexis Nexis eAttorney: http://www.eattorney.com/wnc/owa/eattorney .main
- Minority Corporate Counsel Association: www.mcca.com
- National Legal Aid and Defender Association: www.nlada.org
- United States Department of Justice Recruitment: http://www.usdoj.gov/ oarm

NONPROFIT/PHILANTHROPY RESOURCES

- American Society of Association Executives: http://asaenet .jobcontrolcenter.com/search/results
- Chronicle of Philanthropy: www.philanthropy.com
- Council on Foundations: www.cof.org
- Foundation Center: http://www.fdncenter.org
- Guidestar: http://www.guidestar.org
- Idealist: http://www.idealist.org

- Independent Sector: http://www.independentsector.org
- Interaction: http://www.interaction.org
- National Council of Nonprofit Associations: http://www.ncna.org
- Nonprofit Oyster: www.nonprofitoyster.com
- Opportunity NOCS: www.opportunitynocs.org
- Philanthropy News Digest: http://www.fdncenter.org/pnd/jobs/index .jhtml

PUBLIC RELATIONS/MARKETING/COMMUNICATIONS/ SALES RESOURCES

- Ad Age: http://www.crain.com/classified/adage/index.cfm
- Ad Week: http://www.adweek.com/aw/classifieds/index.jsp
- American Marketing Association's Job Center: http://ama.jobcontrolcenter .com/search.cfm
- Careers in Marketing: www.careers-in-marketing.com
- CommArts Network: http://www.commarts.com
- Communications Roundtable: http://www.roundtable.org/jobs.html
- Creative Freelancers: http://www.freelancers.com
- Direct Marketing Careers: http://www.the-dma.org/jobbank
- International Association of Business Communicators: http://jobs.iabc .com/home/index.cfm?site_id=65
- Job Link for Journalists: http://newslink.org/newjoblinksearch.html
- Marketing Jobs: http://www.marketingjobs.com
- Online Journalism Review: http://ojr.usc.edu/jobsboard/header.cfm
- Public Relations Society of America: http://prsa.org/jobcenter/main
- Retail Recruiter: http://www.retail-recruiter.com/index.htm
- Sales Heads: www.salesheads.com
- Strategic Account Management Association: http://www.strategicaccounts .org
- Talent Zoo: http://www.talentzoo.com
- Work in PR: http://www.workinpr.com

SCIENCE/MEDICINE/HEALTHCARE RESOURCES

- National Institutes of Health: http://www.jobs.nih.gov
- National Science Foundation: http://www.nsf.gov/oirm/hrm/jobs/start .htm

- Aquatic Network: http://www.aquanet.com/busdir/aq_bus.htm
- BIO Online Career Center: http://www.bio.com/careercenter/index .jhtml
- Environmental Careers Organization: http://www.eco.org
- Health Career Web: http://healthcareerweb.com
- MedSearch America: http://www.medsearch.com

SOCIALLY RESPONSIBLE COMPANIES

- Business and Economic Development Impacts: www.economicfootprint .org
- Business for Social Responsibility: www.bsr.org
- Net Impact: www.netimpact.org
- Social Venture Network Jobs Page: www.svn.org

TECHNOLOGY RESOURCES

- Association of Information Technology Professionals: http://www.aitp .org/index.jsp
- Business Software Alliance: http://www.bsa.org
- CIO Magazine: http://www.cio.com/career
- Computer Jobs Store: http://www.computerjobs.com
- Computer Consultant Jobs: http://computerwork.com
- DICE: http://www.dice.com
- Information Technology Association of America: http://www.itaa.org
- Information Technology Industry Council: http://www.itic.org
- Internet Alliance: http://www.internetalliance.org
- TechVentures Network: http://www.techventuresnetwork.org

APPENDIX B
It's More Than Just a Job: Resources for Issues That Are Bigger Than Expected

Work can be overwhelming in so many different ways, affecting your family, your life, and most important, you. Sometimes before you can start developing a career strategy, you need to take a step back. If you find yourself facing a personal challenge that's getting in the way of your career, it may be time to find a qualified professional to help you first address your personal needs. Appendix B provides guidance on understanding what you need, finding the resources to help, and taking the right steps.

LEGAL RESOURCES

Legal Research

- Cornell's Law Site: http://www.law.cornell.edu
- Department of Labor Employment Law Site: http://www.dol.gov/elaws
- Employment Law: http://www.hg.org/employ.html
- Employment Law Resource Center: http://www.ahipubs.com
- Find Law: http://www.findlaw.com
- Law.com: http://www.law.com
- Law News Network: http://www.law.com
- Lexis: http://www.lexisone.com
- LLRX.com: http://www.llrx.com/features/labor.htm
- Mega Law: http://www.megalaw.com
- WashLaw WEB: http://www.washlaw.edu

Selected State Sites:

- California: http://www.leginfo.ca.gov/.html/lab_table_of_contents.html
- Illinois: http://www.state.il.us/agency/idol
- Massachusetts: http://www1.law.com/ma
- New York: http://www.labor.state.ny.us/business_ny/employer_responsibilities/protecting_workforce.html

MENTAL HEALTH RESOURCES

- American Psychological Association: http://www.apa.org
- Depression: http://www.allaboutdepression.com/gen_15b.html
- HealthyPlace.com: http://www.healthyplace.com/communities/ depression/related/work_2.asp
- IMDiversity: http://www.imdiversity.com/Villages/Careers/Career_ Index_List_New.asp
- Job Burnout: http://www.depression-help-for-you.com/job-burnout.html
- Losing a Job: http://careerplanning.about.com/od/jobloss/a/job_loss.htm
- Mental Health.com http://www.mentalhealth.com
- Mental Health Matters: http://www.mental-health-matters.com
- Therapist Finder: http://www.therapistfinder.net

APPENDIX C
The Lowdown on Executive Recruiters: What They Are and How to Use Them

Using an executive recruiter or headhunter is just one of the strategies that should be considered as part of your job search—not your only strategy. However, before you engage executive recruiters or headhunters as tools for your search, it is extremely important you understand how the business works.

Types of Recruiters

Title	Goal	Examples
Temporary agency/ Recruiting firm	Clients depend on these agencies to fill positions quickly. Mostly they run from office administrators and secretaries to data entry clerks. Sometimes they may call at 4PM and need someone for 8:30AM the next morning. The recruiter is expected to have someone fill the position.	Office Team, Todays Temporarys, Randstad, Accountemps.
Staffing/ Placement firms	Placement companies fill positions in middle management and technical support positions and have specialists for major business sectors.	Robert Half, Technalink.
Management consultants	These consultants offer a variety of services, from outplacement and personnel to job description creation and recruiting and are different from recruiting firms that earn money from recruiting fees alone. Clients have long-standing relationships with these consultants and work within the corporate culture to best know the proper fit between candidates and the company.	TalentFusion, Search Strategies Inc., CDI
Executive recruiter	Includes large, worldwide, and smaller specialized recruiting firms focused mostly on director-level and above positions.	Korn/Ferry, Russell Reynolds, Management Recruiters International
Headhunter	Another term for a recruiter/executive recruiter	N/A

Types of Searches

Type	Title	Details
Internal	Direct hire	The organization directly hires the candidate with no middleman.
External	Contingency	The organization works with several search or placement recruiting firms to find good candidates. Each recruiting firm has an agreement with the organization dictating the percentage the organization must pay the recruiting firm if a candidate is hired who was sourced or found by that recruiting firm.
External	Exclusive contingency	Similar to contingency, but the organization works only with one recruiting firm at a time (called a period of exclusivity). However, after that period, if no hire is made, the organization can drop one recruiting firm to work with another.
External	Retained	This is where the organization works only with one recruiting firm exclusively on the search. Rather than being paid a percentage of the hire's salary, the recruiting firm usually receives a flat fee.

Preparation

There are several steps you must take to prepare for and find executive recruiters and search firms:

1. Know the kinds of positions you are looking for and be sure you can articulate well the reasons that you'd be good for those positions. It is also very important to be able to indicate the career path you desire. Prepare a career brief (like a profile), and have your salary history and references ready.

2. Find a specialist in your field. If you are a computer programmer, call a technical recruiting firm. If you're a C.P.A., call an accounting search firm. Most of all, find a good recruiter (or two) and stick with them. A good agency will be able to tell you whether they can help you and can advise you on the best approach to landing the job you want. Be sure to ask about the level of jobs that they handle, that is, the salary level they usually work with. For example, if the level they handle is $100,000 and you're making $40,000, you should not be working with that recruiter.

3. Recruiters have good information about the job market. Ask the recruiter's opinions of the market. How do my skills compare? How marketable are

they? What can I expect in salary for my skill level and background and education? Am I being realistic? Keep in mind, though, that the recruiter is in business and will do what they can to place you and earn revenue.

4. Ask about the jobs that would be a fit. What is the product/service? What essential skills are needed? Which are "nice to have"? How big is the group/company? Why, specifically, are they interested in my resumé? What is the interviewing manager like?

5. Ask about the process they follow. How often can you expect to hear from them? Do they have references? Will they provide feedback to you from the organization?

Note: If you receive an unsolicited call referencing a position, ask how the recruiter found you, what firm or agency he represents, and specific details about the position. Make sure you feel comfortable and do your research on the recruiter. Even if you're not interested, keep the recruiter's name and urge them to call you in the future. You never know when you might be job hunting.

Expectations

Once you decide to work with an executive recruiter or a search firm, the process varies. Typically, for a low or mid-level position, the firm will forward your resumé to the hiring organization. If the organization thinks you're a match, the firm will serve as the middleman and work with the organization to schedule the interview(s). For executive recruiters and higher level positions, the process often goes as follows:

1. *Candidate description*: The executive recruiter will meet with the hiring organization to get an detailed sense of what the needs are. The recruiter will then write up an extensive candidate description.

2. *Sourcing*: The recruiter will source, or find, candidates using various methods, including networking, cold-calling, industry connections, and industry and field research. Interested candidates will be screened by the recruiter.

3. *Interviews*: The recruiter will screen and interview candidates both on the phone and in person, and will likely narrow down the pool to four to six of the best candidates.

4. *Write-ups and recommendations*: The recruiter will then provide a complete write-up and recommendation for each candidate to the hiring organization. Weighing the recruiter's recommendations carefully, the organization

will decide which candidate to formally interview. The recruiter will serve as the middleman in this process.

5. *Offer.* If an offer is made, negotiations and decisions will typically be made through the recruiter. Ask as many questions as you need to make an informed decision!

Things to Avoid

1. Never pay an executive recruiter or headhunter, or work with a recruiting firm that requires you to pay. Recruiters are paid by the organization doing the hiring and make their money that way.

2. Avoid pushy recruiters or those who try to steamroll you into interviewing for or taking a job you don't like or want. It is important to be clear and consistent about the role you're looking for.

3. Don't work with recruiters who want you to lie or mislead readers on your resumé. You're the one who has to perform up to your potential in the role, and lying or misleading potential employers is never helpful.

4. The bottom line: Work only with recruiters and headhunters who make you feel comfortable.

APPENDIX D
The Experts Speak

By now, you may feel like an expert in the job search and offer process. Heck, you read the whole book, right? Don't get on your high horse just yet. Take a moment to read how the experts answered the question "If you could only give one piece of job search advice to a professional what would it be?"

There are so many things in a job search that are out of your control, that taking control where you can is the key to a successful search and to keeping yourself sane in the process. You can't control what decisions a company and/or recruiter make, but you can control how many companies you contact, how large your network is, how prepared you are for an interview, and how well you market yourself to employers—all of which helps you keep a healthy attitude and makes you feel like you are making progress.

Melinda Allen
Executive Director, The Leadership Development Institute
Vanderbilt University, Owen Graduate School of Management

There are two things that anyone looking for a job should remember. First, always tell the truth. If you lacked three credits to graduate, you didn't graduate. If you make $90,000, you don't make around $100,000. Most potential employers run background checks and the truth will come out. You probably will not get the job. Second, don't talk badly about your former employer. The old saying "if you can't say anything nice, don't say anything at all" still works. Future employers don't want to think you might say the same about them someday.

Martha B. Youngblood
Director of Human Resources & Administration
Finnegan, Henderson, Farabow, Garrett & Dunner LLP

NETWORK, NETWORK, NETWORK! Networking is an often overused word that in reality is an underutilized practice by many job seekers. It does not matter where you are or who you are talking with, you should make the most of every situation to network. Not only might you make a great contact, you might just learn something in the process.

Keith R. Stemple
Associate Director of Career Services
The George Washington University School of Business

Too often, job seekers and employees forget that the reason they receive a paycheck is to improve the bottom line of their employer. People are not hired because they really want to work for a particular organization or perform a particular type of work. They're also not hired because they're hard workers or need an opportunity to prove themselves. Rather, they're hired and retained because the employer believes that they will do more to improve the bottom line of the organization than any other candidate. If you do that, and prove to the employer that you do that, then you'll be hired, retained, and rewarded.

Steven Rothberg
President and Founder
CollegeRecruiter.com

Integrity is paramount and nonnegotiable. Once compromised, it cannot be fully recovered. Therefore, protect it, value it, and practice it.

Glenn Richardson
Partner
Deloitte & Touche LLP

Be open. Open to possibilities and the input of others. Open to different industries, locations, and job titles as long as they fit within the boundaries you have set. For example, if you're focused on one type of position, explore what that job might be like in multiple industries. Think big and keep a positive attitude. When you are open to possibilities, you never know what great opportunities may result.

R. Scott Crawford
Director, Career Services
Wabash College

Do the self-assessment work to get some general direction, and then put yourself out there and "experiment." Try to expose yourself to different possible jobs/industries/people to see if there is a fit by doing informational interviews.

Melissa Karz
Partner, Kruz Consulting

You already know the person who knows the person or organization who will hire you (yes, read that again). Utilize your own network relentlessly. By utilize, I mean make your request as simple and easy on the requestor as possible. By network, I mean associates, friends, and family. By relentlessly, I mean steady and polite persistence.

Wendy Person
Senior Director, Talent Management
Corporate Executive Board (Nasdaq: EXBD)

Your network is your most powerful tool for finding/hearing about opportunities and getting an audience with the employer. Build that network and maintain it rigorously—call people out of the blue to say hello; send the occasional e-mail; put them on your holiday card list, etc. One day you will find you travel in a much smaller circle of professionals than you realize. If you are in constant communication with those people, the probability of a fantastic opportunity coming your way is exponentially higher than if you only rely on job posting boards on the Internet and passive searching.

Mike Figliuolo
Managing Director
thoughtLEADERS, LLC

It's not what you know but who you know. It is clear to me after twenty-plus years in recruiting and staffing that experienced professionals succeed in getting their ideal job most often when they combine great job-search skills with the ability to connect with insiders and other professionals—whether it be for an introduction, a referral, or just good advice.

Kip Harrell
Associate Vice President, Career Management and Professional Development
Thunderbird, the Garvin School of International Management

Be careful about taking a job that will require you to compromise your own ideals and ethical standards, no matter how good the pay and benefits are. Jobs come and go. Your own sense of self stays with you forever.

Phil Anderson
Director, Office of Performance Management and Improvement
Transportation Security Administration (TSA), Department of Homeland Security

Understand your "value proposition" and what in it differentiates you from similarly educated and similarly experienced candidates. Make sure it is articulated in your re-sumé, cover letters, and every version of your introduction. Be ready to provide ex-amples of skills applied to previous employers' problems with the measurable outcomes your interventions contributed to or affected. As you research, identify, and talk to prospective employers, tie your differentiators to each organization's current fo-cus and needs. This employer-focus and skills-match analysis will help you to be seen as someone a hiring manager wants on his/her team, often before a hiring need exists.

Carol R. Anderson
Director, Career Development and Placement
Milano, the New School for Management and Urban Policy

My one piece of advice to anyone in a job search is . . . network! If this is not a strong suit of yours, do what you need to do to stretch yourself in this area (get a networking buddy, hire a coach, etc.). No effective job search can be conducted solely from behind a computer screen. You need to get out and talk to people!

Rebecca Zucker
Principal, Next Step Partners

When you are in a job search, be consistent throughout all stages of the search. By this I mean presenting yourself consistently in terms of integrity, personal motivation, and being open to listening while displaying personal capacity to communicate actively.

James R. Calvin, Ph.D.
Associate Professor
Johns Hopkins University Graduate School of Business

Interview. Interview. Interview. While the role might not seem perfect, if you have the chance to get a face-to-face audience, take it. You could be right—the role is not a fit. But they may have another role that is perfect that you were unaware of and they had not previously thought of until they met you. At least create the chance that those discussions will occur. And if it doesn't happen, the time wasn't wasted—you got the chance to practice your interviewing skills so you will be that much more prepared the next time.

Mike Figliuolo
Managing Director
thoughtLEADERS, LLC

Get excited when you are meeting a prospective employer, or a resource, and everyone is a resource. That leads into networking. Network as if your life depended on it, or maybe as if your house payment depended on it, because it does. Get in the habit of asking people "Who do you know?" And if they don't have an immediate answer, ask their permission to call them back in one week, and see if they have remembered two people for you to speak to. Think about it, in over a month's time, you get two new names from each person you talk to. In thirty days, your network has expanded exponentially!

Robert E. Jones
Recruiting Manager
Sherpa LLC

Prepare and practice before the interview. Practice = self-confidence = better interviews = job offers.

Carole Martin
Principal, InterviewCoach.com

Going through a job search is a process. My advice: Trust the process. This is much easier said than done. I consider the transition one experiences in searching for a new job one of the most difficult and challenging endeavors we face during our adult lives. It is frustrating and at times demoralizing. Believing in yourself, maintaining a positive attitude, hard work, and persistence in following up on every potential opportunity will all pay off in the long run.

Vern Schellenger
Vice President of Education and Training
American Association of Motor Vehicle Administrators

INDEX

About the Author

Susan D. Strayer is a human resources and business professional, career development expert, and author. As the founder of University and Career Decisions (www.ucdecisions.com), she works with individuals, companies, and universities in career management, human resource development, recruiting strategy, and employment brand.

Before starting University and Career Decisions, Susan worked everywhere; large corporations, high-growth firms, small start-ups, and nonprofits. As assistant director of career services for Johns Hopkins University she worked with the university's M.B.A., business, and education graduate students. She has also worked in human resources consulting with GWSolutions and the Corporate Executive Board, serving Fortune 1000 clients in research programs that focus on corporate human resources, benefits, recruiting, training, and learning. Susan's career began with Arthur Andersen where she spent several years working in human resources in multiple training, staffing, and recruiting functions.

Susan holds an M.A. in Human Resource Development from George Washington University and a B.A. in Communication Studies from Virginia Tech. She is certified as a Senior Professional in Human Resources (S.P.H.R.), the highest designation of the human resources profession, and is a certified administrator of the Meyers-Briggs Type Indicator. She is also a member of the Society for Human Resource Management.

Susan has made presentations at several national conferences, and has been quoted in print and online publications, among them the *Washington Post,* CollegeGrad.com, *Fast Company, Women's Health,* and the *Washington Times.* She has been a member of the "Ask the Experts" panel at CollegeRecruiter.com, and wrote a career advice column syndicated in several online publications. Susan is also the author of Vault's "Guide to Human Resources Careers."

Originally from Philadelphia, Susan has spent the bulk of her career living and working in Washington, D.C. She currently resides in Nashville, while completing an M.B.A. at the Owen Graduate School of Management at Vanderbilt University as a Dean's Scholar. She completed her Business School internship in corporate staffing for The Home Depot. When not working, studying, or turning general chaos to order, Susan can usually be found watching HBO, buying shoes, or figuring out how to make a career of sleeping late.